# FILMMAKERS SERIES
### edited by
# ANTHONY SLIDE

1. *James Whale,* by James Curtis. 1982
2. *Cinema Stylists,* by John Belton. 1983
3. *Harry Langdon,* by William Schelly. 1982
4. *William A. Wellman,* by Frank Thompson. 1983
5. *Stanley Donen,* by Joseph Casper. 1983
6. *Brian De Palma,* by Michael Bliss. 1983
7. *J. Stuart Blackton,* by Marian Blackton Trimble. 1985
8. *Martin Scorsese and Michael Cimino,* by Michael Bliss. 1985
9. *Franklin J. Schaffner,* by Erwin Kim. 1985
10. *D. W. Griffith and the Biograph Company,* by Cooper C. Graham et al. 1985
11. *Some Day We'll Laugh: An Autobiography,* by Esther Ralston. 1985
12. *The Memoirs of Alice Guy Blaché,* 2nd ed., trans. by Roberta and Simone Blaché. 1996
13. *Leni Riefenstahl and Olympia,* by Cooper C. Graham. 1986
14. *Robert Florey,* by Brian Taves. 1987
15. *Henry King's America,* by Walter Coppedge. 1986
16. *Aldous Huxley and Film,* by Virginia M. Clark. 1987
17. *Five American Cinematographers,* by Scott Eyman. 1987
18. *Cinematographers on the Art and Craft of Cinematography,* by Anna Kate Sterling. 1987
19. *Stars of the Silents,* by Edward Wagenknecht. 1987
20. *Twentieth Century-Fox,* by Aubrey Solomon. 1988
21. *Highlights and Shadows: The Memoirs of a Hollywood Cameraman,* by Charles G. Clarke. 1989
22. *I Went That-a-Way: The Memoirs of a Western Film Director,* by Harry L. Fraser; edited by Wheeler Winston Dixon and Audrey Brown Fraser. 1990
23. *Order in the Universe: The Films of John Carpenter,* by Robert C. Cumbow. 1990
24. *The Films of Freddie Francis,* by Wheeler Winston Dixon. 1991
25. *Hollywood Be Thy Name,* by William Bakewell. 1991
26. *The Charm of Evil: The Life and Films of Terence Fisher,* by Wheeler Winston Dixon. 1991
27. *Lionheart in Hollywood: The Autobiography of Henry Wilcoxon,* with Katherine Orrison. 1991

28. *William Desmond Taylor: A Dossier,* by Bruce Long. 1991
29. *The Films of Leni Riefenstahl,* 2nd ed., by David B. Hinton. 1991
30. *Hollywood Holyland: The Filming and Scoring of "The Greatest Story Ever Told,"* by Ken Darby. 1992
31. *The Films of Reginald LeBorg: Interviews, Essays, and Filmography,* by Wheeler Winston Dixon. 1992
32. *Memoirs of a Professional Cad,* by George Sanders, with Tony Thomas. 1992
33. *The Holocaust in French Film,* by André Pierre Colombat. 1993
34. *Robert Goldstein and "The Spirit of '76,"* edited and compiled by Anthony Slide. 1993
35. *Those Were the Days, My Friend: My Life in Hollywood with David O. Selznick and Others,* by Paul Macnamara. 1993
36. *The Creative Producer,* by David Lewis; edited by James Curtis. 1993
37. *Reinventing Reality: The Art and Life of Rouben Mamoulian,* by Mark Spergel. 1993
38. *Malcolm St. Clair: His Films, 1915–1948,* by Ruth Anne Dwyer. 1997
39. *Beyond Hollywood's Grasp: American Filmmakers Abroad, 1914–1945,* by Harry Waldman. 1994
40. *A Steady Digression to a Fixed Point,* by Rose Hobart. 1994
41. *Radical Juxtaposition: The Films of Yvonne Rainer,* by Shelley Green. 1994
42. *Company of Heroes: My Life as an Actor in the John Ford Stock Company,* by Harry Carey, Jr. 1994
43. *Strangers in Hollywood: A History of Scandinavian Actors in American Films from 1910 to World War II,* by Hans J. Wollstein. 1994
44. *Charlie Chaplin: Intimate Close-Ups,* by Georgia Hale, edited with an introduction and notes by Heather Kiernan. 1995
45. *The Word Made Flesh: Catholicism and Conflict in the Films of Martin Scorsese,* by Michael Bliss. 1995
46. *W. S. Van Dyke's Journal: White Shadows in the South Seas (1927–1928) and other Van Dyke on Van Dyke,* edited and annotated by Rudy Behlmer. 1996
47. *Music from the House of Hammer: Music in the Hammer Horror Films, 1950–1980,* by Randall D. Larson. 1996
48. *Directing: Learn from the Masters,* by Tay Garnett. 1996
49. *Featured Player: An Oral Autobiography of Mae Clarke,* edited with an introduction by James Curtis. 1996

50. *A Great Lady: A Life of the Screenwriter Sonya Levien,* by Larry Ceplair. 1996
51. *A History of Horrors: The Rise and Fall of the House of Hammer,* by Denis Meikle. 1996
52. *The Films of Michael Powell and the Archers,* by Scott Salwolke. 1997
53. *From Oz to E. T.: Wally Worsley's Half-Century in Hollywood—A Memoir in Collaboration with Sue Dwiggins Worsley,* edited by Charles Ziarko. 1997
54. *Thorold Dickinson and the British Cinema,* by Jeffrey Richards. 1997
55. *The Films of Oliver Stone,* edited by Don Kunz. 1997
56. *Before, In and After Hollywood: The Autobiography of Joseph E. Henabery,* edited by Anthony Slide. 1997
57. Ravished Armenia *and the Story of Aurora Mardiganian,* compiled by Anthony Slide. 1997
58. *Smile When the Raindrops Fall,* by Brian Anthony and Andy Edmonds. 1998
59. *Joseph H. Lewis: Overview, Interview, and Filmography,* by Francis M. Nevins. 1998
60. *September Song: An Intimate Biography of Walter Huston,* by John Weld. 1998
61. *Wife of the Life of the Party,* by Lita Grey Chaplin and Jeffrey Vance. 1998
62. *Down But Not Quite Out in Hollow-weird: A Documentary in Letters of Eric Knight,* by Geoff Gehman. 1998
63. *On Actors and Acting: Essays by Alexander Knox,* edited by Anthony Slide. 1998
64. *Back Lot: Growing Up with the Movies,* by Maurice Rapf. 1999
65. *Mr. Bernds Goes to Hollywood: My Early Life and Career in Sound Recording at Columbia with Frank Capra and Others,* by Edward Bernds. 1999
66. *Hugo Friedhofer: The Best Years of His Life: A Hollywood Master of Music for the Movies,* edited by Linda Danly. 1999
67. *Actors on Red Alert: Career Interviews with Five Actors and Actresses Affected by the Blacklist,* by Anthony Slide. 1999

# Hugo Friedhofer:
# The Best Years
# of His Life

*A Hollywood Master of
Music for the Movies*

edited by Linda Danly

*Filmmakers Series, No. 66*

The Scarecrow Press, Inc.
Lanham, Maryland, and London
1999

SCARECROW PRESS, INC.

Published in the United States of America
by Scarecrow Press, Inc.
4720 Boston Way
Lanham, Maryland 20706

4 Pleydell Gardens, Folkestone
Kent CT20 2DN, England

British Library Cataloguing in Publication Information Available

Library of Congress Cataloging-in-Publication Data

Danly, Linda.
    Hugo Friedhofer : the best years of his life : a Hollywood master of
music for the movies / Linda Danly.
      p.  cm. — (Filmmakers series ; no. 66)
    ISBN 0-8108-3582-7 (cloth : alk. paper)
    1. Friedhofer, Hugo.  2. Composers—United States—Biography.
  3. Motion picture music—United States—History and criticism.
I. Title  II.  Series.
ML410.F87D36   1999                            98-50959
781.5′42′092—dc21                           CIP
[B]                                               MN

To the memory
of Tony Thomas

# Contents

*Acknowledgments*     xi

1   Introduction by Tony Thomas     1

2   A Portrait of Hugo Friedhofer by Linda Danly     3

3   AFI Oral History (interview by Irene Kahn Atkins)     27

4   Correspondence with Page Cook     159

5   Epilogue by Gene Lees     175

6   In Memoriam by David Raksin     185

7   Filmography (compiled by Hugo Friedhofer, Clifford McCarty, and Tony Thomas)     189

*Index*     205

*Contributors*     211

# Acknowledgments

I wish to acknowledge members of the Friedhofer family, Karyl Gilland-Tonge, Jenifer Williams Angel, and the late Louise Friedhofer Vadetsky, who helped me piece together the character of a man I have long admired but never met. Many of the stories and quotations that follow are from these three bright and interesting women to whom I owe many thanks.

My appreciation extends to Earle Hagen, Gene Lees, David Raksin, Mike Lonzo, and Bruce Babcock for their excellent interviews, to James D'Arc for his assistance at Brigham Young University, and to Lance Bowling, Jon Burlingame, Pete Candoli, Betty Bennett Lowe, and Ned Comstock for their kind assistance.

For portions of my research for this book, I want to thank A. Scott Berg for his superb biographies, *Goldwyn* (Ballantine Books) and *Directed by William Wyler* (a PBS documentary for the *American Masters* series). I'd also like to thank J. S. Lasher for the program notes to his Entr'acte soundtrack recording of *The Best Years of Our Lives*.

For permission to publish an abridged version of Hugo Friedhofer's oral history, taken by the late Irene Kahn Atkins, I wish to thank Jean Firstenberg, director of the American Film Institute.

And lastly, my heartfelt thanks go to my good friend and mentor Tony Thomas, who suggested this book and helped me stay on course. Tony died unexpectedly on July 8, 1997, shortly after the book was completed. I greatly miss my friend of twenty years, our weekly luncheons, and our endless discussions. I feel honored to have worked with the man who did so much to bring film music out of the background and into the foreground of public awareness.

· 1 ·

# Introduction

## by Tony Thomas

$\mathcal{O}$f all the composers I have known, the only one I would describe as diffident was Hugo Friedhofer. Composers, especially successful film composers, tend to be people of considerable confidence, as well they might be. What they do calls for talent, skill, and intelligence well beyond the norm. Friedhofer had every reason to be confident because he had all these qualities in abundance. Yet, he seemed ill at ease when praised, particularly when it was pointed out to him that he was the composer all the others considered their superior. It was not a case of being modest. Friedhofer was aware of his ability, and certainly aware of the ability of others; indeed, he was a most critical assessor. He simply felt that he should have been better than he was, that the industry in which he worked should have been far, far better in terms of its product and its ethics, and that the world itself left a lot to be desired. In short, Hugo was a curmudgeon, albeit a rather warm and kindly one. Such a viewpoint would, of course, have caused him to snort with disgust.

Hugo is long gone, but what is not gone is his work, his music, and the influence it has on anyone interested in the art and craft of film scoring. He truly was a master. His whole output can be viewed as a course in film composition. Nothing that he wrote is out of date and his techniques are as valid now as ever. He had, whether he cared to admit it or not, a perfect understanding of the function of music in film, how it should be used and how it shouldn't, where it can be of value and where it isn't, and how music can add a comment to film that no other contribution can. He knew about the inventiveness of film composition, the need for understanding of drama; he knew

1

about the curiosity it takes to find the right way to marry sight and sound; and he knew that there was no end to musical education. Perhaps it was the fact that Hugo knew so much that caused him to be modest. Or as he once put it, "No matter how much you know, it isn't enough."

For any student of film music, the career of Hugo Friedhofer makes for a perfect case study. He came to film at the start of the sound era and he grew up with the industry. He was there at the time of pioneering and he was there all through the years when film scoring developed into an art. And if it is an art, then Friedhofer had something to do with it being so. He was a remarkable composer and an extraordinary man.

# ·2·

# A Portrait of Hugo Friedhofer

## by Linda Danly

𝓗ugo Friedhofer was an American composer who devoted his immense talent to writing music for films. With his arrival in Hollywood in 1929, he helped forge a new creative form, that of composing music specifically and effectively for motion pictures. He worked among the best musicians Hollywood has ever offered to the collaborative art of the motion picture, yet the name Hugo Friedhofer is often less recognized than Max Steiner, Alfred Newman, Erich Wolfgang Korngold, Franz Waxman, Victor Young, Bernard Herrmann, and other contemporaries in his field. Why is this? Perhaps because he worked as an unsung arranger and orchestrator for the first fourteen years of his Hollywood career. Perhaps because he didn't always get the biggest and best pictures to score. Or possibly because it was against his nature to promote himself.

Among his peers, Friedhofer was recognized as exceptional, "the most learned of us all and often the most subtle," according to his friend David Raksin. Hugo was unequaled in his musical knowledge. He could quote musical works ranging from the most obscure chamber piece to the latest jazz arrangement. He was the composer other composers looked to for answers. Henry Mancini wrote, "An affirmative nod from the man is worth more than all of the trinkets bestowed by the film industry."

Hugo's colleagues loved him, not only for his musicianship but for himself. They enjoyed his lively mind, his humor, and his wit. Yet Friedhofer rarely sought company. He was a loner and, like the well-respected Badger in *The Wind in the Willows*, "he simply hated Society." Hugo could be the gentlest and most generous of men, yet an

3

irascible pessimist whose cynical view of life came not from a mean spirit but from an impatience with the stupidity of mortals. His somewhat gruff exterior belied a very passionate and romantic heart. And though he professed atheism, he could not deny the divine music that poured from his disowned soul.

## THE EARLY YEARS

When Hugo was a child he was given two dachshunds. People would see the boy with his pets and say, "What adorable little dogs. What are their names?" Hugo had a habit of putting his hands into his trouser pockets and taking a stance with his feet apart. He'd look up and reply, "Why, Castor and Pollux, of course, the Heavenly Twins."

Hugo Friedhofer was an individualist. He was his own man by the time he could walk. Driven by an inquisitive intellect and a consuming passion for the arts, he sought to learn everything he could, and retained it all by way of an extraordinary, near-photographic mind.

The Friedhofers were, for generations, strong-willed, educated Germans, making their livelihoods in the arts and sciences. Hugo's grandfather, Friedrich Friedhofer, studied to be a doctor in Heidelberg when political revolution broke out in 1848. Leaving medical school and his native Germany, Friedrich traveled to parts of Europe, then on to America. He crossed the rugged country in a covered wagon and settled in San Francisco. A big, robust man of many skills, he set up shop as a blacksmith, wheelwright, carriage maker, and veterinarian. He married a German musician, a pianist he knew from the Conservatory in Mannheim. They had four sons and one daughter. The youngest of the boys was Hugo's father, Paul Mathias Friedhofer, born November 17, 1872.

Paul and his brothers were sent to Europe for their education. The older sons went into medicine and engineering. Paul, who loved music, studied the cello in Dresden, Germany, for ten years. When he returned to America, he briefly joined the orchestra of the French Opera in New Orleans, then moved back to San Francisco and, like his father, married a musician he had met in Germany. Her name was Eva Koenig. Her father and brothers were professional violinists and Eva, a talented singer and pianist, studied at the Conservatory in Dresden. When she married Paul, she left her dreams of an operatic career behind and moved to America. Paul and Eva had their first and only child, born in San Francisco on May 3, 1901, Hugo Wilhelm Friedhofer.

Soon after Hugo was born, relations between Paul and Eva became strained. Deciding they could not afford another child, Eva withdrew from her husband. She turned her affections toward Hugo, becoming very possessive of him. As tensions mounted, the couple separated. Eva took Hugo to Germany for several months in 1906, just missing the great San Francisco earthquake. Paul moved to Los Angeles and joined the orchestra at the Orpheum Theater. Three years later Paul returned for a reconciliation but it didn't last. They divorced about the time Hugo entered high school, and Paul remarried. His second wife, Elise, was a musician. They had a daughter, Louise, who became a cellist.

Hugo spent most of his youth alone. Growing up, he had one or two close friends but generally kept to himself. Even at large family gatherings, Hugo was conspicuously absent. He was in his room doing homework or reading poetry, studying music, art, and literature. He spent hours in the public library or browsing secondhand bookstores. At home, he loved to listen to his mother sing and play the piano. He sat and listened for hours, deeply moved by her music.

Hugo began cello lessons with his father at age thirteen, but it was art that Hugo chose as his major when he enrolled at Polytechnic High School. With a talent for drawing, he joined the art staff and contributed illustrations to the school yearbook. He excelled in English composition and played the cello in the school orchestra. Then, suddenly, in 1917, Hugo dropped out of school. The world was at war and Hugo associated with a group of pacifists at Polytech who quit school in protest over the forced resignation of an English teacher condemned for radical, antiwar beliefs.

Hugo found work doing odd jobs at the Schmidt Lithograph Company in San Francisco while studying art at night at the Mark Hopkins Institute. Within a couple of years, his interest in an art career faded and Hugo threw himself full time into music. He took cello lessons at Berkeley, and studied composition with the Italian composer Dominico Brescia.

Brescia had been a fellow student of Respighi in Italy. He joined the faculty at Mills College and later became head of the music department. Hugo learned the works of all the great masters, tucking them away in his incomparable memory. One time, after listening to a piece by Purcell, he was greatly affected. "My God," he lamented, "after Purcell, music got worse as time went on." He engrossed himself in the orchestration techniques of Debussy, Ravel, Respighi, and Berlioz. Hugo was nineteen when his skill as a cellist won him a chair with the People's Symphony Orchestra, a rival of the San Francisco Symphony Orchestra. As a cellist, he discovered the advantage of sitting in the middle of the orchestra, where he could hear what the other instruments were doing around him. This fascinated him.

It was also at age nineteen that Hugo got married. He was introduced to a professional concert pianist named Elizabeth Barrett, who performed with a rare and beautiful touch. They played sonatas together. Infatuated, Hugo spoke to his father about her. "I'm going to marry that girl," he said. "She plays such beautiful Debussy." When Eva learned of this, she was firmly against the marriage. She disapproved of the fact that Elizabeth was six years older than her son and bluntly accused her of robbing the cradle. Hugo and Elizabeth eloped on a Friday the 13th, in 1920.

For the next few years the young couple enjoyed a Bohemian life together, playing music and getting by on a musician's salary. Their first daughter, Erica, was born on February 26, 1923. Hugo worked in various theater orchestras, playing for silent films and stage shows between features. He began writing arrangements and eventually went to work downtown at the opulent Granada Theater, where he wrote occasional incidental music. Performing gave way to composing and arranging until Hugo gave up playing the cello professionally altogether by the end of the decade.

Paul, who remained in close contact with Hugo, had a tremendous respect for his son as a musician. Hugo resembled his father in many ways. They were similar in build and height. Both men were orderly and dressed meticulously. They had the same deep, rolling voice, so similar, in fact, that they were indistinguishable on the telephone. Both were witty and strong-willed. They argued vehemently at times but never held a grudge. Although Hugo described himself as apolitical, he inherited his strong social conscience from his father. Paul reportedly took a buggy whip once to a man who was beating his horse. At the end of World War I, Paul devoted several hours a week to the Musician's Union, volunteering his time every day after lunch to meet immigrants arriving in San Francisco. He learned about their backgrounds and helped them register, sometimes even bringing a newcomer home to dinner.

In 1923, Paul moved with his wife and daughter to the growing city of Los Angeles. He played in theater orchestras and concert halls for the next few years. Coming home from rehearsal one evening around 6:15, he was standing at the intersection of Sunset Boulevard and Golden Gate Avenue, his cello next to him. A drunken motorist, speeding by at 60 mph, ran him down, injuring him so badly that he died the following morning at White Memorial Hospital. A colleague, C. L. Bagley, wrote an obituary in the L.A. Local 47 Musician's Union newsletter stating, Paul Mathias Friedhofer, who died September 27, 1927, "had lived 54 years, 10 months and 10 days . . . Brother Friedhofer was a good man, a splendid musician, and had been my personal friend for many years. His passing has been a shock to everyone who knew him."

Six days after the funeral, *The Jazz Singer* premiered at the Warner Theater in New York. Silent pictures had come to an end. Musicians were dismissed from theaters across America. And in San Francisco, twenty-six-year-old Hugo Friedhofer was out of work.

## HOLLYWOOD

Hollywood boomed with the arrival of sound in motion pictures. Enormous sound stages were built on studio lots. Music departments recruited composers, arrangers, and orchestrators from musical theaters and cities across America and overseas. Hugo's friend, violinist George Lipschultz, left San Francisco to become a musical director at the Fox Studio in Los Angeles. He wired Hugo to tell him the studio was looking for an arranger. Hugo applied for the job, got hired, and moved to Los Angeles in the summer of 1929.

For a while the Friedhofers moved in with Hugo's mother-in-law, Libby, who ran a boarding house just above Sunset in the Silver Lake district. Elizabeth's sister had a daughter about the same age as Erica named Jenifer. Jenifer came to the boarding house for extended visits and became Erica's best friend, and, in later years, Hugo's cherished pen pal. Jenifer can remember afternoons when her uncle would be at the Everett grand piano in the parlor working on composition lessons for his teacher Ernst Toch, or sitting at the table copying music. Libby, "tough as old boots," kept the boarders out of there while he worked. Hugo's second daughter, Karyl, was born that autumn on November 13, 1929. The following year Hugo was making enough money to build a house in Glendale and move his family to 854 Kenneth Road by the end of the year.

Karyl remembers a warm and balmy quality to the house. Part brick and part stucco, it had a nice pitch roof and a bay window with leaded glass. The house was surrounded by walnut and sycamore trees and looked out on the San Fernando foothills. A badminton court was set up in the backyard, where Hugo—a fanatic for the game—played competitively with his daughters. He didn't do any work around the house with the exception of helping his wife construct a formal rose garden.

Hugo's day began as he shuffled heavily into the kitchen. "Coffee!" he'd gasp in his deep voice as he headed for the percolator. He loved the Charles Addams cartoons in the *New Yorker* and could be heard chuckling to himself as he took his coffee into the living room and sat down with his magazine. His opinions on anything (particularly music) could be summed up efficiently in one of two words: "Jesus!" when he was impressed and "Stinks!" when he was unimpressed. His tastes in literature and art were broad. He had an abiding love of Shakespeare and treasured the works of the Brontës, Edna St. Vincent Millay, A. A. Milne, Lewis Carroll, Wallace Stevens, William Carlos Williams, Balzac, Anatole France, James Joyce, Charles Lamb, and e.e. cummings, saying, "I can get as high on cummings as I can on alcohol." He collected paintings from the Pomona School by Millard Sheets, Milfred Zorn, Paul Landacre, and Thomas Craig. For his own amusement, he sketched a little and wrote witty and sometimes bawdy limericks. He admired the letters of Robert Louis Stevenson and became an accomplished letter-writer in his own right.

Whether or not he went to the studio that day, he bathed, dressed, and got ready for work. He wore an expensive aftershave and favored a brown suede jerkin vest, well fitted over a clean shirt and wool trousers. He bought Bally shoes, which he kept in shoe bags, neatly lined up on his closet shelf. Hugo was extremely fastidious, everything in its place. He drove to work in a 1932 Ford V8. (A decade later, he drove a Chrysler convertible, bashed in on one side—he was known to fall asleep at the wheel.) In the evenings, he would often invite string players to come over and play chamber music with him. The music of Beethoven, Bach, Schubert, and Brahms, gloriously performed by professional musicians, filled the house. Members of the Hollywood String Quartet, namely Felix Slatkin, his cellist wife, Elinor Aller Slatkin, and pianist Victor Aller were frequent visitors to the Friedhofer home, as were Ira Gershwin and Oscar Levant, who entertained the children with piano pranks.

A studio was built in back for Hugo, where he worked when he was at home. On occasion when Erica and Karyl were playing too loudly, the studio door would fly open, Hugo would thunder at them to be quiet, and then he would shut the door. Under the pressure of studio deadlines, Hugo frequently worked there through the night. He sat on a piano stool, leaning over his music, poorly illuminated from a goose-neck lamp. The ashtray was filled to overflowing with unfiltered Camel cigarette butts. Elizabeth would come in with hot towels she had prepared to put over Hugo's aching shoulders.

The studio was Hugo's domain. Sometimes when her father had left for the day, Karyl would go inside to read. There was a smell of manuscript paper, leather and tobacco, and her father's own attractive scent. The room was orderly. Thirty or more Venus pencils were sharpened and in their holder, ready for work. Stacks of music and score paper were about the room. He had a black, Steinway upright, later to become hers, bearing a deep scar to the left of the keys where years of unattended cigarettes had burned into the wood. Sitting quietly in his studio, Karyl could feel close to her father.

Hugo was not by definition a family man. He was married to his music. He never took his daughters to the studios even though Warner Bros. was only twenty minutes down the road. When he did take time for his family, it was usually on holidays. His favorite was the 4th of July. He set off firecrackers and rockets in tin cans with the glee of a naughty child. He also loved Christmas. During a time when families were struggling everywhere in Depression-era America, Hugo provided well for the Friedhofers. His girls had kittens and puppies, dancing lessons, and summers in the mountains. He was always gentle with them, but it was hard for him to relate to them. His world was music. It was his religion and he devoted himself to it.

Hugo worked at Fox for five years, arranging, orchestrating, and writing occasional cues. When Fox merged with Twentieth Century Pictures in 1935, Hugo was fired along with most of the music department in a general housecleaning. The same year, Warner Bros. signed the most prestigious composer to date, the Viennese opera and concert composer Erich Wolfgang Korngold. Korngold was about to score his first motion picture, *Captain Blood*, when his assistant recommended Hugo Friedhofer as a choice for orchestrator. Friedhofer could speak fluent German and that may have been what launched their long association. But Friedhofer's work so impressed Korngold that he chose him as principal orchestrator on most of his sixteen scores.

Max Steiner also came to Warner Bros. in 1935 after seven years with RKO, and Hugo orchestrated Steiner's first Warner film, *The Charge of the Light Brigade*. He orchestrated over fifty films for Max. The head of the music department at Warner Bros., Leo Forbstein, knew he had a good thing in Hugo, and for eight years kept him orchestrating for his two most valuable composers, never offering him a job as principal composer. Between features at Warner, Hugo's time was his own and he would pick up work at the other studios, primarily at Twentieth Century Fox, where he orchestrated for composer Alfred Newman, head of the music department from 1940 to 1960.

It was Al Newman who gave Hugo his first opportunity to score a film by recommending him to Sam Goldwyn for *The Adventures of Marco Polo* (1937), starring Gary Cooper. The score was a success, but it did not sway Forbstein to offer any features to Friedhofer. Finally, in 1943, Hugo chose to leave Warner Bros. to go to Fox, where Newman offered him steady work as a composer. In the next three years he scored fifteen films, winning an Academy Award nomination for *The Woman in the Window* (RKO, 1944). Hugo, who had been in Hollywood for sixteen years, was finally receiving recognition as a composer. His days and nights were mostly devoted to his work. His friends were other composers and people he knew from the studios.

Life at home, however, became increasingly remote, and Hugo announced to Elizabeth that he wanted a divorce. He had fallen in love with a woman he met in Hollywood, a fashion model and designer. She was called "Ginda," a nickname for Virginia. Hugo got his divorce and married Ginda. Elizabeth stayed in Southern California for a few years, living in North Hollywood, then moved back to San Francisco, where Karyl finished high school. Erica married and stayed in Los Angeles with her husband and two sons. Thereafter, whether by guilt or by pressure to honor a new allegiance, Hugo had little contact with his daughters. In 1954 Erica went to the doctor with what she thought was the flu. It turned out she had leukemia. Erica held on for a year and died in September 1955 at the age of thirty-two. Hugo never got over the grief and he lived with guilt for the rest of his life.

Friedhofer's family life ended about the time his composing career was taking off. He was about to embark on a project that would launch him into the Hollywood spotlight, William Wyler's blockbuster film about three returning World War II veterans, *The Best Years of Our Lives*.

*The Best Years of Our Lives* opened at the Astor Theater in New York on November 22, 1946, and in Los Angeles at the Beverly Theater during Christmas week. Audiences and reviewers were elated. *Variety* called it "one of the best pictures of our lives." The *New York Times* stated that the film "sets the highest standards of cinematic quality and meets them triumphantly." Among the many telegrams sent to producer Sam Goldwyn, he most cherished the one from his daughter that read, "I HAVE JUST SHED THE BEST TEARS OF MY LIFE, YOUR LOVING AND VERY PROUD DAUGHTER, RUTH."

Within a year the film became the second highest money-maker in Hollywood history, second only to *Gone with the Wind*. It won the New York film critics' best picture of the year award, the British Academy's award for best foreign or domestic picture, several international awards, and seven Academy Awards: Best Picture, Best Screenplay (Robert Sherwood), Best Actor (Fredric March), Best Supporting Actor (Harold Russell), Best Editing (Danny Mandell), Best Director (William Wyler), and Best Scoring of a Dramatic Picture. Lana Turner announced the winner in that category, Hugo Friedhofer.

Music critics and fellow composers praised Friedhofer's score. Excerpts were published in *Film Music Notes* along with a lengthy analysis by music critic Louis Applebaum. He wrote, "The Academy Award for a dramatic musical score was bestowed in 1947 on a work about whose merit there can be no question. Not always does this recognition fall on the most deserving of the year's efforts—nor does it always reflect studied judgment and unbiased critical reflection. Film fans, students, and critics can find no quarrel with the fact that Sam Goldwyn's and William Wyler's *The Best Years of Our Lives* swept off most of the important Academy prizes, and those interested in film music can be especially happy that Hugo Friedhofer's remarkable score for that film was included in the sweep."

Composer Lan Adomian wrote "An Appreciation," which was published in the February–March 1947 issue of *Film Music Notes* a month before Friedhofer won the Oscar: "Any composer charged with the great responsibility of supplying a score for so important a human document as *The Best Years of Our Lives* would have to approach his task with the same honesty of purpose, with the same seriousness as did the writer, director, actors, and all concerned with the making of this film . . . The story of three returning veterans is uncommonly warm and human . . . Such a story calls for a composer whose sensitivity will infuse the film with a poetic feeling which is only implied by the action. Mr. Friedhofer's score abundantly demonstrates that his talents and richly varied skills were equal to the responsibilities imposed by this film.

"Given the enormous technical equipment of Mr. Friedhofer, many another composer would have trotted out the bag of orchestral tricks that are the hallmark of most film scores today. 'Passionate' sweeps and harp glissandos, harmonics, celesta, and the whole paraphernalia of 'impressionistic' and 'mood music' would have cluttered up the score—thus making it another slick job in complete disregard for the basic quality of the film. One searches in vain to find these tricks in the score of *The Best Years of Our Lives*."

The subject of adjusting to civilian life after the war was one in which director William Wyler took a personal interest. Lieutenant Colonel Wyler served his country by making wartime documentaries about fighter pilots and the perils of flying bombing missions. On one of his filming excursions involving a one-seat fighter plane, he operated the camera himself. The engine noises and blasting winds caused him to lose hearing in both ears. He was sent to several hospitals for treatment. In time, he recovered only partial hearing in his left ear. Afraid he would never direct again, he remained depressed for months. His spirits were restored when a sound engineer rigged up a device for the director to hear dialogue on the set. However, Wyler was literally tone deaf and was never really able to appreciate music.

When it came time to call in a composer, Sam Goldwyn consulted his former musical director, Alfred Newman, for advice. Newman suggested Hugo Friedhofer and meetings were set up between director and composer. Wyler and Friedhofer discussed every aspect of the score, deciding it should have a homey, Americana feel to it in the style of Aaron Copland. The score was recorded and everyone was satisfied with it except Wyler. He felt it was all wrong (just as some years later he would consider Jerome Moross's score for *The Big Country* all wrong). He had no confidence in the score until a former army buddy of Wyler praised the music. The Oscar sealed his faith.

Film music critics and musicologists recognize "The Best Years of Our Lives" as one of the outstanding scores in American film. Several scenes have become textbook examples of what music can do for a film, including the "catharsis scene" where former bombardier Fred Derry (Dana Andrews) climbs into the nose of a junked plane and relives the nightmare of a bombing mission, and the moving "homecoming" scene when Seaman Homer Parrish, whose hands were burned off in a submarine fire, is reunited with his family. Producer-director Billy Wilder considered *Best Years* the best-directed film he had ever seen. "The picture started and three minutes later I was dissolved in tears," he said, "and I cried for two hours plus after that. And I'm not a pushover, believe me. I laugh at *Hamlet*." Hugo's score had more than a little to do with eliciting such a reaction.

The following year Friedhofer was nominated by the Academy for his score to another Goldwyn picture, *The Bishop's Wife*, and the next year for RKO's *Joan of Arc*. He scored only two films in 1949 and then entered the busiest decade of his career in feature films, working for ten different studios, composing over forty film scores. Five of them were nominated for an Academy Award, making a total of nine:

| | |
|---|---|
| 1944 | The Woman in the Window |
| 1946 | The Best Years of Our Lives |
| 1947 | The Bishop's Wife |
| 1948 | Joan of Arc |
| 1953 | Above and Beyond |
| 1956 | Between Heaven and Hell |
| 1957 | An Affair to Remember |
| | Boy on a Dolphin |
| 1958 | The Young Lions |

Friedhofer's music stood apart from much of the mainstream Hollywood sound. He explained, "As an ardent lover of chamber music, I had grown up with an economical approach to the orchestra. Not that I don't like a big, fat, healthy sound when it is called for, but I don't like it to be muddy. Even with a big sound in the orchestra, I like a certain transparency. I like the air to come through."

His harmonies drew from more contemporary sources: "David Raksin and I underwent a period of total immersion in the music of Copland, Hindemith, and Stravinsky in an effort to find our own way out of the current late nineteenth-century morass; a striving for simplicity of line, clarity of texture, and an avoidance of over-lush chromaticism. In short, something that didn't sound as if it had just gotten off the boat from Europe (no disrespect intended)."

Even with five nominations, an Oscar, and the abundant praise he received from the industry, Friedhofer, ever the self-critic, felt he had not really mastered his craft until 1954 when he scored the western *Vera Cruz*.

"My Mexican experience on 'Vera Cruz' was most beneficial," he wrote, "in that it was the first 'big' score with which I felt completely secure, having (at long last) learned how to expand my material, with minimal repetition and little (if any) padding."

As Hugo's career flourished, he was encouraged to promote his career through publicity: "I somehow got conned into putting myself in the hands of a public relations outfit, which was about as close as I ever came to 'going Hollywood,' " he confessed. "After about eighteen months of the phony garbage they were perpetuating in the name of publicity, I paid them off telling them that I much preferred the relative obscurity which I had been assiduously cultivating to the unlikely image they were trying to perpetrate."

The last notable film Friedhofer scored was Marlon Brando's *One Eyed Jacks*, released in 1960. The film, deemed too long by Paramount, was cut down to standard running time and Hugo's score was sliced, pasted, and shifted around within the film. Nevertheless, the finished product is stunning despite its flaws, and the score is considered among Friedhofer's best. The trumpet soloist on the recording session was Pete Candoli, who praised the score and added, "You should have heard what they took out! He had a thing going with four cellos, all open strings—kind of like a bagpipe—a drone, during the prison break. It was fantastic." Although the score was not nominated for an Academy Award—an oversight in the opinion of many—a long-playing record album was released and the love theme, with its uniquely beautiful melody, was a popular instrumental and received considerable radio play.

After *One Eyed Jacks*, Friedhofer's film scoring career came to a disturbing halt. He scored only six features and one documentary over the next twenty years. Times and tastes were changing radically. The studio system was breaking down. A new generation of composers was rising in popularity. Yet the '60s were not the end for Hugo. On the contrary, his life was busy and even more hectic as he threw himself into the fast-paced profession of scoring for television.

Before beginning work on *One Eyed Jacks*, Hugo scored two television pilots, *Outlaws* and *The Blue and the Grey*. The pilots sold and Hugo was requested as composer on both series. Choosing one, he went to work on *Outlaws* after finishing his ten weeks on *One Eyed Jacks*. Hugo scored the entire first season of *Outlaws,* but only half of the second, bowing out due to stress and related health problems.

For budgetary reasons, Hugo conducted the recording sessions. Conducting was an area he had previously avoided, saying, "I used to be a pit musician; I like to keep my friends." Orchestras loved to play Hugo's music, but following his direction was another matter. A colleague joked, "When Hugo came at the orchestra waving a baton, they ran screaming from the room." In time, Friedhofer's skills improved and he even enjoyed conducting. Another area of his profession in which he was equally inept was playing the piano. George Duning remarked, "If you've never heard Hugo demonstrate something on the piano, you haven't heard anything. His fingers would get all tangled up and we'd have more laughs on Hugo demonstrating a theme."

Although *Outlaws* was his first TV series, it was not his maiden voyage into television scoring. In 1953 Hugo paid a visit to Earle Hagen, former arranger and orchestrator at Fox, who had started a business with Herbert Spencer writing and packaging music for television. The film industry was in a slump and Hugo's spirits were low. It seems he had run into some trouble at Fox. Al Newman had put him on a film, and one week before the music was scheduled to go to the scoring stage, no score had been turned in and Hugo wasn't answering his telephone. To those who had worked with Hugo before, this meant he was hopelessly behind and was in hiding. Newman assigned several composers to jump in and write cues. Hugo's name was mud for a while with Al. Years later Hugo feebly punned, "Miss a couple of deadlines and you're a DEAD LION."

Earle put him to work on *The Ray Bolger Christmas Show*. Hugo also worked on various assignments for Hagen and Spencer over the years, including *The Danny Thomas Show, The Joey Bishop Show*, and *The Dick Van Dyke Show*, plus lending a hand to whatever was needed, especially during a period of time when Hagen had five shows going at once. A friendship developed that was mutually respectful and long-lasting. A year after Hugo was hired by Earle, he sent a letter of thanks to Hagen in which he wrote:

"You'll have to take my word for it being 7:30 A.M. and that I am, as a result, cold sober, not having, as yet anyway, gotten to the point of having the jug handy on the bedside table as a specific against the horror of still another day. We are well into the beginning of the second year of a fairly close association both business and social wise and one which I hope is going to continue for a good long time to come. It has been a shot in the arm for me and a welcome one for sure because around November 1953, what with the state that the business was in at that point plus the business that I had been getting from a certain quarter, which shall be nameless, my free-flowing morale was at a low ebb. The tide was way out and the beach was a litter of empty beer cans, dead starfish, and gutted clam shells. Then came *The [Ray] Bolger Christmas Show*. The rest, to coin a cliché, is history. Thanks, friend."

Hugo admired Earle's talent for arranging, and praised him with his customary wit: "it is my considered opinion that you are one of the half dozen of arrangers in this country who really knows their brass from their oboe." He also recognized Earle's gift for composition and encouraged him to stay with it, rather than "spending the rest of [his] life in dressing up other peoples' ineptitudes."

Hagen's admiration for Friedhofer began long before he hired him. In 1945, after coming out of military service, Hagen orchestrated for a composer at Columbia. Hugo was at the studio working on *The Jolson Story*. The music department had a table at a local restaurant where composers gathered frequently. Earle joined a group there one day and among them was Friedhofer. As Earle tells it:

"I didn't know Hugo. Somebody would say to him, 'Have you ever heard of an operatic composer by the name of Throckmorton Hepplewaite?' and he'd say, 'Yeah, he lived in 1526 and he wrote two operas, both of which had bad reviews . . .' and he'd go on, you know, and finally on the way back I said to George Duning, 'What's the joke with this guy that I'm not in on?' And he said, 'Well, it's no joke. Every night we go home and we look up something in *Grove's Dictionary* and try to stump him and we never can, 'cause he has total recall.' Hugo remembered everything he'd heard, said, or read since he was two, which was a hangup, because every time he put two notes down on paper, he knew where they came from. A lot of people have the impression that Hugo was a slow writer. He wasn't. He was an incredibly slow starter."

In 1965 Hugo and Earle worked on the series *I Spy*. The theme was composed by Earle and the shows were divided between the two composers by alternating weeks. They worked together on the show for three years. Sometimes Hugo would run into deadline problems, and when he did he locked the gate to his house and wouldn't pick up the telephone. Earle would call his orchestrator, Carl Brandt, and say, "We're going over the fence tonight." They would scale the wall and bail out Hugo by finishing cues for him. Pages went to the scoring stage still wet with copyist's ink. Earle forgave Hugo this sin and continued to hire him.

"Hugo had the ability that I think separates the men from the boys," says Hagen, "and that is, it's easy to make an eighty-piece orchestra sound pretty good, 'cause you can just say to somebody, 'hit a C chord' and give a down beat, and anybody can pick a note and it's going to sound pretty good with eighty men. When you're down to twelve or fourteen or ten, you've got to know what you're doing. And Hugo was absolutely a master orchestrator. He could make anything sound good. I don't think there was a better orchestrator who ever lived."

Hugo worked on a variety of TV shows through the '60s in addition to his work with Earle: *Voyage to the Bottom of the Sea, Rawhide, Lancer, The FBI,* and *My World and Welcome to It.* The hectic pace and the constant deadlines took a toll on the seasoned composer. "Lord," said Hugo, "I've seen younger men than I am who are involved with television come out at the end of a season looking like their own grandfathers." His last television score was written in 1973 for an episode of *Barnaby Jones* called "Echo of a Murder."

## THE LAST YEARS

As the country changed drastically in the '70s, so did Friedhofer's world as he knew it. The studio system was dead. The trend in film scoring was toward experimentation with electronic scores and rock and pop music, and sometimes no music at all. Alfred Newman, who had been in declining health, passed away. "When Newman died on February 17, 1970," wrote Tony Thomas, "it was—for many of us— the official parting knell of Hollywood's Golden Age." Max Steiner died the following year. Calls stopped coming in for work, with the minor exception of a film called *Von Richtofen and Brown* in 1971, which Hugo considered to be his worst score (although he later altered his opinion), and the psychosexual slasher *Private Parts* in 1972, a score he enjoyed writing even though the film was, in Hugo's words, "very sick and altogether revoltingly decadent." Hugo turned to serial music for the score. Typical of Friedhofer's unending quest for knowledge, he was studying composition in atonal and serial music with various teachers, including Milt Thomas. He incorporated these principles into his last scores.

Over the years, Hugo had been approached several times by soundtrack enthusiasts urging him to record his score to *The Best Years of Our Lives*. The score was lost or thrown out and it meant Hugo would have to reconstruct his music. He decided to take on the task in 1972 and wrote about it in a letter to his friend Charles Boyer (pen name Page Cook), a film music critic who wrote a column for *Films in Review*.

> Dear Charles,
>     I am taking off for Europe on or about the 10th of September for the purpose of settling down somewhere and getting the long-delayed "Best Years" suite out of my hair. Radio Cologne wants it as does Muir Matheson in London, and John Lasher has long been promoting the thing on this side of the water. So I've got to plant myself firmly down and try to recapture the warm, humanistic mood of 1946. And that, my friend, ain't going to be a breeze. Things have undergone a few alterations in the past quarter century, but somehow it'll get itself done. Do wish me luck, won't you?

Hugo struggled with the music for a few weeks then gave up, finding the chore impossible. Three years later he tried again and wrote to Cook: "Meanwhile, I sweat and strain over the goddamn 'Best Years' and not enjoying it at all. Mind you, I am quite aware that it's a hell of a fine score, within the context of the film, but I am torn with doubt as to its validity as music per se. At bottom it's practically monothematic and repetitious as all get-out, something one isn't particularly aware of when listening to it in the film, since the silent stretches are spaced out so that the thematic repetitions and their variants take the curse off the monotheism—practically nothing but a bunch of triads with 'wrong note' bass lines."

Somehow the music got written, orchestrated by Anthony Bremner, and turned over to producer John Lasher. Various delays prevented recording the score until years later. Hugo's career slowed down to nothing and, at the end of 1973, Hugo wrote, "It's getting to be sort of lonesome out there, but Hell! I'm by temperament, as well as by inclination, an archetypal loner."

1973 was indeed a bleak year for Hugo. In the autumn of 1972, Ginda ended their marriage, although there was no divorce. She held on to the big house on Woodrow Wilson Drive but lived in Mexico much of the time. Burdened by financial obligations, Hugo moved in for a while with composer Paul Glass in the San Fernando Valley, then rented a two-room apartment in a rather ordinary building on Bronson Avenue in Hollywood. He fell into a severe depression. In a letter dated October 15, 1973, Hugo wrote:

> My dear Charles,
>
> My abject apologies for this unwarranted silence. It is the result of an emotional and physical tailspin during the past year which necessitated a complete withdrawal from just about everything, human contact, creative activity, etc., etc., in order to find out just who and what I am and what I want to do with the all too few years remaining to me. Fortunately the clouds are lifting and life, which seemed hopeless and futile for the better part of ten months, is gradually becoming meaningful once more.

Some of Hugo's melancholia was lifted through his relationship with Jeri Southern, a well-known jazz pianist and singer who lived in the same apartment building in Hollywood. He loved going over across their "cell blocks" to listen to Jeri perform Schumann. She was his loyal and loving companion for the remainder of his life. Hugo rekindled his relationship with his daughter, Karyl, visiting and corresponding with her in Cupertino, California. He also formed warm relationships with his grandchildren. Hugo started teaching composition to students in his home, and he embarked on his extensive oral history for the American Film Institute. In addition, a Canadian lumber company hired Hugo to score a half-hour documentary about timber cutting and reforestation entitled *A Walk in the Forest*. Life picked up for the seventy-three-year-old composer, although he continued to suffer spells of depression and self-doubt.

As a teacher, Hugo was generous with his time and expertise, going well over the allotted time per student. One of Hugo's pupils, composer Bruce Babcock, claimed he got more guidance and practical instruction from Hugo than all of his years in music school. He was awed by Friedhofer's knowledge. One day Babcock brought in a twelve-tone piece he had written for clarinet, flute, and cello. They sat and looked at the piece. The first statement of the theme was in the cello. Hugo played the first three notes on the piano and said, "Well, you've selected the same three notes that Beethoven selected in one of his string quartets." He reached up and pulled the score off the book shelf, opened it to the page, and said, "but for some reason you've written yours down a tone."

Composer David Shire attended some of Hugo's seminars held in Friedhofer's living room. "The classes were suffused with Hugo's wit," he commented, citing, as an example: "A proper score for *The Hunchback of Notre Dame* should be quasi-modal." Shire also pointed to Hugo's modesty, observing that "the majority of musical examples he referred to were taken from the works of others, rather than his own."

Hugo was respectful of his students as long as they respected him. He received a letter from a young man who had never studied music but seemed impressed with his own latent talent. He asked Friedhofer to tutor him for the summer. This riled Hugo and he sounded off in a letter to Boyer: "Does this dolt believe that he is capable of absorbing, in one brief summer, what has taken me some forty-odd years of constant application to learn? This reeks of dilettantism."

In the end, Friedhofer believed it was impossible to teach anyone to compose music. He advised Earle Hagen when Hagen was just starting out as a composer: "Remember, always, that nobody in God's world can teach you how to compose. In all the history of music there isn't one composer who is not, in the final analysis, a self-taught man. True enough you can benefit from guidance (and I don't mean the kind that is handed out you-know-where); I mean to what is lying all around to be picked up free for nothing by anybody who is interested enough to avail himself of five centuries worth of the best damned kind of tuition I know."

*A Walk in the Forest* was an expensively produced public relations documentary, beautifully photographed by Michael Lonzo and narrated by actor Richard Harris. When it came time to consider a composer, Lonzo, very knowledgeable about film music, recommended Friedhofer for the job. Meeting with director Randall Hood, Friedhofer had doubts whether he could handle the project, which called for thirty minutes of wall-to-wall music. But he had three months from the finished cut to work on it, so he accepted.

When the recording date was a week away, Hugo had not finished the score. He began working around the clock and received "vitamin" shots, a concoction known to Max Steiner and other composers under tremendous pressure, consisting of vitamin B-12 and Benzedrine, to keep him going. On the morning of the recording date, the orchestra assembled at Sound Stage One at M-G-M with Carl Brandt at the podium. Hugo still had about six minutes of unfinished score to write. Mike Lonzo, who attended the session, relates what happened:

"Randy said, 'We're going to start recording and we still gotta get stuff finished—can you finish it?' Hugo said, 'Oh, yeah, I can finish it.' So Hugo was set up in a little office in the music department with a piano where he could compose. Well, by that time he was so burned out he couldn't even think straight. It was sad in a way, and I said to Randy, 'He's not going to work anymore here, this is ridiculous. Have him come over and sit in on the session.' Randy went over to the office where Hugo was behind the piano working. Hugo looked up and said, 'Be with you in a minute, Alfred!' In his mind he thought it was Alfred Newman, who must have cracked the whip at times, I guess. It was touching, really."

The score was recorded that day by a thirty-five piece orchestra. The missing six minutes were written later and, for budgetary reasons, recorded by a smaller chamber group.

*A Walk in the Forest* received over fifteen awards, including one for the music. Page Cook praised the score effusively in the December 1975 issue of *Films in Review*: "So brilliant is the music," he wrote, "so dazzling and subtle its impact, that the impulse is to write *around* the score, to avoid the superlatives it evokes. It reaches to the heart of the poetry and subject of the film, i.e., 'Man as Nature's partner': few short subject features have been graced with such music."

Cook chose it as the best film score of 1975. He added, "Fried-hofer's score for *A Walk in the Forest* is so brilliant it is a cultural crime he is not writing music for today's better films."

Hugo was called on once more by Randall Hood, who was about to produce and direct a murder psychodrama called *The Companion.* Hugo liked the script and was excited about writing the music. The limited budget required a chamber orchestra. "That means less notes," wrote Hugo, "but more thinking about the notes that I put on paper." He started work in the spring of 1976, but was slowed down after spraining his ankle coming out of a theater.

"I've been feeling much below par ever since that stupid mishap with my right foot and ankle; also the advent of still another birthday tended to depress me not a little. At age seventy-five one begins to ponder and the certain faith in one's own indestructibility gets to be a little shaky. 'The Companion' is inching along at a tired snail's pace. Nevertheless, I'm not unhappy about what's going down on the score paper . . . It's neurotic as all get-out, post-serial and polytonal without a pure consonance in a carload."

Hugo finished composing and orchestrating music for *The Companion* on June 30, 1976. (The film had distribution problems and was released years later as *Die Sister, Die.*) Randall Hood, who had been battling advanced stages of cancer, died before the recording of the score. This depressed Hugo profoundly and he admitted that, quite selfishly, he also worried about what was to become of his own career. Carl Brandt flew to London to record the music. Hugo remained in California, not feeling well enough to travel. He wrote to Boyer in August to say that Warren Barker, his music copyist, and his assistants considered the score to be his best to date. "I hope that they're correct, since it is my firm resolve to bid film music a not-so-fond farewell . . . a half-century (almost) of servicing the flicks is more than enough."

For the next few months Hugo tried writing concert music, but nothing stirred him. "Everything sounds tired and twice-told," he wrote, "and that goes for everybody else's music as well as my own pale efforts." He complained in a letter to his niece, Jenifer, that most of the new concert music he was hearing was "sterile and attenuated stuff consisting of one wind instrument (generally flute) and various percussion instruments, with little wriggly bits for harp and piano, and it all got to sound pretty much alike after a while. It's like a perpetual diet consisting of nothing but broken crockery and crystal chandeliers." He added, "A lot of the boys are still chasing up the Anton Webern alley, which in my opinion gets them nowhere. It's the same cul-de-sac in which the Debussy epigonoi found themselves some sixty years ago. Poor Claude-Achille had exhausted that particular vein and was making a determined effort to spring himself. What's more, he was succeeding—witness the three sonatas, the ballet 'Jeux' and 'En Blanc et Noir.' " Hugo attempted to write some violin duets that were not coming off. He wrote, "I'm going to roll up my sleeves, spit on my hands, and start again from scratch. Although 'Scratch' isn't le mot juste for violin duets—or is it?"

In another letter: "Composing in a vacuum isn't for me. I'm one of those unfortunates who requires the stimulation of the visual in order to get rolling. Without that incentive, everything in the way of ideas which may come to me seems utterly blah and useless."

He organized his studio. He went down to the pool and lay in the sun. Back in his apartment, he sat at his typewriter and wrote letters. "Sometimes I wonder if it was really worth the effort," he wrote to Boyer. "My striving for that which is virtually unattainable to the neglect of practically everything else has, to date, loused up two marriages and poisoned a lot of friendships . . . all of which goes to prove that the single-track mind is for the birds. But at my age it's a bit late to change. So I'm stuck with it to the bitter end."

To his niece: "I'm still hibernating and have been, ever since last July. I am totally bereft of any inclination to work, either for money or just for fun. I've had notions (purely speculative) for three or possibly four pieces of music, all of which stubbornly refuse to budge. Could be that I've lived too long and heard (let alone written) far too much. This all sounds pretty downbeat and defeatist. Not so. Like our Mr. Micawber, I've got the feeling that something's bound to turn up and the septuagenarian syndrome be damned!!! Just writing to you, my dear niece, nudges this hibernating groundhog into wakefulness."

Nothing did turn up in the way of writing assignments, and Hugo lamented: "I seem to be the totally forgotten man . . ."

By summer, Hugo was still languishing and growing concerned over money. In his letter to Boyer on August 6, 1977, he confided, "My financial situation appears slightly toward the grim side since I haven't done any work since *The Companion*. A year of idleness is a bit too much. And the worst aspect is that I really haven't felt like doing much of anything, be it writing, looking at new scores, listening to records, or going to the movies or concerts."

That was the last letter Charles received from Hugo for nearly two years. An explanation arrived, dated May 15, 1979: "It has been forced upon me by illness in the form of a partial paralysis, which has kept me hospitalized, immobilized, bed-ridden, unable to read, write, walk, talk, or think straight for more than five minutes at a time. Recovery has been slow and painful, and the bad days outweigh the good by a considerable number."

That year, the long-awaited recording of "The Best Years of Our Lives" was released by John Lasher on his label, Entr'acte, in honor of Friedhofer's fifty years in Hollywood. The album contained a seven-inch bonus disc with a tribute to the composer, written by Gene Lees, spoken by actor Richard Hatch, plus a souvenir booklet with extensive score analyses by Louis Applebaum and Royal S. Brown. Page Cook contributed a summary and biography, and no less than ten composers paid their respects to their beloved colleague through loving and humorous tributes. Hugo was very pleased with the finished product and the brilliant performance of his music by the London Philharmonic, conducted by Frank Collura. A dinner party was given in Hugo's honor, celebrating his seventy-eighth birthday and the release of the album. The film critic Arthur Knight was invited and wrote about it in *The Hollywood Reporter*.

"It was one of those evenings when you just wished you had a tape recorder going. Guests included John Green, Bronislau Kaper, Henry Mancini, Alex North, David Raksin, Lalo Schifrin, and David Shire—all there to honor Friedhofer, not as part of some fraternal or institutional organization, but because they honestly like and admire the man (as do I)."

Among the many accolades was this one from composer John Green, head of the M-G-M music department: "Korngold, Steiner, Herrmann, Newman, Waxman are but five of the many significant names among the roster of those who have contributed in major ways to the development of film music in America as a genuine art form. But there is one composer's name that has a peculiarly 'institutional' quality about it . . . Friedhofer. He is, somehow, different from all the rest; he is unique, in many ways a phenomenon. A remarkably gifted creator, a super musical craftsman, the arch enemy of excess, a master of good taste and restraint, equally blest by an unerring sense of dra-

matic values, most particularly as they pertain to the delicate relationship between music and filmed drama. His humor, his wit, his dedica-
tion to truth, his merciless decimation of sham and pretense have all
been thoroughly explored by others. Mine but to salute him as a peer
among peers, and to be grateful that his magnificent talent has graced
a profession to which several of our most admired and respected colleagues have dedicated their professional lives."

Bronislau Kaper honored him with these words: "When you say
'Hugo,' nobody will ever ask you, 'Which Hugo?' If you say 'Hugo
Friedhofer,' people will look at you as if you were a tourist. Hugo is
unique and individual, both as a musician and as a personality . . .
Here is a man with a fantastic background in any category of music,
be it so-called classical, romantic, post-romantic, impressionistic, contemporary, popular, jazz, film, or stage. But he never tries to impress
anybody with his knowledge. This is taken for granted. He would
rather tell some exquisite anecdotes about music and musicians, and
he does it with this charming twinkle in his eyes, which is a characteristic part of his personality. I am sure I will never meet another Hugo,
and to tell you the truth—I don't want to. Stay well, dear friend! We
love you and your music."

In the spring of 1981, Hugo knew he was dying. He had fallen
and broken his hip in his apartment and was failing quickly during his
stay in the hospital. His lungs were diseased from sixty years of heavy
cigarette smoking. Unable to write any longer, he telephoned his
niece. Hugo was lucid and calm and stayed on the phone reminiscing
with her for nearly two hours. He told her, "I've had such a good
life." Jenifer knew this telephone call was his farewell to her.

Both Karyl and Jenifer believe that Hugo willed himself to die as
his mother had done when she was in her nineties. Eva had been
blind for twenty years and decided she had had enough. She made
appointments with everyone dear to her and said her goodbyes, then
she stopped drinking water and died. Hugo's death took place in the
early morning hours of Sunday, May 17, 1981, two weeks after his
eightieth birthday.

# ·*3*·

# The American Film Institute's Hugo Friedhofer Oral History

*interview conducted by Irene Kahn Atkins*
*edited by Tony Thomas*
*and Linda Danly*

$\mathscr{I}$rene Kahn Atkins, daughter of famous lyricist Gus Kahn, grew up among celebrated musicians. George Gershwin, Harry Warren, and Richard Whiting were frequent guests and collaborators in the Kahn apartment in Chicago during the 1920s. Irene's family moved to Hollywood in 1933, where her father wrote songs for the movies, primarily at M-G-M until his death in 1941. Irene's interest in music led her to studies in theory and composition, and work as a music and sound editor at RKO and Paramount. She regarded Hollywood in the '30s and '40s as a unique period in film music history, a period she experienced firsthand as she frequently "ditched school" to spend days on the colorful sound stages where her father worked. In her efforts to document those days, she interviewed several composers and writers, creating extensive oral histories sponsored by the American Film Institute. She interviewed Hugo Friedhofer in 1974. There were eleven meetings spread over a period of six weeks, from March 13 to April 29. In Ms. Atkins's words:

> "All of the interviews were conducted at Mr. Friedhofer's home, usually starting at about ten in the morning, and always with my host providing a cup of coffee to get things going. Most of the sessions lasted about one and a half hours, but occasionally the energetic and enthusiastic Mr. Friedhofer continued for about two

hours without fatigue. I think we both enjoyed the interviews; certainly Mr. Friedhofer was a most cooperative and informative oral history subject."

What follows is an abridged version of the original oral history, which runs over four hundred pages. It is available for reading in its entirety by contacting the American Film Institute in Hollywood, California.

## ORAL HISTORY

ATKINS: I understand both your parents were professional musicians.

FRIEDHOFER: True. They were. My father was a cellist. My mother played piano and sang. She had a beautiful alto voice, and did a lot of recital work, things like that, around the northern part of the state—East Bay, California. And I think that the reason I fought shy of music for so many years was that in my youth it had such a tremendous emotional effect on me that I just couldn't bear it. I remember at night, when I was a wee one, after I went to bed my mother would play the piano in the living room in the flat where we lived. And certain things I can't hear today without suddenly doing a complete throwback in time. She was, of course, a complete romantic. It was Schubert and Schumann and Chopin and some Beethoven, and the rest of it, you know. But sooner or later the pull toward music got too great. And I had the unfortunate thing happen to me, in that there was a state law to the effect that you had to write with your right hand, regardless of whether you were left-handed or right-handed.

ATKINS: An actual law?

FRIEDHOFER: Actually. Sure. The old superstition about left-handedness—if you were left-handed, there was something odd. As a matter of fact, the Latin word, as you know, sinister, which means left-handed, right away has, you might say, sinister implications. But that made for a certain awkwardness in playing a stringed instrument. My left-hand technique was fine, but I always had a certain difficulty with my bow arm, for a long time. And then, besides, I was interested in other things, as a child, you know. And my father was not the most patient man in the world. Actually, it wasn't until I got into high school, and was sort of drafted into the high school orchestra, that I began to take a real interest in anything musical. I know that at that time I started going to symphony concerts with my mother, and immediately a whole new world opened up to me, and I began to take it rather seriously. My mother and father were divorced by that time. He was in New York for a while, and when he came back, I really started to work very hard with him. In about three years time, I was able to work professionally. And that was the beginning of my contact with films.

By the time I got into the business, practically every motion picture theater had small orchestras. They were about the size of the average vaudeville orchestra. I was very fortunate in my first actual position with one of these orchestras, in working with a very fine man by the name of Maurice Lawrence. He later went to work for Paramount, in the thirties. Maurice had a vast library, and we used to change programs about three times a week, and that meant covering an awful lot of music. It wound up with my becoming, if I do say so myself, with undue immodesty, a pretty good sight reader. I also cultivated a memory at that time, in that once I played a show, I used to sit there and watch the film—which naturally is a source of great annoyance to—no, but I think I managed to get by without too many reproaches.

ATKINS: What was the theater?

FRIEDHOFER: The first theater—what the devil was the name of it? I know it was on Polk Street, in the Polk-Larkin district. Then I moved out after that, into another one out in what much later became the center of the hippie kingdom, the Haight-Ashbury district, where I lived as a boy when I was in school. From there, where did I go? Oh, there was a theater over in the Mission District where I worked also, at the Castro. By that time, I had begun studying composition, orchestration, and what not, and I began making arrangements for Oliver Alberti and our little combo at the Castro Theater. Oliver sort of gave me a big push in the right direction and I ultimately wound up at the Granada, one of the bigger palaces downtown, the first theater that had a hydraulic platform on the stage. It was a stage and pit band combination.

ATKINS: Did the orchestra play for the silent film and then play for the stage show, too?

FRIEDHOFER: Yes. We had brass men and reed men who played legit, and they played saxophone, and they all doubled. We had, I think, four violins, one of whom doubled on viola, fortunately for me, and cello, which was yours truly, and a bass player, who also doubled tuba, on the stage. Let's see: the combination was two or three trumpets, two trombones, two horns, tuba, four saxes—all of them doubled woodwind—and, as I say, this kind of poverty-stricken string section. And we also had, strangely enough, two pianos.

The house leader at the time was a very fine musician by the name of Andrea Setaro. He was very much interested in what I was doing in the way of writing. I made my first stage band arrangements for Andrea. Then, later on, a picture would come up for which he couldn't find exactly what he wanted, so he'd say, "Look, could you write something to cover such and such a scene?" So I did. So, actually I was writing for silent pictures before I ever got into the sound end of it. At that time, I was beginning, in the course of my studies, to get extremely interested in what happens with the orchestra. My teacher, Dominico Brescia, recommended that I take this position, because, he said, "If you can learn to write effectively for a combination of eighteen or twenty men, you'll have no problems, and thereafter have no problems." And it turned out that he was right. Which was of great value to me. He was a fine gentleman. He had sort of a Renaissance profile, a very handsome man to look at. He was thorough, and progressive in his ideas. I owe a great deal to him.

ATKINS: You certainly had an opportunity that a lot of students of composition don't have, that is, being able to hear what you're writing.

FRIEDHOFER: True. And if you made a mistake, you either knew how to correct it instantaneously, or else you never made it again—because to goof off on an orchestration or a cue or a scene in a picture is kind of an unpardonable sin.

ATKINS: It sounds as if the orchestra in a silent movie house was awfully busy. When did you have time to rest?

FRIEDHOFER: Well, you must remember that there was always a theater organist who worked on shifts. We generally did four stage shows a day, and five on Saturdays and Sundays. And then we played a certain amount in the pit, and then the relief organist would take over. There was a long break after the afternoon stage show of about two hours. Then we came back in and did the first night show, and then went into the pit and did part of the feature. Then the organist took over again and we had a short break before going on the stage for the last stage show. That was the end of it for us. We were generally out of the theater by ten o'clock.

We had a drummer who lived across the bay from San Francisco, in Oakland. He used to very carefully cut himself a hole in the scenery, hidden by the drums, of course, so that he could sneak out the minute the curtain came down and catch his street car to get down to the ferry building and across the bay. Some of the guys in the band used to take great delight in trying to hold him up and make him miss his boat. It was kind of a dirty practical joke, but you know, fun-loving musicians. It was a wild scene at times because that was, of course, right in the middle of the Prohibition era. We had, I think, two bootleggers in the band and one regular who used to come around with so-called gin, still warm from the bathtub. I can still remember this chap. He wore a double-breasted suit always, with pockets on the inside where these square bottles of Gordon's Gin were stored. Oh, it was wild sometimes. But I survived it somehow.

ATKINS: It seems as if you did.

FRIEDHOFER: With the advent of sound, in 1927, all the theater orchestras were little by little dismissed. So I was sort of living hand to mouth for a long time, what with playing all kinds of casual engagements, and I had a hotel job for a while. I coined a phrase for that kind of music, which Lawrence Morton later appropriated: "potted palm music," which has become the standard for the little trios and quartets that play in hotel lobbies at tea time and at dinner time. There I made the acquaintance of another man who was of great assistance to me, a man by the name of George Lipschultz. He was a very fine violinist and he got this offer to come down to the old Fox Studio here and become a musical director. George came down and I sort of hung around San Francisco for awhile longer. I suddenly got this wire from George. He said, "Come on down. They need another arranger." So I don't know what prompted my ultimate decision, but I came down and went to work for Fox.

ATKINS: What was Hollywood like when you arrived here?

FRIEDHOFER: Well, all the activity was down on Hollywood Boulevard, not the kind of activity that we have now, certainly. I used to commute. The first year I was down here, I lived with my at that time mother-in-law, around Silver Lake. I used to commute, on the big red cars, out to what was known as Fox Hills. Now it's West Los Angeles. I worked at the studio there. I don't remember much about it actually, except that it certainly has changed. Well, good Lord, the biggest building in Beverly Hills at that time was the Beverly Wilshire Hotel, which had just gone up. And it was a sleepy little community, which ended there. And beyond that, it was grain fields and small houses and very little going on, except for this new studio, which had originally been Tom Mix's horse ranch. Most of it is now the site of Century City.

ATKINS: Were they also using the Fox Western Avenue Studio?

FRIEDHOFER: That's now a thing of the past. Yes, they were still using that, but they had just built the first four sound stages, and the executive building that housed the music department. Then there was a later one that was put up four or five months after I came down here. Originally we were in a building that later became the research library. It was one big room with half a dozen arrangers in it, and a big room with one piano, where if you needed a piano—which I do—there was always a fight about who had first dibs on that piano. Not a fight, but a friendly argument, let's say. And when I first came down here there were loads and loads and loads of songwriters, because it was just the beginning of the end of the first wave of the songwriting thing.

ATKINS: Were musicals still popular?

FRIEDHOFER: Musicals were still . . . well, they were just on their way out. I know the first commitment I had down here was the last big musical that Fox made at that particular time, a picture called *Sunny Side Up*, with Janet Gaynor and Charles Farrell, and songs by DeSylva, Brown, and Henderson. But there were, I don't know just how many songwriters were on the lot at that time. There was Con Conrad—Conrad, Mitchell, and Gottler. Of course, it was the big exodus from the East, out to this new gold mine on the coast. But by the end of 1929, you could shoot a cannon down any one of the studio streets and never hit a songwriter. There was one who remained for a long time after that, Jimmy Hanley, who wrote any number of standards: Just a Cottage Small by a Waterfall, Home in Indiana, and Lord knows how many others. He was a friend of Winfield Sheehan, who was executive head of the studio then.

Of course, what put the quietus on the big musical was the Depression. You remember that thing, or you've heard about it. We don't call them depressions anymore. We have all kinds of fancy names for them—slumps, recessions, what not. To me it's always a depression.

ATKINS: What happened to the music department when the songwriters left?

FRIEDHOFER: You might well ask, "What happened to the music department when the crash came?" It was cut down very drastically to—let's see—there was a musical director, George Lipschultz. There was a contractor, Frank Tresselt. There was a composer-arranger-copyist by the name of Hugo Friedhofer. And I think Jimmy Hanley still stayed on for a while, and another songwriter named William Kernell was there. That was the music department for some time.

Of course, the period after that was kind of a chancy one for everybody. Oh! I know what happened. On the recommendation of Jimmy Hanley, Fox hired a man named Arthur Lange. You remember Arthur, at one time considered America's foremost dance arranger. Arthur came over there and worked, and he and I became very close friends. He had come from New York and worked at Metro-Goldwyn-Mayer. Then he worked at RKO and at Paramount. Then he came out to Fox. Arthur, incidentally, brought Ray Heindorf to the coast, and also another good arranger by the name of Charles Maxwell, who stayed on at Metro for quite a number of years. Arthur stayed on at Twentieth and conducted, and arranged and composed. We remained very good friends up to the time of his death.

ATKINS: Reginald Bassett is one of those names that's forgotten, or unknown, and yet his name is on so many films.

FRIEDHOFER: Oh, yes. Well, I knew him from San Francisco. In age he sort of stood midway between my father and myself. He came down here when films were still in the silent stage, and he was one of the men behind the very celebrated musical director at the Carthay Circle Theater, Carli Elinor.

ATKINS: Carli Elinor's name is associated with *Birth of a Nation.* I think he wrote a score.

FRIEDHOFER: Well, Carli couldn't write his name, frankly. And I know that he had on his staff a pianist, and a couple of arrangers, and a copyist. Reginald Bassett, or Rex, as he was known, used to do all the writing. He used to compose the incidental music that was required that they couldn't find in the library, and used to orchestrate.

Rex Bassett was quite a character. He was an independent cuss, in a way, and very much admired for his work. But you couldn't get him to work after, let's say, five o'clock. At five he was off. Forget it. He also was an ardent flyer. He owned his own plane at one time—this is a long time ago—during the mid-thirties. When he had a day off, let's say, he used to go out and get his plane and then he'd come in and he'd buzz the studio.

ATKINS: His name is on several pictures.

FRIEDHOFER: Oh, yes. He did a beautiful, outstanding score for a picture that was originally called *The Paul Street Boys.* It was about a gang of kids, a sort of gang war in Budapest. It was a very subtle anti-war preachment, actually, and Rex did a truly magnificent score for it. This was under the direction of Lou Silvers at Columbia. Then later, Lou came out to Twentieth Century Fox.

ATKINS: I don't believe there were contract orchestras at that time, but were there regulars?

FRIEDHOFER: Yes, yes. One of the first musical directors at the old Fox studio was Arthur Kay. He had formerly been musical director of the pit orchestra in Grauman's Million Dollar, the old theater downtown. I think he brought the bulk of the pit orchestra out to Fox then. I think we had a nucleus of about eighteen, nineteen men, which was augmented when occasion demanded.

ATKINS: By the way, this was all standard recording at that time?

FRIEDHOFER: Oh, yes, it was. Playbacks didn't come in until some time after that. The first primitive playbacks came in in the 1930s.

ATKINS: At the same time that they were standard recording the musical numbers, were they postscoring the dramatic films?

FRIEDHOFER: Oh, they were postscoring them. Sometimes, I recall a couple of occasions when we were not only postscoring, but there was a crew in front of the orchestra doing sound effects. Or else there would be a crew in a separate room doing sound effects and listening to the music over a speaker from the recording stage—which was kind of a cockeyed way of doing things. I remember walking on the—into the recording—it wasn't a stage. It was a room actually, that later became Projection Room One before they built the big thing out at Fox. It was crammed with musicians, and in front of the musicians were three or four sound effects men. It was a nightclub scene, and they were clinking glasses and pouring water out of jugs and making "hubba-hubba" conversation noises, at the same time. Kind of confusing! But it was fun.

ATKINS: With dramatic films, would someone, the producer or director, come in and have a screening with you of the rough cut of the picture?

FRIEDHOFER: Occasionally, but they never said much. Sometimes they would show up on the scoring stage and say, "I like this," or "I don't like this." But we were left pretty much to our own devices, except that we knew that there were certain things that they demanded should be done.

ATKINS: Did you decide which sequences to score?

FRIEDHOFER: This was generally up to the musical director for whom I was working at the time.

ATKINS: But could he decide without consulting the producer?

FRIEDHOFER: Yes, pretty much. And then maybe he would go up and consult later. Or maybe he had a consultation before. At that time, as I told you, we were all jumping about from one project to another, quite at random. One day I'd be doing a vocal background for some lady baritone, who had maybe two good notes above middle C, and the next day I'd be orchestrating something for somebody else, or else writing dramatic cues or some atmospheric music, or a main title or something of that sort. So it was a sort of an overall experience which hasn't, I believe, hurt me in the long run.

Then, a little after that, that old demon, typecasting, was starting to affect the music end of it, too. You were typecast as a great guy for love scenes, or a whiz at main titles, or you made great string arrangements. In my case, it was the music that covered all scenes dealing with machinery and that sort of thing—motors, airplanes, locomotives, typewriters, you name it. Anything that went clickety-click was my bag. But I fortunately managed to spread myself around, finally.

ATKINS: Did you do any conducting at Fox?

FRIEDHOFER: No. There was a sort of hierarchy out there, and nobody conducted except the Newmans. Except I think the only people who conducted there outside of Alfred were Victor Young and Bernard Herrmann.

ATKINS: It seems that everybody shifted around from studio to studio.

FRIEDHOFER: Yes, we did, because hardly anybody was under contract except the musical directors. Nobody in those days got screen credit except the musical director.

ATKINS: Do you recall what was your first freelance job?

FRIEDHOFER: Yes, I do. I did some work for Roy Webb at RKO on *The Last Days of Pompeii*. And right about that time, my friend at Paramount, Andrea Setaro, whom I notified that I was available, called me in to do some work on a film that was sort of the forerunner of *Gone with the Wind*. It was a picture called *So Red the Rose*. And there was also a film called *Rose of the Rancho*, a western with Gladys Swarthout. As I recall, she was a sort of female Mark of Zorro type. I wrote some things for that, including an interminable chase, which Irvin Talbot became so enamored of that he used it to do preview track jobs and in some cases actually recorded it over for various films that had western chases in them. *So Red the Rose* was actually a composite score that was written partially by W. Franke Harling and Frederick Hollander. And I was pulled in to do some things on it.

ATKINS: *Rose of the Rancho* was produced by William Le Baron, who was also a songwriter.

FRIEDHOFER: Well, you know, I feel about producers the way most people feel about the Chinese. They all look alike to me. No, my association with producers has been fairly scanty. I exclude, of course, Darryl Zanuck and Sam Goldwyn—only to mention the best, you know. And later on, a charming man by the name of David Weisbart. He started over at Warner Brothers as a film editor and later became attached to Kazan, and they finally promoted him to producer over there. He made several very fine pictures, including *Rebel without a Cause*. Then he finally left Warners and came to Twentieth. This was in the '50s, around the time I was doing my third tour of duty at Twentieth.

ATKINS: When you say that producers look alike, do you categorize them as far as musical taste is concerned?

FRIEDHOFER: That's a little difficult to do. I don't know exactly what their musical tastes are. Their musical tastes are, in many instances, dictated by the kind of phonograph records that their wives buy. I know that Dore Schary was a very difficult man in that respect. I've never done any work for Schary, but I have friends who've worked very closely with him. And he was invited as a guest speaker, once, at an annual dinner given by the Screen Composer's Association. And in his book, he sort of very lightly dismissed the underscore as part of what he called "the mop-up operation." And he didn't win any friends for himself at the dinner. I was sitting with Elmer Bernstein, and at one point Elmer nudged me and said, "Why, this boy's got to go."

ATKINS: He did go, as you say.

FRIEDHOFER: Finally, he did. Although I will say he made some very good pictures out there.

ATKINS: Getting back to the 1930s, what about *Last of the Pagans*?

FRIEDHOFER: That was a picture at M-G-M. It was a Polynesian idyll that starred Jon Hall, I believe.

ATKINS: Was this some sort of "epic?"

FRIEDHOFER: It was supposed to be, but in the last analysis it didn't amount to much. So consequently it was loaded with music. I know that it was split up between two or three, or possibly four composers. I think I wrote about three reels of it. We were all in a hurry, one of those things. I had a slight exchange with Nat Finston one time, together with the chief librarian at Metro, George Schneider, who called me shortly after I put in my bill for my services. He said that Nat asked him to see if I couldn't shave my price a little bit on what I had done, on account of the fact that the score was a little thin, he said. So, I don't know, I guess I was rather feisty at that time—I must have been prosperous—I told George, "Would you please tell Nat that I am not charging for the notes that are on the score paper. I am charging for the notes that I had the good sense to leave out." Well, there was no further discussion about it. I got my money.

Then I was back at Fox, and then back at Paramount. And it was while I was at Paramount, doing a picture called *The Trail of the Lonesome Pine*, that a man who had been a bass player at Fox gave me a call. He was a copyist, as well, and I got to know him fairly well. He was a big Czechoslovakian by the name of Jaro Churain. And Jaro had—from the time that Korngold first hit Hollywood in connection with *A Midsummer Night's Dream*—been Korngold's amanuensis and copyist. You see, Korngold was born in Brunn, in Czechoslovakia, which is Brno, actually. And I think he had probably known Jaro from Europe, or at least they got together over here, and they were very closely associated from that time on. Jaro became Korngold's amanuensis, as it were, and also chief cook and bottle washer and the rest of it. Also, he used to make the conductor parts from Korngold's sketches because Korngold's handwriting, while it was perfectly legible, was very small. He knew exactly what he was writing, but you could ruin your eyes trying to read the manuscript. Very, very small. On Korngold films, with one exception, when we were in a terrible rush and I had to work right from a sketch of Korngold's, I always worked from Churain's sketches.

But, anyway, Korngold was at that time doing a film called *Give Us This Night* over at Paramount. It was a musical with Gladys Swarthout and Jan Kiepura. Kiepura had sung a big role in one of Korngold's operas in Vienna. So he probably suggested that they pull in Korngold because there was a long operatic sequence that ran for some seven or eight minutes in the thing. And Korngold was having difficulties with the man who had been assigned to him to make his orchestrations, who shall be nameless. Korngold wasn't very happy with him because the guy was always giving him arguments. And, after all, Korngold is a superb orchestrator, and the only reason he needed an orchestrator was because of the pressures of time. Anyway, Korngold had finished the prescore—the vocal backgrounds for Swarthout and Kiepura—and he had time on his hands. Then, in the interim between the prescore and the final "mopping-up operation," which just had a little incidental music, Korngold got this call from Warner Brothers, having worked there before on the Reinhardt picture. And he was unhappy with his orchestrator or arranger at Paramount, so Churain, for whom I had done a couple of favors out at Fox, suggested me. We got together and seemed to hit it off, so Korngold suggested to Leo Forbstein that I do the orchestrations on *Captain Blood*, which I did.

ATKINS: Did you do any on *Give Us This Night*?

FRIEDHOFER: Finally, we went back and I did just the clean-up stuff, and the main title, and a couple of things.

ATKINS: Then, *Captain Blood* was Korngold's first dramatic score?

FRIEDHOFER: Yes, because the *Midsummer Night's Dream* music was the Mendelssohn, plus some other Mendelssohn music that Korngold found that they needed. He got it out of Songs without Words, and, I think, Rondo Capriccioso, and some other things. He orchestrated those himself.

   After that, owing to the circumstances, I was pulled in, and orchestrated just about all of *Captain Blood*, with the exception of the main title. I don't know whether Leo didn't trust me to do a main title or not, but Ray Heindorf did the main title, and brilliantly.

ATKINS: There are all sorts of questions I can ask you about working with Korngold, beginning with what it was like working on that first picture.

FRIEDHOFER: Well, it was a very, very close association. He always liked to look at the scores. We'd discuss the sketches very thoroughly. He had a fantastic way of playing the piano with an orchestral style, so you could almost sense what he was hearing in the orchestra. He did not make an orchestral sketch, in four or five lines, as some do, and as I do personally. He wrote a piano part, actually. And sometimes there was a large hole in the middle, you know. It would be what lay conveniently under the right hand. You had to sort of be possessed of a certain clairvoyance, a kind of a musical crystal ball, to figure out whether that was the way he really wanted it, because sometimes he *did* want that wide open space in the middle. And sometimes the whole set-up, in the piano part, would have to be to a certain extent, revoiced, or else filled out.

   But the first few, he gave me half a dozen of his sketches, we discussed them, and then I took them home and orchestrated them. He seemed very pleased and he made an extraordinary remark. He said, "You must be very well acquainted with the music of Gustav Mahler." And at that point, while I had heard considerable Mahler, and liked it, I had never made an intensive study of his methods of composition and/or orchestration. I guess it's probably part of my middle-European background. But he said, "That's extraordinary, because you have a way of distributing strings and the rest of it in the orchestra that is extremely like Mahler." And that he liked, because there was much of Mahler in Korngold. Mahler was one of the first people to whom old Julius Korngold showed any of his young prodigy's music, and Mahler was tremendously excited.

ATKINS: He was a child prodigy?

FRIEDHOFER: Yes, he was, and I've seen music that he wrote at the age of ten or eleven that is fantastic, a set of piano things, Fairy-Tale Pictures. The invention, and the harmonic daring of them for that time—Good Lord, Korngold was born in 1897, so these things were written up to 1910 let's say, all these early things, and some of his first published things, a couple of piano sonatas and things like that. Then, of course, he burst into prominence as a composer of operas.

Anyhow, I started talking about Ray Heindorf and his contribution to *Captain Blood*. Korngold was very, very pleased with the score and with my work on it. And strangely enough, at that particular period in time, Max Steiner came over to Warners to do *The Charge of the Light Brigade*. There I was, and so Forbstein, who had become sold on me as an orchestrator and arranger, proposed that I do *The Charge of the Light Brigade*. And very fortunately for me, my association with Steiner became just about as close as my association with Korngold had been. So, my principal job over at Warner's was to service these two gentlemen. I never had a written contract with Warner Brothers, strangely enough. It was on a gentleman's agreement basis; it was a handshake thing. As far as Leo Forbstein was concerned, I could stay there as long as I wanted to. This was all very well, for awhile.

ATKINS: Was that on a weekly basis, or per picture?

FRIEDHOFER: No. I was on a guarantee, against pages, which was spread out over a period of time. So it was actually an annual, fifty-two weeks a year deal. Outside of taking care of Steiner and Korngold, I could do what I wanted in my spare time. And what I did in my spare time was rush right over to Goldwyn, and do some work for Alfred Newman. It was a very cozy arrangement.

ATKINS: You were working for Hollywood's three top composers.

FRIEDHOFER: Yes. Of course, I didn't do all of Al's work. Edward Powell was Al's orchestrator by that time. Before Powell, Conrad Salinger came out here for a short time to work for Alfred.

ATKINS: You mentioned that Steiner and Korngold had very different methods of working.

FRIEDHOFER: Oh, yes. Steiner, after running the picture once—at the most twice—would depend entirely on the cue sheets which were supplied to him by his music editor—who was really not a music editor, in that there were some union restrictions at that time that specified that nobody except a film editor could touch a foot of film at any time. So what he did was simply to time the stuff on the movieola and make up the cue sheets. The so-called "music editor" was actually a part of the music department—a very nice chap who originally had been with Steiner over at RKO. I think it was Steiner who brought him into Warners when he went over there. This was a boy named Hal Findlay. Hal was a very good all-around musician.

Korngold did all his work in the projection room—just improvised to the film. After seeing the film the first time, without fooling around at all, he would go home and start inventing themes. Then his next running would be in the projection room with a small upright piano, and he improvised on the material that he had dreamt up, to the film as it was run. He'd start making very rough sketches which he'd take home and refine. Then he'd come back the next day and check and double-check for timing and what-not. Never any marks on the film until he was about ready to record. Then he would go in and sit with the film editor and have the punches and what-not put on the film, the warning signals and so on, and also certain interior cues, to indicate changes of tempo. And his scores were always marked sort of in synchronization with the marks on the film, itself. He had a way always of indicating changes of tempo or changes of meter, if he were moving from four to three or what-not.

Korngold had a way of writing, you might call it a sort of written-out rubato. It all sounded very free and relaxed, but it was all metronomically on the paper that way. So that called for innumerable changes of time signature. It was always indicated. When he'd move from four to three, let's say, he would always give the conventional "one, two, three, four," marked that way on the score.

ATKINS: Did he put metronome markings?

FRIEDHOFER: No. The tempos he knew. He had them in his head and was infallible about it. He had a built-in sense of speed at which something should move. Steiner, on the other hand, always worked, as I say, to cue sheets, and also utilized the click track a great deal for tempos—but utilized it in very ingenious ways, so that you would never be aware that there was a mechanical beat going on in the background. He had a way of writing across the bar line so that it sounded very free. And then he had a very neat trick which later became sort of common practice in this town. Say something started in one tempo and remained in that tempo for a considerable length of time, and then there would be a change of mood or a change of action. He would find a place where he could hit a fermata, that is, a hold. And the old click track would go out, and it would be held long enough for warning clicks for the new tempo to start. And away we go! Everybody has done that since.

ATKINS: Was there any utilization of variable clicks?

FRIEDHOFER: Variable clicks we did not have at that time. They came in later.

ATKINS: When you did your orchestrations, were they on a full score sheet?

FRIEDHOFER: Yes, they were on full score sheets. I worked directly from Max's layouts, which were generally on four lines.

ATKINS: How about from Korngold's piano sketches?

FRIEDHOFER: Oh, there were certain places where I believe I used to lay out certain things on an expanded sketch, so that there wouldn't be too many erasures on the score page. But not often. I generally worked pretty well from Churain's copy of Korngold's sketch.

Steiner used to always indicate his harp parts, and used to use different colored pencils, you know. He was very cute, in a way. He would write out the harp parts, which were always quite florid because of the fact that his wife at that time, Louise, was a harpist, and an excellent one. But when the pedal changes and the chromaticism got a little bit too intricate, he would start writing wavy lines and saying, "Et cetera. You know what I want."

As a matter of fact, a great deal of our conversation about what we were doing, from about the middle of *The Charge of the Light Brigade*, was entirely confined to telephone conversations. And we never saw each other from the day we ran the picture until the time that we went on the stage. We used to have these wild telephone conversations, sometimes at two, three, four o'clock in the morning. I don't know whether I could still take that sort of thing, but the hours that we used to put in were simply fabulous. I remember one year, I think we did something like eleven pictures in the space of one year. Of course, not all of them were full, enormous scores, but still, it was an awful lot. Occasionally, when the pressures got overbearing, I would go to Forbstein and say, "Look, I've got to have some help on this. There's just too much, and you want it on such and such a date. I'll never get it finished by myself." He said, "Okay. Get whoever you want." So I did. But I still kept close supervision over everything that was done.

ATKINS: Who were some of the people who worked with you?

FRIEDHOFER: Well, Leo had a great fondness for Eddie Powell, among other people. And there was a young man named George Parrish, who came out here who had been in radio somewhere around Kansas City. He didn't, at that time, know much. He'd done some very nice things for radio, but he didn't know much about the full orchestra. So Max suggested that I sort of take him under my wing—the one that isn't broken, you know—and work with him whenever I needed assistance or whenever it was feasible. George developed into a very good orchestrator, and then later fell into the clutches of Dmitri Tiomkin, and worked with Dmitri. He was always a little bit confused by Dmitri's sketches, and so we carried on a sort of long-distance correspondence school. You know, he'd ask me how certain things should be done. So I'd try to clarify it for him. But in the main, the bulk of that avalanche of notes flowed off the end of my own pencil.

ATKINS: Everyone talks about the big music staff at Warners.

FRIEDHOFER: Oh, there was a big staff there. There was Steiner, Korngold; before that, Bernhard Kaun had been there. Heinz Roemheld, Ray Heindorf. Then in 1937, Adolph Deutsch was added to the staff. But my main association at Warners was with Steiner and Korngold, and occasionally with Heinz Roemheld. And my little excursions over to Alfred Newman, between assignments. I would go to Leo and say, "Have you got something coming up for me?" And he'd say, "Get lost. I'll call you." So I'd call Alfred.

ATKINS: Were there any problems when you worked with Steiner?

FRIEDHOFER: We never had any problems. Max and I—I remember once, only, that we had problems. It was on a picture called *Green Light*. It was one of Lloyd Douglas's little ecclesiastical lollipops. There was a character played by Sir Cedric Hardwicke. He was a bishop who had a slight limp in one leg. And Max was, to a certain extent, a Mickey Mouse man, and he had sort of made a reputation with the music he had written for *Of Human Bondage* where I think the principal character has a limp, or a club foot. Max wrote this kind of limping theme, and he had indicated in the score, "This is for the bishop, who limps. He's a cripple, but," he said, "don't make him as heavy-handed as the one in *Of Human Bondage*. He's a pretty cripple." And that's all he told me, so I fooled around with it. For some reason or other, I was not on the stage when this episode was recorded. Max read it through and was very unhappy, for some reason or other. He said, "No, this is all wrong." And he started tinkering with the orchestration, and apparently spent about two hours, trying this way, trying it that way, adding, subtracting, et cetera, et cetera, and always going up in the booth to listen up there. And that used to be a considerable climb over at Warner Brothers in those days, with that long staircase up. Finally—I got this report later—he said, "All right, fellows. Let's forget all about that. Let's try the original version again." So they did, and then he liked it. But he was very sweet about it. He called me at home that night. He said, "You know, you won a great moral victory over me today. You were right all the time." Which was sweet, I thought. But that's about the only time that Max and I ever quarreled about a concept—my concept of something he had written.

But, Lord, there were so many pictures that I did with Max that it's hard for me to pick those that really stand out in my mind. One of them is a score that he wrote for *All This and Heaven, Too*. That was a beautiful picture, from a Rachel Field story, with Charles Boyer and Bette Davis. There was another picture that wasn't a big, wide, expansive score, but it was a very, very good one, and made its points very well. It was called *A Dispatch from Reuters*. A very good picture. Another standout of Max's, for me, was *We Are Not Alone*, a picture that Paul Muni made with Flora Robson and a young girl who did all too little at Warners—Jane Bryan. It was a very sad picture about this Austrian refugee girl, and about the shrewish wife who takes poison, instead of a sleeping pill, by accident. And Muni is accused of murdering his wife. It winds up with them being executed. No, but a beautifully made picture. And Max did a lovely score for it. Also, he did a lovely score for *Tovarich*, with Claudette Colbert and Charles Boyer, and I know that Rathbone played the part of the Russian commissar. That was the story of the two aristocrats who fled Russia during the revolution and got jobs as butlers and parlor maids in this establishment.

ATKINS: And you worked on all these?

FRIEDHOFER: Yes, I did. Oh, Lord, I must have done sixty or seventy pictures for Max. I know that at the time that I made up the list for either Tony Thomas or Cliff McCarty, both of them pointed out that I had omitted several.

ATKINS: After Max Steiner and Erich Korngold became so prestigious on the Warner lot, when either of them did a movie, did they have pretty much carte blanche as far as where they wanted music?

FRIEDHOFER: Well, they always sat with the producer, but by that time, they were left to their own devices pretty much. I know Korngold had this sense of theater and of timing, and of stagecraft that began in his childhood, actually, from the first thing he ever wrote for the stage. It was a little children's pantomime called "The Snow Man," a ballet which was finally performed at the Vienna opera. I can recall many instances when Korngold would go to the producer and say, "Look, can you give me a little more footage at the end of—" whatever scene it was. "I feel that as the end of an act. I feel that there's a first act curtain there." And he would always get his way. In some instances that I recall, he would suggest transpositions of scenes.

He was acting like a producer, actually, saying "I think that this would be more effective if it would occur after such and such happened." And they listened to him, much to their own advantage.

ATKINS: There are very few composers who have enjoyed this sort of treatment, I would guess.

FRIEDHOFER: That's true. We're mostly hampered by time elements, and also by a timorousness about suggesting to a producer that he should do so and so. On the other hand, we have our moments where we'll suggest mildly that we think perhaps something would be better this way, or that we shouldn't have music here, or that the music should not start at the beginning of the main title, but at so and so, or else the music should be solid from the beginning of the main title up to a certain point, but no sound effects. And at that point, if we can make a dramatic entrance of sound effects to take over from music, that's the way we do it. And, very fortunately, on the few occasions when I have asked for something like that, I've gotten my way about it.

But there is a strange thing that I pointed out in a seminar one time, about the strange mystique that surrounds the Academy Awards. You can sit in on a conference and make some very valid suggestions, but nobody listens. But the minute you've got that Academy Award, you can at times talk the most errant nonsense—you might do it deliberately, just to see if there's a reaction, and there will be a pause, and someone will say, "Well, maybe you've got a point there." That's why this business, as much as I love it, has handed me considerable laughs through the years.

ATKINS: You worked on several Max Steiner films that were either nominated or won awards.

FRIEDHOFER: Only one Award winner, *Now, Voyager*.

ATKINS: Anyway, I wondered, when Steiner or Korngold won an award, was it beneficial to you, even though you didn't actually share the award?

FRIEDHOFER: As a matter of fact, my whole association with Steiner and Korngold was beneficial. But it was kind of a two-edged weapon because when I finally left Warners to go to Twentieth Century Fox in 1942, and was there for two years, the pressures of wartime got to be too great. We were turning those things out like McDonald's turns out hamburgers, because the riveters on the night shift wanted to go see a movie after they got through with work. And the product was pretty miserable. Of course, the industry was making a lot of money, but I just couldn't take it any more, so I went back to freelance.

★   ★   ★

ATKINS: You whizzed by the first picture that you did for Samuel Goldwyn. I wanted to ask you a little more about that.

FRIEDHOFER: I'm sorry I whizzed by that one. There was one period when things got a little slack over at Warners, and Goldwyn had three pictures in production at the same time, one of them being the celebrated *Goldwyn Follies*. That was the picture that Gershwin did. Another was *Hurricane*, with Dorothy Lamour, Jon Hall, and Mary Astor, and the Canadian actor, Raymond Massey. The third one was *The Adventures of Marco Polo*. I had done considerable writing for Alfred before this, when he would occasionally get into a bind with a lot of work, starting way back with a picture that Fritz Lang directed, *You Only Live Once*, or *You Live Only Once*. I never know which it is—a very sad little picture, with Fonda and Sylvia Sidney. Then there were various things, like the original sound for *Prisoner of Zenda*. I did several things for Al on that. I can't remember all of them. So Al pegged me to do the score for *Marco Polo* because there was just too much to handle. He recommended me very highly to Goldwyn, and there I wound up with the *Marco Polo* picture, which was my first screen credit. And while I was waiting for *Marco Polo* to be finished, I jumped in and assisted Eddie Powell on *Hurricane* and also on *The Follies*.

ATKINS: Did you know George Gershwin?

FRIEDHOFER: Oh, Lord, yes. I had met George in 1931 on the *Delicious* picture. And we became quite close, because George loved to have somebody around when he was writing. I used to take his original—what were really piano parts, or two-line sketches, and blow them up. In the case of the Second Rhapsody, originally called Rhapsody in Rivets, I laid out the first orchestral sketch on it, from sitting alongside him and discussing orchestration as we went along. I think it was about three months that he was out here. I was with him practically every day, let's say from eleven o'clock in the morning until three or four in the afternoon.

ATKINS: Was he working on the Rhapsody while he worked on the film?

FRIEDHOFER: The Rhapsody was part of the score. There was a long scene in *Delicious*, where this little stowaway girl runs away because the immigration department is after her. She wanders through the streets of New York. George thought it would be a good idea to write another extended piece, because it had been some time since the Rhapsody in Blue and the Concerto and An American in Paris. This was the next one. He took my sketches and went back to New York and orchestrated the whole thing back there, but he wanted to hear parts of it to see how it worked out, and also parts of certain sequences in the picture. There was a long dream sequence that she has before she gets off the boat that's bringing her over to the United States. He wanted to hear that, which I had arranged and orchestrated, and some of the songs in the thing. So we called an orchestra session, and George, who liked to conduct, did so. And he was very pleased with the results. When he got finished orchestrating the Second Rhapsody, he sent it out here. We had, naturally, to make cuts in it to fit to the film.

But it was through George that the following year I got acquainted with Oscar Levant, because Oscar, in the interim, had come out here and was doing I don't know exactly what, over at the Western Avenue Studio. Somebody said he was largely Mrs. Sol Wurtzel's court pianist. I know he was in a projection room when I went over to run *My Lips Betray*. And I saw this quiet young man sitting in a corner. Sol Wurtzel introduced Oscar and me. Oscar, who, come to think of it, was still fairly naive at that time, jumped up and he got all flustered and excited and came over to me and said, "I'm so happy to meet you. I've heard so much about you from George," which was very nice. And then he came to all the scoring sessions on *My Lips*

*Betray*. And from that time on we were very close friends, and became even closer when Eddie Powell and Herbert Spencer came out here, because they both knew him from New York. We used to get together up in his—believe it or not, he had a suite in the Beverly Wilshire Hotel, and was being subsidized by, I think, S. N. Behrman and Irving Berlin, and one of the Marx Brothers—I think Harpo. Oscar had come out here and was working very diligently with Arnold Schoenberg, studying.

ATKINS: Do you think he had aspirations to being a film composer?

FRIEDHOFER: Not to be a film composer—I think he had great aspirations to being a composer, period. But I think the shadow of George Gershwin lay rather heavily upon him all the time. And it's a pity, because he had great talent.

In connection with *The Goldwyn Follies*, that tragic year which saw George's demise, unfortunately, Vernon Duke came out here to finish up and that was the beginning of my acquaintance with Vernon. The two ballets, and I believe, the verses of a couple of the tunes that George had written, and one tune that George had never gotten around to writing, were from the pen of Vernon. The second ballet, the one with Zorina, called "The Water Nymph," was one of those last-minute things. I recall that Edward Powell and David Raksin and I split the piano score in three parts and then retired to our own little cubbyholes and orchestrated the thing overnight. The only communication we had concerned certain doublings in the woodwind sections, or, "should the violins or the string section have mutes at this point?" That was the only communication we had, by telephone.

ATKINS: In a case like this, when three of you are orchestrating the same composition, can you notice the "seams?"

FRIEDHOFER: No. The style was Vernon's and we knew what to do with the thing. Actually, Vernon's orchestration was a little bit, shall we say, spotty, until sometime later when he became a disciple of Schillinger's. It was pianistically conceived and needed some doctoring. Not any violent changes or anything of that kind, but sometimes there were holes in the texture that needed either plugging up,

# SCARECROW PRESS

4720 Boston Way
Lanham, Maryland 20706
(301) 459-3366

We are pleased
to provide you with the
enclosed book(s) for review.

*(Please send us two copies of your review
for our files. Thank you.)*

Nancy Hofmann
Marketing and Promotions
Scarecrow Press

or else it was too thick and it needed thinning out. But that is why arrangers are born.

ATKINS: Going back, one question about the Second Rhapsody— were your orchestral parts very like the final orchestrations?

FRIEDHOFER: George followed the indications in the sketches I made, my blown up orchestral sketches, pretty closely, except that, being a pianist, he strangely enough did not have a complete under-standing, at that time, of the sustaining powers of the instruments. So there were a lot of fills which are derived from keyboard manipula-tion that actually are superfluous in the orchestra. I'm not saying that it isn't good, but I can show you—I have a copy of the original pub-lished score of American in Paris, that he gave me. And he gave it to me rather apologetically, saying, "Look, this has got all of Rodzin-skis's markings in it. Do you mind? I can get a new one." "No," I said. "I'd sooner have that. It has certain historical value."

So, because of his extreme pianist feeling, there were a lot of su-perfluities, which really don't matter. They don't interfere with the musical quality of the work. But they are a purely pianistic concept, which you can take or leave alone, actually. That's the trouble with being that kind of a facile pianist—to translate your pianism into terms of the orchestra is a thing that is given only to very few men, like Maurice Ravel, for instance, who could translate from one idiom into the other without any trouble.

ATKINS: Stravinsky is supposed to have written within the span of his hands.

FRIEDHOFER: Not within the span of his hands, actually, but he was a piano thumper. He had a very valid reason for that: he said he wanted to keep in physical contact with the medium of sound. Ravel, of course, pushed that point just a little bit farther. He said, "Look, without the piano how do you discover any new harmonies?" There are some men who write at the piano. There are some men who never touch the piano. Me, I touch the piano, unless I'm driven to desperation. I know that I've turned out bridges and cues in the ten-minute intermissions on the sound stage for TV and that sort of thing. It's a good discipline and I like to divorce myself from it, and yet I still want to test. Another one was Puccini, who tinkered with the keyboard constantly, and yet there's a glow about his orchestration that certainly does not smack of the keyboard. So I don't know actually. Stravinsky tells the story about how, when he was studying with Rimsky-Korsakov, he asked Korsakov about this business of writing at the piano. Korsakov said, "Some men write at the piano. I don't ever touch the instrument. You," he said to Stravinsky, "will write at the piano." Period. That was it. And certainly if there was ever a contemporary master of instrumentation, it was Stravinsky. But orchestration is not something that is merely plastered on top of a composition. It's an integral part of it. And the principal difficulty of being an arranger, unless you disregard the songwriter's intent, is to become an alter ego, to literally crawl inside the skin of whatever songwriter he's working for. He's got to constantly be saying to himself, "Now, if so-and-so could orchestrate, how would he do this?" And you've got to assume a personality. Of course, with some very, very few songwriters, that problem doesn't exist. For instance, Jimmy Van Heusen, although he doesn't orchestrate, writes like an arranger. His piano parts are those of a very gifted arranger. Lennie Bernstein, to go into that particular groove, orchestrates and orchestrates brilliantly. I don't know about Sondheim, whom I associate with Bernstein. I don't know how much of his concepts are his or whether they are those of his arranger. But if it's the latter, in the case of A Little Night Music, he's found the ideal alter ego. And I can never think of the man's name who did those [Jonathan Tunick].

ATKINS: When you see a film that you're going to score and you "hear things," do you hear them as they would be orchestrated?

FRIEDHOFER: I do, in an overall fashion. And so much of what becomes orchestral color is dictated by a visual element. What you write is governed by atmosphere, that is, atmosphere that is created through camera angles let's say, or through lighting, or through color sometimes in the case of color film. So it actually influences what you write. What you write actually becomes a third dimension to what is primarily a pretty flat medium.

ATKINS: Getting back to *The Adventures of Marco Polo* and Alfred Newman—

FRIEDHOFER: Well, it was at that time, 1937, that Al—well, this thing had kicked around a long time, and finally, when the United Artists thing dissolved, and Goldwyn was really the trigger man in that whole operation over there, he acquired the script of *Marco Polo*, which was originally designed for Doug Fairbanks Sr. and was a straight-away swashbuckler. And then Ben Hecht worked on the script, and it became a sort of wise-cracking vernacular type of thing, which wasn't right, either. And then Bob Sherwood was called in, and he injected little shots of social significance along the way. So, as a script it was kind of a mess. But it was a spectacle, and Richard Day did some simply magnificent art direction on the thing. Some of the casting was very good; some of it was not. Every hero in those days, every Don Quixote, had to have his Sancho Panza. Ernest Truex was Marco's companion. The girl was Sigrid Gurie. I think she was known as "the Swede from Brooklyn." Oh, and naturally, Basil Rathbone was the heavy. This was my first excursion into the field of what you might call a big costume epic. And not one note of the score remains in my possession. I don't know what became of it.

ATKINS: Did you have much contact with Goldwyn?

FRIEDHOFER: No. He sort of took me on good faith, owing to the fact that Al was interested in having me do it. And Goldwyn had his hands full with the other two films. So my actual personal contact with him didn't occur until 1947 when I did *Best Years of Our Lives*. After that, the next picture I did for him was *The Bishop's Wife*. That was a very pleasant experience, except—just to give you an idea of how Goldwyn operated—the minute that your name was mentioned, and he'd agreed that you were to do the picture, from that moment on, you were on the lot and working on the picture, even though you may not have seen it at the time. So, it so happened that I was busy over at the now defunct Enterprise Studio. I was doing a film called *Body and Soul* with John Garfield and Lilli Palmer. I was just finishing that job up when the word came through that *Bishop's Wife* was finishing and that Goldwyn wanted me for the score. I still had some cleaning up to do in the way of dubbing and so on, so when I walked into Goldwyn's office to confer with him and Henry, or "Bob" Koster, who was the director on it, I came in, and Goldwyn glared at me and said, in that strangely high-pitched voice of his,

"You know, I saw last night a picture with the worst score I ever heard in my life." I said, "What was that, Mr. Goldwyn?" He said, "A picture called *Body and Soul*. Score was terrible." So I started to get up out of my chair and say, "Well, Mr. Goldwyn, in view of the fact that you don't like the score, perhaps I'm not the right man to do the score for *Bishop's Wife*." And Bob Koster was sitting there as I started to get up. Goldwyn waved me down, and then he turned to Koster with this strange grin on his face, and pointed to me and said, "You know, he's a very sensitive man." And from then on, everything was fine.

ATKINS: Was he very specific about what he wanted, scene for scene?

FRIEDHOFER: No. No, no. As a matter of fact I don't think I ever discussed a scene-for-scene approach. I know that I had worked for a few days on thematic material and couldn't come up with anything, and all of a sudden, he wanted to bring Koster down to my office and hear the themes. Well, I had some very, very, very vague ideas, and I was panic-stricken because, you know, I'm a lousy pianist. But do you know, I actually, by the grace of God or somebody, I winged it. And what he heard he liked. I had a vague recall of it and I said, "I hope this is something like what I improvised." It turned out that it was, and after that everything was okay. He didn't show up at the recordings or in dubbing, except on the final recording on *Bishop's Wife*. It was the end title, the sermon, and he loved it. After that I did a picture called *Enchantment*, a nice picture, very warm. I enjoyed it very much.

Since we're speaking about Goldwyn, I think I should interject that there was a certain prestige connected with working for Goldwyn, because even his unsuccessful pictures had a certain patina, a certain aura, a certain quality. There were always great, great production values. There was a certain aristocratic quality about them that made one rather happy to be associated with an output, a product of this kind, because this was the Tiffany or Cartier of producers.

ATKINS: Would you say that part of his success was attributable to the fact that he surrounded himself with very good people?

FRIEDHOFER: I think that this is the secret of the success of any producer who really makes it. A producer who has the intelligence and the innate taste to surround himself with whoever he thinks are the best people he can find. And Goldwyn did. He had, starting with Alfred Newman as his musical director, Richard Day as his art director, Gregg Toland, a magnificent cinematographer, and other men, and top-flight film directors and top-flight writers. There was a time when Dorothy Parker did a lot of work there, Ben Hecht, Bob Sherwood, and countless others. That was the secret, I think, of Goldwyn's success. Of course, sometimes it was agonizing working for him. And he had one of the greatest editors of all time, Danny Mandell. He was just great, and the only man who could stand up to Goldwyn in an argument and win. He had an uncanny ability to imitate Sam's voice on the telephone, which he used to do every once in awhile. He played practical jokes on several people. He'd call them up and chew them out in this Goldwyn voice. Then the guy would come running in to Danny and say, "My God! Sam really gave it to me. I'm afraid I'm going to be fired."

The next thing I worked on was *Roseanna McCoy*, which was the old feudin' and fightin' Hatfields and McCoys. He wanted David Buttolph. David is a very fine composer, but for some reason or other, Goldwyn didn't like the score very much. So I had to rewrite about half of it. I can't remember to this day if I got screen credit. The theme song was written by Frank Loesser, which was used partially as thematic material in the score. *Roseanna McCoy* was 1949. I think there was something I did before that.

ATKINS: When did you do *A Song Is Born*?

FRIEDHOFER: Oh, that was before that. That was a remake of *Ball of Fire*. Instead of making it a group of encyclopedists, made it a group of musicians. And we had an all-star band—Goodman, the Dorsey boys, Mel Powell was playing piano, Satchmo and one of the fine drummers, Louis Bellson, and Lionel Hampton. There were two songs written by Don Raye and Gene DePaul. Howard Hawks was the director. They needed an underscore for *A Song Is Born*, so I came in and did that job. Did I mention the rows that took place on the stage during that? The Dorsey Brothers, who, when they weren't fighting amongst themselves, would fight with somebody else. There had been bad blood between them and Benny Goodman for a long time. And there was this terrific row on stage, with the mike open. Anyway, the news got all over town in no time. Louie Bellson reminded me of it when I saw him some time later. It was a laugh to think of in retrospect—Emil Newman, who weighed about ninety pounds dripping wet, stepping in between these combatants, and getting slammed into the mike. That, naturally, was the end of the thing, but the whole argument and everything had been picked up. I'd like to have an acetate of it.

ATKINS: I have another Goldwyn film, 1950, *Edge of Doom*.

FRIEDHOFER: Ah, yes! *Edge of Doom*, with Farley Granger and Dana Andrews. It was a very strong, very powerful picture about a young boy who lives alone with his mother in sort of a slum part of Los Angeles. And his mother has devoted herself to sort of good works for the church and she finally dies. They're very poor and so the kid feels that the church owes his mother a fancy, bang-up funeral. And he goes to see the priest who loses his temper with the kid. And the kid loses his temper and picks up a brass crucifix off the desk and clobbers the padre with it, which is not the sort of thing that one could get away with very neatly in 1950. I must say I liked it and was very happy with what I did. There was one sequence when the kid staggers out of the parish house and into the church, and all of a sudden the avenging God is in the music. It was very effective.

ATKINS: Was it a success?

FRIEDHOFER: No. It was a dismal flop. It was strictly an art-house product. I recall to this day the quality of Phil Yordan's script, which was a very good one. *Edge of Doom* was 1950 and that was sort of the end of my association with Goldwyn because I got busy elsewhere.

★    ★    ★

ATKINS: After you did *The Adventures of Marco Polo*, did you go back to Warners?

FRIEDHOFER: Well, I never really left Warners. It was just one of those periods when there was nothing for me over there. And as I told you before, Leo always closed his eyes to whatever I did in the way of moonlighting. Then Korngold came back from Europe, much against his will, strangely enough, to do *The Adventures of Robin Hood*, which was one of the biggest of the costume epics that Warners made, and a magnificent picture. The color, to this day, is something to marvel at. Korngold had some sort of a contractual agreement with Warners at the time, that in the event that he should have to go back to Europe, they would let him go, and somebody else would finish the score with his thematic material. But as it turned out, shortly after he got over here, the Hitler takeover of Austria occurred. Korngold had come here with just his wife and one of the two sons. But his father and mother and the younger son remained behind, in Austria. Very fortunately, they managed to get out before the takeover. But I saw Korngold actually lose about twenty pounds in the weeks that elapsed before news got to him that his mother and father and his other son were safe. It was a bad time for him.

Anyway, *Robin Hood* was finished, and very successfully. And we know what happened with the thing. As a matter of fact, it's sort of a classic of that particular swashbuckling type film. I don't remember much about the cast, except Errol, and the girl who always referred to herself as "Errol Flynn's straight woman," Olivia de Havilland. And Alan Hale, and the arch villain of all time, Basil Rathbone. Strangely enough, *Robin Hood* was shown on a double bill with *The Adventures of Marco Polo*. In both pictures, Rathbone was the conniver, the arch villain, and had practically the same dialogue. He said, "The people have to be taxed more." And it got to be kind of a laugh.

ATKINS: Did you know him?

FRIEDHOFER: No. I've killed him innumerable times, but I never got to know him. As a matter of fact, Korngold killed him in the first picture he did, and I helped orchestrally to do him in, in *Captain Blood*.

ATKINS: What interest would someone like Flynn show in the music?

FRIEDHOFER: I don't recall Flynn having any particular interest in what was done in the score. Of course, he may have been in contact, not as a critic, but just a friendly contact, with Korngold. Because Korngold had that aura of being the great Viennese operatic composer, and I know that a tremendous fuss was made over him when Reinhardt first brought him over to adapt the Mendelssohn music to *Midsummer Night's Dream*. And I know that there's a still of him someplace playing various themes for various members of the cast. It said something about his tailoring the Mendelssohn music to fit Jimmy Cagney, who played Bottom, the weaver, and also Mickey Rooney, who played Puck. And probably de Havilland. But I don't know whether that went on in subsequent pictures, or not.

ATKINS: Was *Robin Hood* treated any differently musically, on a larger scale?

FRIEDHOFER: No. We worked pretty much the same way. That large sequence, when Flynn invades Nottingham Castle, the scene where he comes in with the deer slung across his shoulders and dumps it on the table; they attempt to seize him, and he fights his way out, and there's a long chase after that—because of the enormous amount of music in the picture, Korngold helped himself to a symphonic piece that he had written for the Vienna Philharmonic, a thing called Sursum Corda, Lift Up Your Hearts. We adapted it for the picture. But outside of that, and the duel in *Captain Blood*, which was actually conceived and orchestrated overnight—I don't know whether Korngold was tired or what, but anyway, he decided that except for an introduction to it, a play into the actual duel, and a play-off at the end, we adapted something from a symphonic poem of Franz Liszt called Prometheus. It had a fugue. And fugues make an excellent background for duels because that's the conflict—one voice against the other. I think I still have a miniature score of the Liszt piece, with the markings in it that we discussed the night I went over to his house at about eight o'clock in the evening, and left around midnight and went home and orchestrated. The copyist picked it up in the morning, and that afternoon it was recorded.

ATKINS: Was your orchestration very different from the original Liszt version?

FRIEDHOFER: Well, yes. It was gutsier because of the situation, the duel and all that. Then, of course, it had to be adapted to the orchestra that we had, which was different from the original orchestral score—which was probably not orchestrated by Liszt, either, because Liszt was primarily a pianist. When he first started writing orchestral works, he was dependent upon contemporaries who knew more about orchestration than he did.

ATKINS: You've brought up a very good point, because people are always very surprised that Steiner and Korngold didn't orchestrate their films. Just how general a practice is this in serious, nonfilm music?

FRIEDHOFER: It happens. It happens sometimes because of an uncertainty on the part of the composer, as regards his knowledge of instrumentation. But it happens mainly because of a time element. There is a certain snobbery about Hollywood, mainly felt by composers who have not been asked to write for films. They say, "Well, they don't do their own orchestration." But they don't say a word about the fact that Prokofiev didn't, not because he was incapable of orchestrating—we know better than that. He was a master. But simply because of the time element, he used orchestrators.

No, there was no reason that Korngold, had he had time, couldn't have orchestrated his own music. But when you've got seven, eight weeks to do one of those monster epics, you just have not got the time. And I know that in my own case, there are very few of my own scores that I have orchestrated myself. They were always under strict supervision and I've used as many as sometimes three orchestrators.

ATKINS: To the best of your recall, just how long would you say you and Mr. Korngold worked on a film like *The Adventures of Robin Hood*, from screening to finish?

FRIEDHOFER: Oh, I should say, at the outside, about seven weeks. But you will notice in the credits, not in the screen credits, but in the book credits, you will find "additional orchestrations by" a man by the name of Milan Roder. He was a sort of freelance orchestrator around town who used to be called in. Well, Korngold was very sweet about it. He said, "Here comes another duel," or another—what was the word he used—"messer-kampfe," knife combat. He said, "I'll give this to Roder because I want to save you for the re-finements—"die feinheiten." We spoke a strange mixture of German and English.

ATKINS: In the late 1930s, there seem to be a lot of Steiner and Korngold pictures all mixed together. That brings us up to *Gone with the Wind.*

FRIEDHOFER: Oh, *Gone with the Wind.* Yeah. That was a heroic job. That was in 1939.

ATKINS: When did the music preparation really begin on that film?

FRIEDHOFER: The picture was finished, and I know that I must have seen it through at least five times, and then piece-meal innumerable times after that to refresh my mind on things. So I actually have never seen *Gone with the Wind* in the theater. By that time, I had had it. This is not putting down the picture which is still a monument of its kind, but I've never had any desire to see it again.

ATKINS: Did you go to any of the previews?

FRIEDHOFER: There were no previews actually. We scored it right up against the deadline of the premiere in Atlanta, Georgia. And I don't think there were any changes made afterwards. No major changes. I know that I would still have the sound of Max Steiner's screams resounding in my ears in the event that there had been any, because there's nothing that he hated more than having to go back and do something over. Well, we all do. Sometimes it's part of the hazards of the business.

ATKINS: Just how much back-and-forth discussion was there on this picture? Was Steiner given a pretty free hand?

FRIEDHOFER: Oh, Steiner was given an absolutely free hand in the thing. And because of the pressure, I started as Max's arranger-orchestrator, and the pressure was so great that Max finally decided that we'd better call in some other people to orchestrate. And he put me on the job of sort of supervising these guys, and writing some of the score—based on his material, of course.

ATKINS: There doesn't seem to be any general agreement about who these people were. Could you give an accurate listing?

FRIEDHOFER: Well, I think that Maurice DePackh was one. Reginald Bassett was following me on the stuff that I was writing. Heinz Roemheld did one or two sequences. I don't know who orchestrated for him. And Adolph Deutsch did one very striking sequence, the whole thing, the siege of Atlanta, with all the wounded lying around and the fire and the whole bit. But the score was fundamentally—the material—was all Max's, really. And even what I wrote, with a few minor exceptions, was based on Max's material, because, after all, if you are pulled in, in that capacity, you forget your own personality and you try to forge a little Steiner—or whoever you're working for. And, I might mention, incidentally, that forging Steiner is more difficult than forging anybody else's style in the business.

ATKINS: Why?

FRIEDHOFER: I don't know. I know I always found it difficult. I could forge Alfred Newman with a great deal more ease than I could Max. And I could even forge Korngold, not that I ever had to. But what I learned from him came in handy in later years on some pictures that were in that particular groove. And I think I got most of my middle-European proclivities out of the way on those things.

ATKINS: When you say that it was difficult to forge his style, was it possibly because it changed? Or was it consistent?

FRIEDHOFER: No, it was consistent, but—I have never quite been able to put my finger on it—Max had a way of pushing whole blocks of chords around in a way that is not particularly germane, shall we say, to my own musical temperament. It always sounded fine, but when I was doing it, it always sort of bothered me, for some reason or other. It worked great for Max, but it just was one of those things that didn't work for me. So I had to force myself into that particular style of writing.

ATKINS: Didn't most of the instrumentation involve the larger orchestras at that time?

FRIEDHOFER: The producers had an idea, at that time, that a big important picture needed a big, important, expensive-sounding score. Of course, that is particularly the case with producers who grew up in the days of silent film and the big movie palaces which had large-sized orchestras in San Francisco, in Chicago, in Los Angeles, and New York. So they were used to that sound as an accompaniment for silent films, and there was a long period where producers had not gotten used to the fact that we now had dialogue and sound effects. So they still wanted scoring, for instance, in the battle scenes, which is a drag, because then the sound effects department would load them up with cannon shots and rifle fire and screams of the wounded, et cetera. So what was the use of music? It was just an interference. It was always so amusing to me that this din of battle, plus music would go on and all of a sudden there'd be a close-up of somebody falling wounded, and a couple of lines of dialogue, and everything would drop out of sight to clear these two lines. And then whammy, up again. It got to be pretty silly.

ATKINS: Was Selznick a man who would want everybody in the orchestra playing all the time?

FRIEDHOFER: Not necessarily, but they wanted a big sound. It had to sound expensive. That's where a certain Hollywood style got a bad name among the highbrow composers who rather contemptuously looked down upon Hollywood. So we took the money and ran, and paid no attention particularly. You have to give them what they want and little by little do a little cultural boring from within, so to speak. And it was a very slow, subtle process of musical indoctrination and sort of stimulating good taste, and little by little, the whole character of the thing changed. Alfred Newman was very important in that respect, in that when Zanuck first started his own production company, which was Twentieth Century, Darryl wanted music you could tap your feet to. But Alfred sort of broadened his musical horizon and by the time I got to working for him out at Twentieth, he gave the composer a pretty free hand, based in the beginning on Alfred's recommendation. Then later, if he got to trust you and like what you did, you had pretty much a free hand.

But that's general, down the line. Goldwyn was different. Goldwyn, while he was a nonmusician, certainly, seemed somehow to have the kind of good taste that is confined to a mere handful of producers. There's another school of thought, too, in that connection. Take an admirable director like Capra. Capra was averse to music, in that he felt if a scene required music, he had somehow failed. I can't hold this against him because he's got a pretty good production record over the years. But it was a very strange thing, that he had that built-in notion that maybe there was something unreal about the idea of underscore. One could very well have pointed out to him that there's something unreal about a sixteen-foot head close-up. This isn't realism.

ATKINS: By the time you were writing the score for *The Best Years*—that's seven years later—there is a chamber music sound there.

FRIEDHOFER: Yes. Well, I don't say that I was responsible for it, but it was my conditioning as a string player and an ardent player of chamber music in my spare time that sort of got me into a very economical approach to the orchestra. Not that I don't like a big fat healthy sound when it's called for. But I don't like it muddy. Even with a big sound in the orchestra I like a certain transparency. I like the air to come through somehow.

ATKINS: Are there any sequences that you did in *Gone with the Wind* that you particularly remember?

FRIEDHOFER: Yes. I remember two very distinctly. There's a very famous scene, one of the first really bloody scenes on the screen—the Yankee deserter who gets shot by Scarlett. That was mine. Also, the famous seduction scene which started with Gable standing behind Scarlett. I remember his hands around her neck. He ultimately picks her up and carries her upstairs, and fade out, fade in to next morning, with Scarlett sitting up in bed with this complacent, pussycat smile on her face. And there were some other minor things I did throughout.

ATKINS: Were you around the dubbing of *Gone with the Wind* ?

FRIEDHOFER: No, because we were recording and dubbing practically simultaneously. Max put in a certain amount of time in dubbing. I know we recorded over on Stage 7 at Goldwyn. But that whole thing had a nightmare quality because we were really under pressure. We never started recording until after dinner, and we'd record until two, sometimes three in the morning. This was before the "golden hours," as they were called, set in. Then we would go home, grab a couple of hours' sleep, get up and write, with orchestrators and copyists breathing down our necks, and grab a bite before recording, and then start the whole thing all over again. And this went on for—I don't know how many weeks—not many, because it was touch and go as far as making the Atlanta premiere was concerned.

ATKINS: Why such a frantic rush?

FRIEDHOFER: It is the usual thing that everybody steals time from the composer. In the first place, there's been a delay in the starting date, perhaps. There've been script changes. Then come retakes, and going over schedule on shooting, and all these imponderables which nobody figures on. But they never *extend* the time, regardless. The schedule is set up and that is it. There's a famous saying. It's pasted up on walls in cutting rooms: "The difficult we do immediately. The impossible takes a little longer."

ATKINS: Anything else about *Gone with the Wind*?

FRIEDHOFER: No, except that I was very much impressed with the picture. It was a phenomenal picture for that time, and for now, even. I don't know what else I can tell you, except that with my ill-gotten gains from it, I built a studio detached from the house, bought a new car, and put in a badminton court.

ATKINS: Then you went back to Warners?

FRIEDHOFER: Right back to Warners.

ATKINS: Did you have any greater stature when you got back?

FRIEDHOFER: No, I don't think so. You see, I don't think I had any screen credit on it. But I was getting credit as arranger-orchestrator at Warner Brothers. My first credit was on *Robin Hood*. I think Leo threw me that as sort of a sop, so I wouldn't start bothering him about writing my own scores.

ATKINS: There are a lot of films in 1940—again, the Steiner films alternated with Korngold—*The Sea Hawk.*

FRIEDHOFER: Yes, I was jumping from one assignment to the other. Part of *The Sea Hawk* I orchestrated sitting on the beach at Laguna, and picked myself up a magnificent sunburn down one side of my body.

ATKINS: Was that to get in the mood of the sea story?

FRIEDHOFER: No, no. I just wanted to get away. It was very nice. The seacoast down there wasn't quite as built up at that time as it is now. It sort of left certain things in my mind that I later utilized.

ATKINS: Did you have much contact with Michael Curtiz?

FRIEDHOFER: No. I never got to meet him personally. But we all knew what Curtiz stood for in the business: a man of stature, definitely.

ATKINS: There is a string of Steiner pictures; I'm looking for credits on *The Letter.*

FREIDHOFER: Oh, that was a fine picture. I have a story in connection with *The Letter.* There's a scene where Bette Davis goes to see a woman who is blackmailing her. There was a very important thing in the film, one of these beaded curtains, which was being agitated by the wind or somebody walking through it. Max persuaded the sound effects department to eliminate all this physical beaded curtain noise, and then we proceeded to make a loop of a contrived beaded curtain. We used something like eighteen percussion instruments on it: two celestes, a harp or so, a tiny gamelan, bells, and other things. It made a fine mish-mash, but we were able to control it in dubbing and mixing—mix it in with the underscore track as well. And we worked several hours to get just the right balance of sound on it. And somebody said, "That's like Max, that here he could have done the same thing with a small electric fan and a set of Japanese wind bells; instead he spends three hours with an eighteen-piece percussion section, getting the same effect." It was a bit of light irony that I don't think was entirely valid, even though it was funny at the time. And of course it was one of those things that enhanced Max's reputation for this sort of thing. But it was very, very effective in the picture.

ATKINS: There are so many Steiner films. *Virginia City*—

FRIEDHOFER: Yes, that was one of the standard Westerns that Warners was turning out in living Technicolor.

ATKINS: *The Sea Wolf*—

FRIEDHOFER: That was Jack London. A fine, fine picture, a little different than anything else that Korngold did over there. As a matter of fact, it was the picture on which he did me the honor of saying, "Look, you know a great deal more about how to orchestrate this kind of music," because it was edgy, quite dissonant for the time. So he said, "I'm not going to tell you a thing about what to do with it." So he left it entirely up to me, and fortunately, it turned out very well. I think that the only thing we really discussed in enormous detail was a scene right at the beginning of the picture where this fog-bound San Francisco Bay is shown, and I think it's two ferry boats that collide, or something like that. He had a beautiful texture laid out on this descriptive fog bit, with a million notes in it, but fun to do. And then there were some very sparse things. I remember there was one thing, sort of a folk thing, played by a harmonica, with kind of a string haze surrounding it—a little like the sailors' song on the masthead in Tristan, not that kind of music, but that concept.

ATKINS: Was it an original of Korngold's or a folksong?

FRIEDHOFER: It was something he wrote in the manner of a folksong.

ATKINS: In almost all these movies, including *The Sea Wolf*, Ray Heindorf's name appears.

FRIEDHOFER: Korngold would hand out certain things to Ray, just as he did in the case of Milan Roder. Ray's sense of the orchestra is, not only in my estimation but in the estimation of Erich Korngold and God knows how many others, a true mastery. As a matter of fact, when I first went over to Warner Brothers to do the *Captain Blood* score, Leo Forbstein, who would always play it safe, had Korngold turn over the main title to Ray Heindorf. And Ray did a brilliant job. And it was at that moment that Korngold said, "Das ist ein riesentalent," which, translated, meant that this is a colossal talent. And then he added, "Und so schnell!" And so fast! Because Ray had a tremendous technique and wrote like a streak. On some of those Busby Berkely pictures, he'd sit in the music library, or in among the copyists in their little quarter. And you'd hear that pencil going, and it sounded like a machine gun. Rat-ta-ta-tat. That fast, because he knew what he was doing. He did the main title on *Captain Blood* and one thing in particular on *Kings Row*. It was the theme for Ann Sheridan and Ronald Reagan. Also, he did the main title on *Sea Hawk*.

Ray was one of those natural talents—all he had to do was hear something once, and he got it, like that. Ray was actually apprenticed to Arthur Lange in New York, who was at that time considered America's foremost dance arranger. When Arthur came to the Coast to go to Metro-Goldwyn-Mayer, he brought Ray along with him. Then Ray worked for Alfred Newman at United Artists and from there he went to Warner Brothers. His going to Warner Brothers was instrumental in the importation of two very fine arrangers, Conrad Salinger, who later wound up at Metro, and Edward Powell, who went to work for Alfred Newman and later went to Twentieth Century Fox and was there for many years.

Another arranger who came out just about that time, in the early '30s, was Herbert Spencer, who also went to work at Twentieth Century Fox before Alfred went in there. Herbert was, for a long time, sort of court arranger for little Shirley Temple. He used to make all her vocals and dance routines at that time.

ATKINS: Had all these men come from New York?

FRIEDHOFER: Yes. Herbert originally came to this country from Santiago, Chile. He studied at the University of Pennsylvania, and suddenly discovered jazz. He played saxophone, and played with the Vincent Lopez band in New York. At that time he encountered young David Raksin, who was also attending the University of Pennsylvania. So, as we say, it's a small world, and ultimately they all wound up on the coast.

ATKINS: What had Conrad Salinger been doing in New York?

FRIEDHOFER: He was a show arranger, and a very good one. He was a graduate of Harvard and more or less a contemporary of John Green's. When Ray left Alfred Newman to go over to Warner Brothers, Salinger came out here for a while. But on his first trip, he just couldn't stand Southern California. So he was here for about six months and went back, after which Eddie Powell joined Alfred. Then Connie came back and finally wound up at Metro-Goldwyn-Mayer, and did so many musicals over there that I wouldn't even venture to count them.

ATKINS: A lot has been said about the "M-G-M sound" and that Salinger was largely responsible for it—

FRIEDHOFER: Salinger was.

ATKINS: How would you describe it in terms of orchestration?

FRIEDHOFER: The only word I can think of is "lush." Beautiful. He had a way of writing for French horn, in particular. He had a very—the only word I can think of to describe it is a very *sexy* horn line wandering through perhaps a big haze of strings. And he also had a way of surrounding the voice. I know he did some beautiful work back of Judy Garland.

We have strayed a little bit from Korngold and Ray Heindorf. But, as I say, for real flair and brilliance, Ray, I think, topped just about anybody. Powell and Spencer and, later, Earle Hagen were three other men to be reckoned with as far as supplying the proper sounds for the musicals that were made, particularly at Fox. Later on, somewhere after the windup of World War II, Earle Hagen joined the Twentieth Century Fox staff, and he and Herb Spencer worked as a team. Eddie was largely confined to making all of Alfred's orchestrations. He worked for Alfred and he also orchestrated for me, and that kept him pretty well occupied.

Just one more thing I'd like to ring in, and that is David Raksin, who was originally brought here by Alfred Newman on the recommendation of Edward Powell, to do the score—or rather, act as musical amanuensis to Charlie Chaplin—on the score of *Modern Times*. I know there was a big hassle about it because Charlie was fairly dictatorial about his music, to the point where, when they were recording, Alfred walked off the podium and told him in no uncertain terms to forget it.

ATKINS: There's been much speculation about just how much Chaplin contributed musically to his films. What would you say?

FRIEDHOFER: I wouldn't venture to guess actually, except that I don't know if Chaplin was capable of notating anything. I daresay not. Maybe all he had was melodic ideas that somebody like David Raksin blew up into orchestral dimensions. So now, let's get on with it.

ATKINS: We're about up to 1941.

FRIEDHOFER: That's sort of approaching the end of my first tour of duty at Warner Brothers.

ATKINS: How did you decide to leave Warners? Was it an amicable parting?

FRIEDHOFER: It was. Actually, it came as kind of a shock to Leo. I didn't leave Warner Brothers until the fall of 1942. I was getting a little bit restless and a little bit impatient over the fact that I was not getting to do my own scores. I think I mentioned that occasionally Max, with those giant economy-sized Westerns they were making—it was just too much for one man to do, so I would jump in and do maybe a couple of reels of this or that or the other. I even forget the ones I worked on.

ATKINS: The general impression here is that you must have been very busy—

FRIEDHOFER: Oh, good Lord!

ATKINS: —and that the Warner music department must have been very well organized.

FRIEDHOFER: Oh, it was. Beautifully organized. And Leo was a master at running a department. He ran it so beautifully it could run itself. I can do no better than to quote from an interview I did with Tony Thomas several years ago. "Forbstein was no musician to speak of, but he was a good executive and organized Warner's music department so well it could practically run itself. We were all cogs in his well-oiled machine. I was servicing Korngold and Steiner to everyone's complete satisfaction, so why change things? Working conditions were good, I was well paid, and I suppressed my creative ego until I could do so no longer."

ATKINS: Warners was supposed to be a very budget-conscious studio. Was the yearly budget sufficient?

FRIEDHOFER: Oh, Lord, yes. Leo stayed within his limits. I don't know what the sums were because that wasn't any of my business. I got paid, and very well, I might say. And those were prosperous years for Warners, too. So there was no money problem. But I got a little bit weary of not being able to do my own thing, so to speak. The singular part of it, and I think the thing that really led to my leaving Warners, was the fact that I was jumping in sometimes when Max was in a jam, and writing a couple of reels, generally chases, all based, naturally, on Max's material. But in those days, Warners used to actually score their trailers and their advance stuff. Sometimes they were compiled out of music that had been written for the film and tailored in the cutting room. But in some cases, a trailer score was actually composed. There were a couple I wrote, also based on Max's material. I know that Leo walked on the stage one time. I think it was an Errol Flynn picture called *Desperate Journey*. Leo walked on the stage while we were recording the thing. Max was conducting, of course, and I looked at Leo and I detected a kind of speculative gleam in his eye. Maybe it was my paranoia; I don't know. The thought occurred to me, "Good God! Am I going to wind up as a trailer composer over here?" And right on top of that came Alfred Newman's offer to go back to Twentieth Century Fox. So, in view of these two facts, I said "goodbye" to Warner Brothers.

★    ★    ★

ATKINS: Was the first film you did at Twentieth Century *China Girl*?

FRIEDHOFER: That's correct. That's not taking into consideration the amount of ghosting, et cetera, that I'd done there in my spare time. I worked on *Son of Fury*. Alfred and I worked on odds and ends and bits and pieces during that whole period when I was still officially working at Warner Brothers.

ATKINS: How did you find it, working at Twentieth Century after this long period at Warners?

FRIEDHOFER: It was a slightly difficult time for me because both Alfred and I were, each one of us, going through a domestic crisis at the time. And somebody had, unfortunately, quoted me as saying something out of context, which didn't sit so well with either Alfred or some of my colleagues out there. It was not intended as a slap at any of the current methods, but it was so taken. I was, so to speak, in the doghouse for a long time, and the vibes were not good.

ATKINS: Where was this quote? In the newspapers?

FRIEDHOFER: No, no, no. It was something that I said to the effect that at last I would have the opportunity to show what I could do. Certainly you'd have to take an awfully broad interpretation of that to regard it as a put-down of what anybody else was doing, but it was so taken. I had a conference with Alfred, who was at that time living in the Beverly Wilshire Hotel, where he always went during a period of domestic upheaval, and he literally tore the score of *China Girl* to pieces. And if it hadn't been for a certain stubborn streak in my makeup, I would have walked out right then and there. But on sober consideration, I said, "No, I've got to fight this thing out." And the amusing part of it was that in the next issue of *Film Music Notes*, that would be early in 1943, there was a glowing review of the score, which was, however, not credited to me, but to Alfred Newman. Robert Emmett Dolan sent me the clipping because he knew I had done the score.

ATKINS: Was your name on the screen for *China Girl*?

FRIEDHOFER: Yes, it was, but apparently the reviewer just saw Alfred Newman as musical director and that was it. He did conduct that score. And my name, at that time, was relatively unknown, except as arranger-orchestrator. And besides, at that time, the credits were all bunched. It was a kind of photo finish between the wardrobe woman and the composer. In the beginning, even Alfred didn't get solo credit. Then later on, after the Academy Award, I began to get the top half of credit on the screen. But I know that on *Best Years of Our Lives*, I'm bunched in with several names.

ATKINS: *China Girl* and *The Black Swan*, on which you also worked, were written by Ben Hecht. Did you know him?

FRIEDHOFER: I never knew Ben personally. I used to see him around. In my early twenties, long before I came to Hollywood, I read a couple of novels of Ben's. One of them was a thing called *Gargoyles*. They were the very young Ben Hecht. I think he was still working on Chicago newspapers at the time.

There was a time when Ben Hecht was under contract to Sam Goldwyn, and it was at the time when Dorothy Parker was also over there. They tell a story about these two, who were a pair of real cut-ups, sticking their heads out of the window of their offices in their building on the lot and screaming at the passers-by, "Let us out! We're as sane as you are!" I met Dorothy Parker on several occasions, later, and it was unfortunately in the period of her decline, in the merest vestige of what had once been a brilliant, brilliant woman, and a witty one. I'd always been a tremendous admirer of her work and, at the few times that I met her, she just didn't make any sense at all. It was very, very tragic.

ATKINS: Was she still working in Hollywood?

FRIEDHOFER: No. I think she was under suspicion because of the House Un-American Activities Committee at that time. I'm fairly certain that she got on that unwritten Hollywood blacklist out here, which, incidentally, just missed me by about that much.

ATKINS: Would you like to expand on that?

FRIEDHOFER: Yes. I was temporarily associated with an outfit called the Hollywood Educational Center, which dear Louella Par-

sons referred to as "the little Red schoolhouse." Well, being politi-
cally naive, as I still am, I was asked to come over there and lecture
once a week to a class of film students on the function of music in
films. So I did. I was having a rather good time, exercising my vocal
chords, beating my gums, so to speak. And there was an announcement of a faculty meeting at the home of John Cromwell in Beverly
Hills. I got there late and everybody had been talking a lot, and there
was a sudden silence when I came in. I don't think they were quite
sure of me, whether I was a capitalist spy or possibly a likely candi-
date. But it left me with a strangely uncomfortable feeling, so I sort
of bowed out of the whole thing. But, nevertheless, my temporary
association with the outfit, plus the fact that I was a contributor to
several liberal causes, didn't get me in trouble with the FBI or the
House Un-American Activities Committee, but it did get me into
trouble with a man who was at that time president of the Musicians'
Union, Jack Tenney. *Not* a nice man. He immediately slapped a local
Red smear on anybody who didn't vote for him the last time he ran
for the presidency of the union. But that died away.

ATKINS: Do you recall how you set up your classes?

FRIEDHOFER: I didn't actually go into the techniques. I was lec-
turing about the general approach, the reasons for film music and the
general aesthetic, and so on. The People's Educational Center didn't
have an awful lot of money at that time. I know my lectures were
gratis. And on my part, it was beneficial because it got me out of a
congenital shyness about standing up and speaking my piece. It was
psychologically very beneficial to me. I still get moments of clamming
up, but not many.

ATKINS: Getting back to *China Girl*, Arthur Morton has written his
name, and David Raksin's, on my screen credit sheet as orchestrators.

FRIEDHOFER: Yes, they both orchestrated that.

ATKINS: And on *The Chetniks* also?

FRIEDHOFER: Yes. *The Chetniks* was orchestrated by Morton,
Spencer, and, strangely enough, Conrad Salinger, who was freelancing.

ATKINS: *The Chetniks* was released in 1943.

FRIEDHOFER: Yes, it was my next assignment after *China Girl*. Those were the war years.

ATKINS: There's a movie that was made around that time, with a marvelous title: *They Came to Blow Up America*.

FRIEDHOFER: Yeah, which was originally called *School for Sabotage*. I believe it starred George Sanders, who infiltrates the Yorkville Nazi deal and is sent to Germany to study all the methods for sabotaging American industry. He's brought over here via submarine and ultimately exposes the whole Nazi spy and sabotage operation on the East Coast. A typical cops and robbers thing.

ATKINS: Was there any reason why, when you went to Twentieth Century, that you didn't conduct?

FRIEDHOFER: I had always had a sort of a timidity about conducting, and actually didn't really start that kind of activity until I got into television, until I had my own series, which I was doing on a package deal. Naturally, I was paying for orchestra, copying—not the sound stage or any of that—the librarian, and then what was left over was mine. A conductor—at that time, who got double scale—would have meant that much money out of my pocket. So I decided to have a stab at it. As I recall now, I didn't conduct the pilot; Alexander Courage, who was working over at Metro then, conducted the pilot for me. And then, after that, I decided to take over, I think largely because Sandy got busy on something else, and I was stuck. So I did conduct, and the first three or four segments that I did after that were a shattering experience, although I did manage to bull my way through, largely because of the fact that I had the good will of the orchestra musicians. After that, I began to catch on, and finally got so that I really enjoyed it. Then later, when I was working with Spencer and Hagen on various TV series, Herbie always insisted upon my conducting my own stuff. But outside of that, I have actually done very little conducting. I did one feature, around 1961, a picture called *Homicidal*, which I did for Bill Castle—one of his usual horror things. But that was the only feature that I conducted.

ATKINS: Now we have this picture with Mr. Hitchcock, *Lifeboat*.

FRIEDHOFER: Oh! That was a very, very fine picture, but Hitch didn't want any music, except a main and an end title, and a few things—little source things—that Slezak was singing, and that Canada Lee played on the harmonica. And I had approached Alfred with an idea that the picture did, I felt, need music—not a great deal, but sort of in the shape of very classy so-called radio bridges, because there were dissolves and transitions as time went by, and these poor devils were all afloat in this lifeboat. Al agreed with me, but Hitchcock was adamant about it. And this gave rise, incidentally, to that wonderful story that is attributed to David Raksin. He asked Hitchcock, "How come no music?" because David, as I, felt that the picture did need something. So Hitch replied, "Out in the middle of the ocean, where's the orchestra?" So Dave said, "Out in the middle of the ocean, where's the camera?"

So the only thing that I contributed was a main title, and a very short end title. But the main title was rather interesting. The film started with the explosion, and this eternal whistle, or rather this low hooter. And I figured out what the notes were, and it built up into this sort of cluster-like chord. And I wrote the whole main title around that, using that as a sort of multiple pedal point. And then finally, when the liner sinks completely, the music went on without this thing. But it grew out of that, sort of despondent Water Music, you might say, and wound up, as you pan over to the boat and into it, and you see Miss Bankhead's legs, with a large run in one or both stockings. And then you pan up to her face, which has an unforgettable expression on it, which can only be described in four-letter words. But that was it. I wasn't even supposed to get credit on the thing for music. But after Alfred read through the main title and conducted it, he said, "Look, this deserves a screen credit for you." So he went up front, and that's why I'm on the screen on that thing, for the shortest score I ever wrote.

ATKINS: There are some Warner films, such as *Casablanca*, that were released in 1943. Did you go back to Warners to do those?

FRIEDHOFER: No, I didn't go back. *Casablanca* was actually done in, I believe, 1941, as near as I can recall.

ATKINS: Then, *Casablanca, Constant Nymph, Watch on the Rhine* were all done before you went to Twentieth.

FRIEDHOFER: Yes, before the exodus from Warner Brothers.

ATKINS: The next film I have listed is *Wintertime.*

FRIEDHOFER: There's *China Girl, Chetniks, Roger Touhy*—

ATKINS: That was released in 1944.

FRIEDHOFER: Yes, because they had to do a lot of recutting on that. There were some things in the original version that didn't sit too well with the FBI, so we had to recut, and I think they retook some things. So the picture was late in getting out of the studio. It is now called *The Last of the Gangsters.* I have a pretty good recall of that particular period because I was being shoved around into various offices. When I was doing *Roger Touhy,* I was occupying what had once been part of the Will Rogers adobe bungalow, which Will Rogers never really occupied. You know, they had a real set-up there, with cactus and an adobe and that kind of Spanish furniture, and rugs on the walls, and all that sort of thing. And he hated it apparently, because he used to sit out in his automobile, generally parked between two sound stages, and he had a typewriter stand in the car and he used to write his column there. That's way back in the first part of the '30s, when he made a couple of pictures out there at that time. One that I remember was *They Had to See Paris,* with Fifi D'Orsay. I think that was released in 1929, somewhere in there.

ATKINS: Did you know him at all?

FRIEDHOFER: He used to always give me a greeting whenever I saw him. He'd say "Hi." But I never talked with him extensively.

ATKINS: Is that bungalow still standing?

FRIEDHOFER: No, that whole thing was revamped. As a matter of fact, there were two bungalows, one of which had been bungalows, one of which had been built for John MacCormack, when he came over here to do his solo thing for Fox in 1929, a picture called *Song of My Heart*, which brought Maureen O'Sullivan over as his ingenue. It was the real thatched cottage bit, and all that, and it was later occupied for a while by George Gershwin when he was out here doing the *Delicious* score. Then, when Alfred Newman finally wound up at Twentieth, it became his headquarters, and he worked there. When Alfred finally left Twentieth, in quasi-retirement, or to freelance, Jerry Wald took over those two buildings and combined them into one. There was a lot of redecoration. I think they took the thatch off the roof, which was getting kind of moth-eaten by that time. I don't think those two buildings still exist. I know that every time I go on the lot, which hasn't been for a couple of years now, I always have to reorient myself because I don't know exactly where I am anymore.

Anyway, after *Roger Touhy* was *Wintertime*, which was only partially mine. I think Arthur Lange did a lot of work on that. I know that for *Wintertime*, I did two rather back-breaking chores. One of them was a comedy scene, a sort of comedy chase with Cesar Romero being chased all over, through the snow and what not and in and out of hotel rooms and buildings. And the other was probably as tough an assignment as any I've ever had. Sonia Henie wanted a different orchestration on The Waltz of the Flowers, from The Nutcracker Suite. And to try to do something different from what Tchaikovsky had done was not exactly the easiest, or the most rewarding, or the pleasantest task in the world, because you are so conscious that here, in its original form, is a veritable masterpiece or a classic example of how these things should be done. To have to find equivalents that were satisfactory was not the easiest job in the world, and I wasn't happy with it, but everybody else seemed to be, so why should I fight with them. But I remember sitting at the recording and feeling very brought down by the thing.

ATKINS: What was her objection to Tchaikovsky?

FRIEDHOFER: Heaven only knows. As I recall, Arthur Lange was supposed to do it, and I think he said, "Look, Hugo would do a much better job on this than I would," which was a compliment, but I think it was also kind of a cop-out on Arthur's part. He didn't want to fool around with it. Having a great admiration for Peter Ilich, he didn't want to have the onus of lousing up his original score. I wasn't doing anything else at the time, so that was it. But after that, to take the Fox things in continuity, I was given a film called *Paris after Dark*. This was George Sanders, Phillip Dorn, Brenda Marshall, and the Nazi stock company that were playing all the heavies at that time. It was about the Paris underground. Then came *The Lodger*. But actually, it was *Paris after Dark* that sort of restored me to favor out there, you might say. And then came *The Lodger*.

ATKINS: Were there any problems with that?

FRIEDHOFER: No problems at all. John Brahm was the director on that and was very pleased with what I had done on it, as was Robert Bassler, the producer. I liked the score tremendously. I liked the picture and the score, although it was another of what you might call the second unit Fox films, the so-called B pictures, which were under the aegis of Sol Wurtzel and Brynie Foy.

ATKINS: Your name, among many others, is on *The Gang's All Here*, which was a Busby Berkeley production.

FRIEDHOFER: Oh, yes. I think I made a bunch of arrangements of Harry Warren's Academy Award–winning song, You'll Never Know, mainly as background for various love scenes and what not. But that was my entire association with that.

ATKINS: You mentioned that when you worked at Warners, you worked mostly at home, and that you would bring the things in—

FRIEDHOFER: I didn't bring them in. They were sent in. There was a sort of shuttle messenger service between either the music library and my place, or else between the music library and Max Steiner's place.

ATKINS: Anyway, you said that now that you were at Fox, you had an office. Did you do most of your work at the studio?

FRIEDHOFER: I worked partially at home and partially in the studio. During that particular period that we were talking about, my second hitch, you might say, at Twentieth Century Fox, for a while I had an office in what had been the old executive building. Then I was moved into the Rogers bungalow. And then I was in one of the music bungalows, which were on the main street, the one just above the Tennessee gate entrance. Oh, I know, I was pushed out of the Rogers bungalow because Leo Robin and Nacio Herb Brown, I think, were doing the score for a musical called *Greenwich Village*, released in 1944. And in that one, I think I finished the score to *Home in Indiana*. I still have a very warm feeling about that picture. And it was a very pleasant association with Henry Hathaway. And this is a picture that created three new stars: Jeanne Crain, Lon McCallister, and June Haver. The cast also included Walter Brennen and Charlotte Greenwood. She didn't do any musical numbers in that picture. She was strictly a character actress at that time, but good Lord, I remember, as a very small child, her doing musicals, you know, that eccentric dance that she did—those enormously long legs that she used to high kick with. That's going back to my short pants days.

After that came *A Wing and a Prayer*, which was sort of a semi-documentary score. It was the story of one of the strategic turning points in the war in the South Pacific. I worked on several documentaries in that particular period. That was before the thing had gotten established over at the Hal Roach Studio. And we were all throwing in our services for free for the government. There was one that John Ford directed, *The Battle of the Midway*, and there was one documentary about Pearl Harbor that Sam Engel and Gregg Toland did together. I can't recall the name of it. It was about Pearl Harbor and the whole espionage system that existed in the Islands at that time. I think they actually got old Walter Huston to do a sort of a symbolic Uncle Sam bit in the thing.

ATKINS: *Battle of the Midway* is such a famous film and has been shown so many times.

FRIEDHOFER: As I recall, it was rather torn apart by a reviewer who objected very much to the use of "Onward, Christian Soldiers," which I believe John Ford insisted upon. The reviewer said, "So there were no Jewish soldiers in the American army?"

Incidentally, we sort of catered to John Ford, whom we liked and admired as a director. I know that in one place, there was a sky—an aerial shot of the tropical islands—and we referred back to a piece of thematic material of Alfred's out of *Hurricane*, a very ethereal and high altitude schmaltz type of thing that John liked. So we shoved it in because there was hardly time to sit down and write a lot of original music because we not only had our studio commitments to fulfill, but these things, as I said, were done for free, and done to the best of our ability at that time.

ATKINS: Were they recorded on the lot?

FRIEDHOFER: Oh, yes, they were recorded by the studio orchestra. Everybody out there who worked on them was under contract at the time, on salary.

ATKINS: You mentioned that the score for *A Wing and a Prayer* was also a semi-documentary score.

FRIEDHOFER: Well, this was a score that used—it wasn't an original score, really. We used a march that Chuck Wolcott, who was over at Disney at the time, had written for the Navy Air Corps, a thing called Wings of the Navy. And there were a lot of fancy transcriptions of Anchors Aweigh, and a few things like that. It was a score that was literally dictated by Darryl Zanuck. "I'd like this here. I'd like that." So what do you do?

ATKINS: Was this during the period when Zanuck had returned from the war?

FRIEDHOFER: Yes. He'd just come back. And it was just about that time that the pressures began to tell on me very seriously, and I got my release from Twentieth and went back to freelancing.

ATKINS: One of your first freelance pictures was one for which you got an Academy Award nomination, *The Woman in the Window*.

FRIEDHOFER: Yes. That was done for International. This was Bill Goetz and Nunnally Johnson's company. That's the outfit that later became Universal-International. But Nunnally stayed with them but a short time. *Woman in the Window* was my first Academy Award nomination, done in collaboration with Arthur Lange. After that I did another picture, also with Arthur, for which I think I wrote the bulk of it, *Along Came Jones.*

ATKINS: That was released the following year.

FRIEDHOFER: Yes. And it was, incidentally, the first picture in which anybody dared to kid a Western. Gary Cooper and Loretta Young and Dan Duryea, as the heavy, were in it. It was the first one in which the hero—or nonhero, actually—was a goof who couldn't shoot very well, and he couldn't rope very well, and he didn't ride very well, and he couldn't wrestle steers very well. But he had a way with the ladies. And it was kind of an amusing picture, but at the time, not successful because of that old tradition: you don't kid a Western.

ATKINS: There are some films that were released in '44: *Arsenic and Old Lace*, and *Roughly Speaking* in 1945 and *The Man I Love*, also that year.

FRIEDHOFER: Yes. I'm not sure about *Arsenic and Old Lace* and the others. I still think that those were made prior to my leaving Warners the first time. But, that's a long time ago. The two that I recall were *Cloak and Dagger* and the Western *Cheyenne.*

ATKINS: That was released in 1946. It gets very confusing.

FRIEDHOFER: To me, the pictures are always associated not with the release dates, but with the actual writing of the score and the recording. After that, I've generally been on something else. To tell the truth, I have—except in the case of command sneak previews—very seldom seen films in the theater until perhaps long after the fact. My running has generally been confined to studio projection of the final print.

It was right hard on the heels of *Cheyenne* that I got this call from Emil Newman, who by this time had left Twentieth and was musical director for Samuel Goldwyn. Apparently Al had recommended me to Goldwyn to do the score to *The Best Years of Our Lives.*

ATKINS: I think we have to backtrack a little on a few pictures.

FRIEDHOFER: Yes. In that same freelance period, I did two films for Ed Small, *Brewster's Millions* and *Getting Gertie's Garter*. And also, I completely forgot that in 1945, I got a call from Columbia Pictures to do a costume Western called *The Bandit of Sherwood Forest*, which was sort of a Robin Hood deal, and which didn't do me any harm at all. It was a beautiful showcase for music. It was so much like—the film, the whole character of it—was so much like the Korngold *Robin Hood* that I couldn't possibly move in that direction without being accused of plagiarism. So I went very archaic on the thing, you know, the Merrie England bit, with a smattering of Vaughan Williams and that sort of thing. It got me a plaque from the National Film Music Council when it was released. And I think you'll find a review of it in an issue of *Film Music Notes* from around that period. The review, incidentally, was written by Ernest Gold, who was later to become famous for his *Exodus* score, and some other things.

Following *The Bandit of Sherwood Forest*, I worked to a certain extent on *The Jolson Story*, just as an arranger. And in that connection, a very funny thing happened on stage. I had made an arrangement of the celebrated Anniversary Waltz, and when Morris Stoloff, who was the musical director, read through it the first time, he turned to me with a kind of grin, and he said, "It's plain to see that you worked a lot of Jewish weddings when you were a cello player," and he was right, because it had all the schmaltzy cello obbligato in it, and the whole thing.

ATKINS: That picture is famous because of Jolson's comeback.

FRIEDHOFER: It *is* famous. And it's interesting that on account of the passage of years, Jolson lost some of his higher notes, and everything had to be transposed down. He did the actual singing, and Larry Parks did a magnificent job of lip synching to Jolson's tracks.

Also, in that period, I was called in to do what little underscoring there was in a rather well-known Rita Hayworth film, *Gilda*, on which I did the main title and a longish dramatic sequence that wound the picture up. Marlin Skiles actually did her vocal backgrounds and so on, but on the underscoring, for some reason or other—either Marlin was busy, or else Morris Stoloff felt that I should do this particular background thing, the underscoring on the last reel or two of the film—I was pulled in to do that.

ATKINS: Had you known her?

FRIEDHOFER: No. She was Rita Cansino, originally. And I believe that she and Margaret O'Brien's mother and another gal were quite famous as a dancing trio down in Baja, or in Tijuana at one time. But when Rita Cansino got into films, they changed her name to Rita Hayworth, and also changed her hairline. After *Gilda* and *The Jolson Story*, I did one other picture over there, of which I'm kind of fond yet, a picture called *So Dark the Night*. It was a kind of mystery detective story about a detective who commits a murder and then solves the crime himself. It starred a man who'd been a character actor around town and over at Columbia for a number of years, a man named Stefan Geray. He was a singer and dancer in Viennese musicals before he came to this country.

But it was an interesting picture to do, and it was sort of a gamble on my part because we could gamble in those days. We didn't have all the restrictions we have now. I know Morris called me in to look at this thing with him. He asked my opinion on it. He said he had a very low budget and couldn't afford to put a lot of music in it, so he was thinking of maybe scoring about ten minutes of it and doing the rest out of the library. Well, I got a look at the picture and I was intrigued by it. I felt that it was a good opportunity for music. So I made the kind of deal with him that the Composers and Lyricists Guild of America would frown upon now. But the GCLA wasn't in existence then. So I said, "Look Morris, I love the picture. I think it needs a lot of music. We can do it with a relatively small orchestra. And I will *give* you the score. I will orchestrate it myself. All you have to do, to comply with union regulations, is pay me for orchestration and give me a full card on the screen, and you've got it." So he said, "Okay, I'll go up and talk to Harry." He did, and came back laughing and said, "Harry bought the idea. He said, 'What is this guy, an idealist?' " But anyway, it was very successful. The picture was directed by a man who's sort of disappeared from the scene, a very interesting director named Joseph Lewis. He made a lot of Westerns and low budget things. But this was a real gem on his part. The cast was excellent, all unknowns, except for Steve Geray. The picture was quite successful, and occasionally you can catch it on the tube.

ATKINS: Your idea of using a small orchestral group has been picked up by a lot of people since then.

FRIEDHOFER: Oh, yes, I used practically a chamber orchestra, except for, I think, two or three sequences in the picture. We had one special session with a larger group. But even the larger group was small by comparison. It was largely done with a double string quartet, bass, harp, piano, one percussion, some woodwinds, and one French horn. And then for the bigger stuff I added four more violins and some brass, and that was it. But it turned out very well. I had some acetates on it for a long time, but I don't know what has become of them. Those things get lost, owing to my carelessness and my disregard for the past. *So Dark the Night* was just before I went back to Warners to do those two films that we've already talked about, *Cloak and Dagger* and *Cheyenne*. And then, *Best Years*.

★   ★   ★

ATKINS: You were once quoted in an interview as saying that you were influenced by Copland when you wrote *The Best Years of Our Lives*.

FRIEDHOFER: Oh, good Lord, yes. Oh, yeah. That's not an influence that I'm ashamed of, either. I got to know Aaron quite well and was tremendously fond of him. I like his forthrightness, his honesty, and his great musical integrity. He wrote the way that he felt. Actually, the influence was largely in paring, in my weeding out the run-of-the-mine Hollywood schmaltz, and trying to do a very simple, straightforward, almost folklike score. I don't think I actually looked over Aaron's shoulder, but there was a certain use, perhaps a certain harmonic similarity at times. But that was it.

As I recall, there were no troubles except that Willy Wyler, with whom I had discussed every aspect of the score thoroughly, assured me that what he wanted was not a typical Hollywood score. He wanted Americana. And Willy, as you know, has a sad affliction as regards his hearing. It's shot, somehow, with the result that he can't hear low frequencies very well, and when he can hear them, he hates them. But anyhow, the score was done, and we recorded it as we went along. The recording was spread out over a considerable period of time. About halfway through, Willy and Emil Newman, who was conductor, musical director, that is, on the thing, and myself—I forget who else was there—we had dinner up in one of the dressing rooms in the Writers' Building. And Willy said to me, out of a clear sky, "You know, I think this is all wrong. I think we have put music in all the places that don't need music, and we have left music out of all the places that do need music." I forget just what I said, but I had counted ten very slowly before opening my yap, and I think I fluffed it off in a nice sort of way. I said, "Well, Willy, isn't it a little late to reconsider now? Don't forget that you and I sat down and discussed this film foot by foot, and I went exactly according to what you wanted and what I felt was right. Don't worry about the music." Then I got real classical on him. I said, "Remember what Rimsky-Korsakov said to Stravinsky in relation to the music of Debussy. He said, 'You know, it's very dangerous to listen to that kind of music because you might wind up liking it.' So Willy, please try to bear in mind that you might wind up liking this score."

But he hated it! He literally hated that score. He asked me, "Why didn't you give me something like *Wuthering Heights*?" That was Alfred Newman's score and a beautiful one, but I think it would have been highly inappropriate in this film. It's very much like what happened with Billy Wilder when I did *Ace in the Hole*, or *The Big Carnival*, as it was later called. At the final recording session, he said, "That's a good score. Of course, not a note of melody, but . . ." I said to him, "Look, Billy, you've portrayed a set of characters on the screen. Hardly any of them are admirable at all. Would you—did you—want me to soften the blow?" He kind of grinned and said, "No." That was it. But fundamentally, being German, and in spite of that post-World War I cynicism that infuses practically every picture that he's ever made, he's still a kind of a Wagnerian pussycat at heart. He's fundamentally got that schmaltz outlook.

Anyway, Willy hated the score with the result that I was practically treated like an outcast, a pariah, on that lot, because only one man stood up for it. And that, strangely enough, was Leon Fromkess. From Goldwyn I didn't hear a peep. But Leon—after the picture had opened here for a week's showing, in order to qualify it for the Academy Awards—Leon stopped me on the lot and said, "Hugo, I was listening backstage at the Beverly Hills Theater, and it's a beautiful score. Loved it." And then, it was fortunate enough to get a nomination. And then, of course, everything was all right again. And even Willy, who had gone to New York to see the opening at the Astor—I got a telegram from him in which he literally took back everything he had said. But I found out later why—because Marc Blitzstein, with whom he was a buddy, out of the army, spoke very, very highly of the score. And Willy is always influenced by that.

I've got to jump forward here to throw in an anecdote about Miklos Rozsa. I was over at Metro doing I don't know what, and Miki stopped me one day in the commissary. He said, "Look, you've worked for Willy Wyler. What's he like?" And I told him about Willy's vagaries about relying on other people's judgment about whether the music is any good or not. This was just before *Ben Hur*. Shortly after *Ben Hur* was released, I ran into Miki again. He stopped about fifteen feet away from me and started shaking his head. I said, "What's the matter, Miki?" He said, "Well, you remember I asked you about Willy Wyler?" I said, "Yeah." He said, "Well, you didn't tell me half." Apparently Wyler didn't like the score to *Ben Hur* until some aunt of his down in Texas saw it and said she liked it very much. And that made everything okay again. And yet I *love* Willy. To me, he's one of the great directors of all time in this business.

ATKINS: Did you ever work with Wyler again?

FRIEDHOFER: I orchestrated about two-thirds of the score of *The Westerner*. But not as a composer. But those were my only two experiences with Wyler. I see him around once in a while—we're always friendly, and I ask him when he's going to do another picture. And I would do another picture with Willy in a minute.

ATKINS: I saw *Best Years* just the other day, and I was very impressed by the contrast between the small orchestral groups and the scene where Dana Andrews goes to look at the airplanes, which has a large orchestral background.

FRIEDHOFER: Oh, that long walk through the graveyard. I said to somebody, in connection with that, that the volume was up to drown out the screams of pain from the taxpayers. No, but it was a tremendously impressive scene, and in discussing the score with Willy, he said "From here on, this is your baby. This music has got to tell the story. It's got to give the audience the feeling of—" he didn't use the word, but it literally amounted to the catharsis that Dana goes through when he climbs up into the cockpit of this dismantled bomber, and you see him through the plexiglass. And the camera pulls back, and there are four pans to where the motors were in the planes. I actually revved the motors musically. It was a pure musical sound with just the barest smidgen of actual physical motor noise. But the real wallop was in the sound of the orchestra itself. Strangely enough, it was a trick that I had done years before, not as elaborately as this, but a plane taking off, in which I fooled around with the simulation of motor noise. But at that time, nobody paid any attention to it, but here it was so dramatically valid that I think that, rather than anything else in the score, was responsible for the Oscar. Because this was something that the completely tone-deaf members of the Academy could grab onto. The subtleties were, I think, probably wasted on all except the music branch, but who cares? And that is why I've said on several occasions that I attach a great deal more importance to an Academy nomination than I do or did to the Award itself, because this was something that was bestowed on you by a jury of your peers. As for the rest, this was touch and go. I said once that you could do a great score in a picture that didn't quite make it at the box office and get nowhere. And you could do a picture that really made it at the box office, with a fair-to-middling score, and pick yourself up an award.

ATKINS: Getting back to *Best Years*—and this is somewhat tangential—did I see a shot of Gene Krupa?

FRIEDHOFER: Yes, you did. There was a montage, after the boys get home—the nightclub thing—where they wind up finally in Hoagy Carmichael's joint, or Homer's uncle's place, I should say. That was originally a much longer montage. We moved through about half a dozen spots or so.

ATKINS: Were there any other famous jazz names in the sequence?

FRIEDHOFER: No, not that I can recall.

ATKINS: How did he happen to be in that shot?

FRIEDHOFER: I don't know. It may have been a clip from something else that he had done in a Goldwyn film before I got hitched up with this job. But we had quite a time pasting that montage together.

ATKINS: Was the montage postscored?

FRIEDHOFER: It was partially postscored and partly prescored. I know there was some gal, whose name I can't remember, who did a kind of an early bop type thing in it, called "Ee Bop a Ree Bop." I know that was prescored. But the bulk of it was postscored because there were various cuts. They were rather quick, half a dozen bars here, half a dozen bars there. We made them all overlength, and then overlapped them. And then finally, after the first preview, a lot of that was deleted. That was about all the prescoring that I recall in the film. Oh—the scene of Homer and Hoagy, when he plays "Chopsticks" with Hoagy, that was standard, on the stage. I believe all Hoagy's numbers were standard recording in there—when he plays "Among My Souvenirs" for Freddie March and Myrna Loy. A charming scene, that whole thing. And that wonderful confab between Hoagy and his nephew, when he plays "Up a Lazy River," and talks very philosophically to his nephew. There were so many things in that picture that stay with me, that are so touching to this day.

There's one thing. I don't mind, of course, but I'm so indelibly associated with this film and with the music for it, in the minds of so many people, that I find myself feeling very much like Max Steiner did about *The Informer*. Everybody would come to him years later and say, "God, that *Informer*. That was a great score." And Max would sort of break down and weep, that is, to me, and say, "I've done so many things since that I like so much better." So, having this one thing singled out until it gets to be a pain to me—I know there was one fellow, a pianist, and a very good one, named Ray Turner, who, every time he saw me, would always say, "Man, that *Best Years*, that was a score!" I felt like giving him a rap in the mouth, but I'm not a violent man.

★    ★    ★

ATKINS: You seem to have gotten to a lot of different studios in that period. There's *Wild Harvest* at Paramount—

FRIEDHOFER: Now, that was the first after *Best Years*. That was an Alan Ladd deal that had to do with wheat harvesting in the Midwest. *Best Years* had sort of put the Americana stamp on me, so Paramount, actually of their own volition, called me. The Academy Award carries that weight, you know. I could never get a picture at Paramount before that. Louie Lipstone would always say, "Yeah, he's a fine arranger. He's a fine orchestrator, but I don't know." One of those things. And then on the strength of the Academy Award, I finally wound up with a multiple picture deal over there, nonexclusive. But, anyhow, *Wild Harvest*, then came a picture at Columbia, *The Swordsman*. That was done in the spring of 1947. *Wild Harvest* sort of overlapped from 1946 to '47 and *The Swordsman* followed that. And that was not released until late in '47. I know because I went on an extended vacation and they still hadn't recorded it until just after I got back. That was kind of a fun picture to do.

ATKINS: You seem to have had a very good rapport with the people at Columbia.

FRIEDHOFER: I did, with Morris Stoloff. I found him a very pleasant man to work with. As a matter of fact, I think it was around that time he actually offered me a contractual deal over there. But I turned it down for some reason. I think it was a question of money and also being locked into one studio. I had a kind of aversion to that. But anyway, that's the position that George Duning ultimately wound up with. And a very good man George is, too.

   Then, the first thing I did after I got back from the Caribbean was a picture for the long-dead Enterprise Studios, one of the heads of which was the man who had formerly been head of publicity at Warner Brothers, Charlie Einfeld. They made a picture over there called *Arch of Triumph*, which really bankrupted them because they had a lot of faith in it, but somehow it did not come off. And it literally folded the studio. But *Body and Soul* was a big money-maker for them. I don't know just how many pictures they made. I don't think they made more than four pictures, and then they folded. But *Body and Soul* was a success. It was one of my two prizefight pictures, with John Garfield and Lilli Palmer. We had some remakes on *Body and Soul* and I pulled in Emil Newman to conduct for me. But he got tied up with the preparation on the next Goldwyn picture, *The Bishop's Wife*, so this was actually the first time I ever picked up the stick. I did these tie-ins and a couple of additional sequences and managed somehow to get away with it.

ATKINS: What was your reaction to your own conducting?

FRIEDHOFER: Well, I liked it. I was frankly terrified, but all of us who had worked at Twentieth Century Fox were a little bit brainwashed because Al was truly magnificent as a conductor. And nobody ever really conducted out at Twentieth unless you were a Newman. It was sort of gentle nepotism in a way, but it was all right. As a matter of fact, Alfred used to claim that Emil had the best hands of anybody in the family for conducting. The first thing I did with Emil was *The Best Years of Our Lives*.

ATKINS: Did he conduct that?

FRIEDHOFER: Yes. He also conducted *The Bishop's Wife* and another picture of Goldwyn's, *Enchantment*, and also *Roseanna McCoy*, *Edge of Doom*, *A Song Is Born*, and the whole Goldwyn product for quite a period of time. After *Body and Soul*, I went back to Goldwyn to do *The Bishop's Wife*.

ATKINS: That was another Academy Award nomination. Anything to say about that film?

FRIEDHOFER: *Bishop's Wife* was fun. It remains to this day one of my favorite pictures. It's a very warm and very charming picture, with Loretta Young, David Niven, Monty Woolley, and Cary Grant as the angel.

ATKINS: That had some sequences in it with the Mitchell Boy Choir.

FRIEDHOFER: Those were prescored to a certain extent. Charlie Henderson, the very fine vocal arranger, did some very nice things with celestial voices and all that sort of thing. Those were overdubs. I remember the Mitchell Boy Choir very well. They were sort of an enlarged version of the Dead End Kids. A bunch of little devils, actually. After we got through with the recording, the overdubbing and so on, Emil Newman said, "Come on, kids. You're all going to get some ice cream." So they all went over to the commissary and wouldn't you know it, every one of them ordered banana splits, or something like that.

ATKINS: There were quite a lot of them, weren't there?

FRIEDHOFER: Oh, there were. There was a raft of them, as I recall.

ATKINS: Anything else about *Bishop's Wife*?

FRIEDHOFER: Oh, there was one long, long sequence in the film, the ice skating deal in Central Park when the angel gets out on the ice and does all this fantastic figure skating, and finally lures Jimmy Gleason out on the ice. It was a fun thing to do but it was a back-breaker because I think the sequence lasted seven or eight minutes, all told. That was the last thing that I wrote in the score. It was one of these sequences that you look at and sort of hope will go away. But I finally started work on it on a Saturday afternoon and worked all through, late into Saturday night, and then got up very early on Sunday morning and worked around the clock until early Monday evening when the orchestra was called. I staggered over onto the stage to hear it.

ATKINS: That's timing it pretty close.

FRIEDHOFER: Yes, it was. Well, it was one of those things.

ATKINS: Did you ever work with a movieola?

FRIEDHOFER: No. Very fortunately, I was blessed with a fairly long memory. Two shots at seeing a picture screened and spotting it with the music editor and I'm set. Then, of course, a good music editor will always give you—in the more expensive days, that is—would always give you indications as to dialogue levels. And the dialogue would always be typed in red rather than black, so that you could distinguish. And you had your timings down to the split second, and then from that you broke them down, naturally, into larger units because nobody ever scores from second to second. Otherwise you get a pretty choppy affair that goes counter to the function of music in films, the way I see it. Our function is to smooth out the cuts, rather than to accentuate each one.

ATKINS: Do you think that click tracks are a help or a hindrance?

FRIEDHOFER: Oh, I think they're a great help, particularly if time is of the essence, which it always is in television. Most composers who have worked with click tracks for any length of time get into the habit of writing across the bar line, so that you're completely unconscious of the fact that there is a click track. It's largely a matter of experience and gearing your mind to break things up into rhythmic units that run counter to the actual beat. After a while you get so that you can do that without any trouble at all. Then, of course, there's that neat trick which I mentioned was first instigated by Max Steiner. Say he had an enormously long chase to do in one of those Westerns that he was constantly scoring over at Warner Brothers. You know, there's a strange psychology about a steady tempo, that sooner or later, if it goes on too long, it starts to sound slower and slower. So Max would go along at a certain tempo, and he'd find himself a point where he could drop his clicks, and maybe hold on long enough for the old click to leave off, and for a warning click for the new tempo to start. And then away we'd go, at either a faster or a slower click, depending entirely upon the nature of the scene. And that's one of the neatest tricks of the week, which everybody has subsequently adopted.

ATKINS: Do variable click tracks help avoid that feeling of slowing down?

FRIEDHOFER: Well, it's a tricky thing. I have not worked with them myself, but I know it's possible to work with variables. And sometimes, when you're overlaying something that has been pre-scored, say with just voice and piano, or something of that nature where the tempo varies, the only way, really, to lick the problem is to go for a variable click track. But that is in the conducting department.

ATKINS: One other thing about music editing: do you find that the way the music editor has written the cue sheets affects your writing?

FRIEDHOFER: Oh, good Lord, yes. The music editor, who has got a sort of built-in sensitivity and furthermore, knows your style pretty well, will not clutter up the cue sheets with a lot of extraneous detail that he knows you will ignore anyway. He gives you what you want.

There are several whom I've worked with in this business who are simply superb in that respect: George Adams, who was formerly at Twentieth Century Fox; Ken Johnson, who is largely associated with television; John Caper; John Elizalde, who is also a fine musician and composer, and also a fine man for tracking things—which he did on the *Rawhide* series; and Carroll Knudson, the father of the click track book.

When the click track first came in, there was an enormous resistance to the idea on the part of Al Newman. He *hated* the idea of working with click tracks. But he was finally converted later in his career to using click tracks. But ordinarily, he wanted no part of them. He had a very unwavering beat, positively metronomic at times. Going way back to a Selznick picture that I worked on with Alfred, a picture called *The Prisoner of Zenda*, there was a long duel that he threw at me, between Ronald Colman and Douglas Fairbanks Jr., that was one of those tapeworms that ran about seven minutes and was, for the most part, in a very strict and fast tempo. We spent a great many hours on it, and some time might have been saved by the use of click track, but at that time it was a thing that Al wasn't particularly fond of. And it really made things twice as hard for him.

ATKINS: What about scoring *without* picture?

FRIEDHOFER: That has always been a kind of a cheapie technique. But, except for certain things, what isn't these days? I know I could have saved myself a great deal of money, if, when I got into television, I didn't insist on scoring with picture. Of course, Earle Hagen, to this day, works with film, even in television, because he always conceived of a television score as being kind of a film score in miniature. At the time that we were doing the *I Spy* show, I don't think that we tracked more than a couple of things in the entire three years we worked on the show. And these were bridges or something that had been inadvertently overlooked. We, or Ken Johnson, the music editor, would find a piece of track that would cover the situation. But for the rest, every show was scored live.

ATKINS: There are a couple of other films in 1947: *The Adventures of Casanova*—

FRIEDHOFER: I'd completely forgotten that film, which was my sole excursion into the now defunct Eagle-Lion territory. It was a costume picture, a swashbuckler.

ATKINS: *The Man I Love* is from this same period.

FRIEDHOFER: I don't even remember it. Where was it, Warner Brothers?

ATKINS: Yes. Max Steiner.

FRIEDHOFER: I don't know why I should have any credit on that because all I did . . . I think Max called me in to do a couple of arrangements of something of George Gershwin's. What's the name of the picture about Gershwin?

ATKINS: *Rhapsody in Blue.*

FRIEDHOFER: I know I did a couple of arrangements or paraphrases of things. That was also Max's, wasn't it?

ATKINS: Yes.

FRIEDHOFER: Musical direction. He called me to do a couple of paraphrases of hunks of thematic material out of the Concerto in F. What year was that?

ATKINS: 1945.

FRIEDHOFER: That was during my freelance period.

ATKINS: We have talked about *Enchantment,* but is there anything else you'd like to say about it?

FRIEDHOFER: No, except that this was a picture that took place in about two different time dimensions, and it was one of those pictures that unless you saw it from the top, you didn't know just where you were. You didn't know whether you were in the World War II era

or back in the late Victorian era, and consequently, it was very confusing.

ATKINS: Were there flashbacks?

FRIEDHOFER: Well, there were transitions that were done not
with dissolves or with flashbacks as much as with slow pans up out of
picture and then back in, and you'd be in the other time dimension.
One of the things that would trigger off this dimension in time was an
old piano in the drawing room of this house, and there was a crystal
chandelier that responded with sympathetic vibrations to certain
notes on the piano. So I had to figure out a way to make this crystal
chandelier sound, and I did it with overlapping of crystal goblets that
were filled with water, to the point where they gave you various
pitches simply by rubbing a moistened finger around the edge. And
it worked out admirably. It was a nice trick, as I recall.

ATKINS: In 1948, there are some films at Paramount.

FRIEDHOFER: At Paramount, let's see: the first one was *Sealed Verdict*, which was a sort of Nuremberg trials type thing, with Ray Mil-
land and a very beautiful gal who disappeared all of a sudden. She was
the lead in the thing, Florence Marly, sort of the Dietrich type. That's
the only film I ever heard of her doing.

ATKINS: Another one I have is *Bride of Vengeance*, which had another
title, I think.

FRIEDHOFER: It was called *A Mask for Lucretia*, originally. And that
was my first encounter with Mitch Leisen, which developed into a
very pleasant association through three pictures I did for him. Mitch
was kind of a music freak. He always used to come around to recordings and sit in the monitor room and listen, and enjoy. *Bride of Vengeance*, which is a horrible title, incidentally, was quite striking, quite
stunning, and a fun picture to do. I used a lot of closed forms, a sort
of a quasi-Renaissance type thing. There was a long passacaglia in one
place and the Renaissance dance type things. After that, I did another
picture for him, *Captain Carey, USA*.

ATKINS: I haven't seen *Captain Carey*, but I know there's something about the song Mona Lisa.

FRIEDHOFER: Yes. Mona Lisa, which was kind of a throwaway in *Captain Carey*, became very popular before the picture was released, so that actually, it was nominated as best song in 1950, and got it. In the film, it was a sort of signal. It was a tip-off of when there were any Nazi goings-on to warn the underground that they'd better lay low. But somehow the song caught on, and that was their second award—Jay Livingston and Ray Evans—after Buttons and Bows. That was in *Son of Paleface*, still one of the funniest pictures I've ever seen.

ATKINS: When you finally got to Paramount as a composer, how did you feel about it?

FRIEDHOFER: I felt pretty good about it, sure. It was fine. I used to have occasional run-ins with Louis Lipstone who had certain pre-conceived notions. For instance, he couldn't stand the sound of a flute. He'd say, "Why don't you give it to the fiddles?" One of those things. But overall we got along very nicely.

ATKINS: I don't have credits on those Paramount pictures for conductor or orchestrator.

FRIEDHOFER: Everything I did over there was conducted by Irvin Talbot, a gentleman and a fine musician. And a more cooperative man I've never worked with in my life. I never saw this man, but once, lose his temper. And that was on one occasion when Louie Lipstone came on the stage and was trying to get things speeded up, and Irvin laid the baton down and walked off the stage and disappeared. He was white! He walked off the stage for about fifteen minutes, and finally came back and everything was calm. Apparently at one time Irvin had an ungovernable temper.

In connection with Louis Lipstone—we were talking about differences of opinion and certain quirks that he had. For instance, he couldn't stand the idea of anything in the nature of counterpoint. And there was one sequence in *Sealed Verdict* that I scored as a three-part fugal exposition, very slow in tempo, because I didn't want to get into the dialogue. The texture was so that it was very, very transparent, but Louie came on the stage and heard this, and went over to Irvin and stopped him. Then he called me out on the stage—took me over in the corner and said, "What the hell's the idea of writing a fugue?" I counted ten very slowly and said, "Louie, will you please listen to it with the dialogue on the headset?" So he did, and grudgingly admitted that it worked all right.

But these are the things that composers, and I'm not alone among them, run up against. If you're lucky, you win. And if you don't, you just—as a writer friend of mine said—you just take the money and cry all the way to the bank. Something I've never been able to do. I don't, as the saying goes, suffer this kind of foolishness with any equanimity. I'll keep it inside. I don't let go. But it bothers me sometimes. But, by the same token, I don't hold any grudges because that's foolish. You can only get ulcers that way. But, now where are we?

ATKINS: *Joan of Arc*, which won another Academy Award nomination. Were there any problems in scoring *Joan of Arc*?

FRIEDHOFER: No, there were no problems, except that Fleming kept recutting and it got to be a kind of a drag in that respect. Leon Klatzkin was my music editor on the thing, and I was working at home. Leon would call me and say, "What sequence are you working on?" And I'd say, "So and so and so, which you gave me an okay on day before yesterday." He said, "Hold it. Vic has changed his mind about a couple of things." So this went on practically for the whole duration. And, at the very end, Vic got quite ill and wasn't there for the final dubbing. An assistant of his was sort of left in charge and kind of overrode me on several things. But it went along fairly smoothly.

ATKINS: There's an orchestrator's name that I didn't see on the credits of any of your other productions: Jerome Moross.

FRIEDHOFER: Oh, yes, Jerry worked on that. Dessau did some orchestration for me on it, and a man named Harold Byrnes also worked on it. Harold made an orchestration of a sort of curtain raiser, or entrance music, to set the mood before the film came on. This was a last-minute decision on the part of production. And I happened to recall a piece that I had written for my daughter, who was a physical education major at UCLA. One of her graduation projects was to choreograph a thing for a group and herself. So I wrote this thing, in a more or less quasi-modal medieval style for her, and had it recorded on two pianos. And Byrnes orchestrated it from my original two-piano layout, and it became the prologue to *Joan of Arc*.

Then, right on top of that, I went back to Paramount to do *Bride of Vengeance*, and there's a very amusing incident in connection with that. I had come on the stage a little bit early, hoping to hear some of Copland's score for *The Heiress*. But for some reason or other, Willy Wyler objected to Aaron's main title, and used something else, a French chanson called, I believe, Parlez Moi d'Amour, Speak to Me of Love. It's a very popular thing. Everybody knows it. Aaron objected strenuously and would have nothing to do with it. So Van Cleave, who was under contract to Paramount at that time as an arranger, made an orchestration of it and it was recorded and used as the main title for *The Heiress*. And I happened to walk onstage just at that time. Wyler, whom I hadn't seen for some time, came up to me and said, "What do you think of the main title, this substitution?" I said, "Well, Willy, it's none of my business, but I think that Aaron's main title was probably more apt and more fitting, and I'm sorry you did it, but that's your business." And he gave me a kind of glassy look, and he said, "You know, I liked your score to *Joan of Arc* very much," and he walked away from me. And that was it. But that's one of the quirks. And you know, actually, Aaron refused the Academy Award. He refused to pick it up. I don't know who's got it.

ATKINS: At the Academy, there's supposed to be a whole shelf full of unclaimed Oscars.

FRIEDHOFER: Well, that is one of them, I believe, because I don't think Aaron had a change of heart after that. I believe that that was his last film in Hollywood. I've run into him several times since then out here, but not in connection with films. He either came out to visit or to conduct, or something of the sort. Did you ever meet him?

ATKINS: No.

FRIEDHOFER: A charming man, and a very important figure in the history of American music.

ATKINS: People always point to him as one of the very few serious composers who's contributed to American motion pictures.

FRIEDHOFER: Yes. And that brings me back in time again, to my free-lance period when I was jobbing around wherever and whenever. Paramount was making a picture called *Peter Ibbetson*, for which Ernst Toch had been called in to do the score. Ernst had fallen behind in his deadline, or they'd pushed up his deadline, so he told them it would be impossible for him to finish it. So they said, "Well, we can get you some help if you want." And so they called me, as well as a couple of other people, who, for some reason or other, fought shy of the idea of collaborating. But I had heard music of Toch's and some films that he had done in Great Britain, and was very much fascinated by him and wanted to meet him. So I undertook to do several sequences in the *Peter Ibbetson* score. I submitted what I had written to him, which he fortunately liked very much, and the stuff was used in the film. And hard on the heels of that, I asked him whether he would accept me as a pupil. So I put in about two, two and a half years studying with him whenever I had the time, and learned a great deal from him—not so much in the field of film music, but just general cultural infiltration.

ATKINS: What does someone who's been composing and orchestrating for so many years *study* at that stage of one's career?

FRIEDHOFER: Well, it's always like a refresher. I think I can say without fear of exaggeration or successful contradiction, that I've actually been a student all my life. I'm not content with just what I know. I want to find out more about what I don't know. So consequently I've had a fairly long roster of people that I have worked with from time to time: my original teacher in San Francisco, and then, subsequent to that, when I came down here, when Schoenberg first came to Southern California, I attended a seminar that he was holding on variation form. And then after that, Toch. Then after Toch, at the time when Nadia Boulanger was here, I did some work with her. And then, around 1952, I decided to take a refresher course in counterpoint, so I worked with a man who had been on the faculty at USC, Dr. Ernest Kanitz. I believe he was just about to retire from the faculty there at that time. I worked with him from '52 to '54 and then I believe I did some additional work later, in '55. And then things began to crowd in on me, and I didn't have any further time for improving myself.

★     ★     ★

ATKINS: In 1950, there are films from a variety of studios: Goldwyn, Twentieth Century—

FRIEDHOFER: What was from Twentieth?

ATKINS: *Broken Arrow. Three Came Home.*

FRIEDHOFER: Oh, yes. *Three Came Home* was my first return to Twentieth Century Fox after I left there in 1944. That was Nunnally Johnson's picture. The story was based on the autobiographical novel by Agnes Newton Keith, whose husband had been in the diplomatic service. They were stationed in Borneo and were both interned when the Japanese invasion of the British possessions down there took place. It was a beautiful picture. It was my first look at the Japanese actor who was a matinee idol way back in the silent days, Sessue Hayakawa. I can remember him to this day, when I was a small child, this simply beautiful man to look at. And here was this fat, stern-looking, militant character, an excellent actor, incidentally. But the picture was a very warm one, and it was fun to do. It was very moving, an inspiring picture to work on, because it was the first picture after the end of World War II in which the Japanese were not portrayed altogether as arch-villains. Unfortunately, it was still a little bit too close to that, and there were people in whose minds the memory of Pearl Harbor and other things still rankled. Consequently it didn't do as well as it might have.

ATKINS: Did you use any sort of ethnic music?

FRIEDHOFER: No, I made it up. Oh, yes—I used not so much Japanese as Indonesian scales in the thing, but not done with ethnic instruments, because it was all woven into a dramatic fabric. The thing was pretty stark and pretty grim in places.

Right on the heels of that came *Broken Arrow*. I was rather shuttling back and forth between Twentieth Century Fox and Goldwyn and Paramount. *Broken Arrow* was made in 1949 and released in 1950. To me, *Broken Arrow* was a very interesting picture, in that it was the first one in which the Indians were treated entirely differently. They were not the villains. Nobody in the picture said, "Ugh" or "White man speak with forked tongue." It was a lovely picture. It was based on a factual novel, *Blood Brother*, about Tom Jefford, who was the man responsible for cooling the whole situation between the Indians and the white settlers in Arizona through his association with Cochise, the famous Apache chieftain. It was a thoroughly well-made film. That was Delmar Daves; Julian Blaustein produced. In fact, he entered the field of production at Twentieth Century Fox on the strength of that story. But I loved the film and I can think of nothing anecdotal, except that it was a thoroughly enjoyable job. It was later, much later, remade, or the same story line was used, around the end of 1954, after the inroads of television. Twentieth was making a lot of pictures under the title Panoramic Pictures. They were all wide screen. They were all based on old properties of Twentieth. The *Broken Arrow* remake was called *White Feather*. That was after films were beginning to come back. The panic about television had simmered down.

ATKINS: There's a United Artists film in here, too, *The Sound of Fury*.

FRIEDHOFER: Oh, yes. I was in New York and I got this long distance call from Emil Newman, who was going to conduct the thing. The picture was made by Bob Stillman, a charming man. This was a very grim story of a kidnapping followed by a murder and an arrest and a lynching. So this is hardly fun-and-games time. But it was a very strongly made film. The director was Cy Enfield, now living in political exile in London. A very good director. I know Frank Lovejoy was very strong as a returned veteran who couldn't get a job, had a wife and child to support, and was lured away from the paths of righteousness by Lloyd Bridges. They started in a small way, sticking up filling stations and things like that, and finally got into this kidnapping gig, with dire results for both of them. A well-made picture. As I recall, there wasn't much music, but what there was was very, very strong.

I did a subsequent film for Stillman, *Queen for a Day*, based on the television show. It was the story of three different characters—sort of a three-decker. Oh, it was four episodes. I did two of them and the others were done by Arthur Lange. One of the ones I did was about a little boy who lived in a sort of dream world all his own. Every day he woke up being someone else. He was either an African explorer or a railroad engineer or a gardener, or whatever. But it was charming, that particular episode. The other one, I forget, exactly. It was about a Polish family. But the first episode was delightful and I did have a very good time with it. Charles Maxwell should also be listed on that film as co-composer with Arthur Lange. Marlin Skiles orchestrated for me at that time.

ATKINS: There have been many films with separate episodes.

FRIEDHOFER: That started with Somerset Maugham. He made two, *Trio* and *Quartet.* They were excellent, and I don't think that any of the American ones quite came up to his. But they weren't bad. And the thing that Huntington Hartford did that takes us into 1951. It originally consisted of three episodes, one of which was never made. Oh, yes, it was made, but never scored. One was called *The Secret Sharer,* a story of Joseph Conrad's. The other was kind of a light comedy called *The Bride Came to Yellow Sky,* in which James Agee, the famous critic, played a very small part.

ATKINS: He wrote the screenplay.

FRIEDHOFER: Yes. The screenplay was from a story by Stephen Crane.

ATKINS: When you score a film like this, do you consider each episode as a complete entity, musically?

FRIEDHOFER: Well, yes, because they were three completely disparate stories and each demanded a different kind of score.

ATKINS: Going back to the other episodic film, *Queen for a Day:* then there wouldn't be any necessity of coordinating your work with Arthur Lange's?

FRIEDHOFER: Oh, no, because they were completely separate. And the third one, in the Huntington Hartford film, was that famous play, which has been done in colleges all over the United States, a play of Saroyan's, *Hello Out There*. It starred one of my favorite people in the acting end of films, and that's Henry Morgan. My first encounter with him was in *Roger Touhy*, finally called *The Last of the Gangsters*, in which he plays the unfortunate part of a stool pigeon who is murdered behind prison walls. But he was always excellent. Whatever he did was fine.

ATKINS: How far did they get with the Saroyan project?

FRIEDHOFER: They had shot it, but for some reason or other, there was a hangup on it, I think largely owing to the fact that Hartford left California for some reason or other. For some legal reasons, he couldn't come back into the state, and so they never finished it. But it would have been fun to do, particularly because one of my directorial heroes, whom I've never met, from way, way back, James Whale, directed it. He achieved singular fame in the field of the macabre and offbeat. I saw his film for Universal, *The Old Dark House*, and saw it not once, but at least a half a dozen times.

ATKINS: Is it possible that *Hello Out There* is in some vault, waiting to be released for television?

FRIEDHOFER: I don't know what became of any of those projects. I tried at one time, to get acetates of the two episodes that I did. *Bride Came to Yellow Sky* was kind of fun to do. It was a story of the last of the bad men, who is a drunk and always shoots up this town, and is sort of held down by the town sheriff. The sheriff goes off to get married and all hell breaks loose. But the really important one was *Secret Sharer*. I later indulged in a little self-plagiarism there. There was a narration over a flashback about a storm at sea that I later utilized in another film. It's one of the few times that I have actually—of course, in this case, it was a different kind of a storm. It was a sandstorm. But why not? Naturally, there are supposed to be legal restrictions on this sort of thing, but off or on the record, frankly I don't care. Do you expect me, gentlemen, to remember every damn note I have written in the last forty-five years? And probably nobody except a very astute music editor who had worked with me on one or the other, would know. And I'm afraid that they're all gone, too.

I know that one of Alfred Newman's big standard tunes, The Moon of Manakoora, was originally written for a silent film, which later was given a complete soundtrack, a wall-to-wall thing for a picture that Douglas Fairbanks made called *Robinson Crusoe*. They added a soundtrack score which Al wrote, and there were a couple of other pieces of material in that. There was one that dealt with the shore sea birds, the "gooney birds," as they were called during World War II. There was a little theme that he wrote for them that he used in *Slave Ship*. That was a picture with Warner Baxter. It was one of Al's first pictures at Twentieth Century Fox. And later, we both used that particular piece of material in a documentary, *The Battle of Midway*. No matter how inventive you are, or how fertile, there always comes a time when, not through desperation, but because you've run across a piece of material that is valuable to you that can be used in another context, so why not? And there's always a change of a few notes here and there, and a different orchestration. I have never consciously stolen anybody else's music to utilize in a film that I was scoring.

ATKINS: About Huntington Hartford: he had this period of being interested in film production—

FRIEDHOFER: I think it was the lady he was very much interested in at that time, Marjorie Steele, who starred in *Bride Came to Yellow Sky*. She was the bride. I don't know what the legal entanglement was out here that actually drove him out of the state—back alimony or something like that. He was a very strange man. I had one long conference with him on *Secret Sharer*. He had this big estate where he was living, up in the Hollywood hills. He had a house there, and a separate thing, a very beautiful studio with a swimming pool—it would have been an ideal place for a MacDowell colony, which he later established the likes of out in the Palisades. That was a beautiful place, which I think is no longer in existence. It was the Foundation for a while, and as such, probably a fancy tax write-off. Several people I know were there, Ingolf Dahl spent some time there and also Dr. Kanitz got a grant—however you got in.

ATKINS: People like Max Eastman were there at one time.

FRIEDHOFER: Max Eastman. That takes me back a long way. One of the old-line radicals who later wrote a charming book, *The Enjoy-*

*ment of Laughter*, all about the American sense of humor and how it ticks. But I remember reading a very grim book of his, when I was also a young radical, so to speak, about his life in prison at the time they were jailing anybody who was outside the Establishment. Those were the days of the publication *The Liberator.* But, like all young radicals, I got tired.

ATKINS: You have to be careful now, because you said you were apolitical.

FRIEDHOFER: I am really apolitical, except that certain social injustices bug me. I don't go out and carry banners anymore. I just stay home and quietly sulk, which makes a coward out of me, I suppose. But truth to tell, the crown of martyrdom was never made in my hat size.

   To get back to Hartford, I had this one conference with him. I had seen the film and I couldn't quite add up with some recordings that he played for me. It had just been released, a beautiful opera of Rossini's, the Cinderella story, *La Cenerentola,* which is beautiful music, but had nothing to do with the adventures and misadventures of a young sea captain of his first command. Hartford was out of state at the time I was scoring the first one, *The Secret Sharer.* They ran it for him, dubbed, when he returned, and he was, I think, half asleep during the performance. But he suddenly turned to his associate and said, "Have we got time to do this over?" But he got talked out of it somehow. But I don't think he really knew what he was listening to. Anyhow, the music stayed in.

ATKINS: Have you had other times when producers have played records or tapes of what they would like?

FRIEDHOFER: No, no. Of course, the old standard joke about the producer saying to the composer, "I don't care what you write, just so it sounds like Tchaikovsky." No, I've never been pinned down to anything like that. I think it was Alex North, in connection with a film he did at Warners, somebody came on the stage and said, "The music sounds just like Bela Barstow." And I believe I told you the dictum that was laid down by Winfield Sheehan, who said, "Remember, the scene of the action in this picture is Paris, so I want a lot of French horns."

But you hear a lot of that sort of thing. Mostly, these legends sort of grow and some of them are true. Oh, and once, I don't recall what picture it was, a man said to me, "You know, it was a choice between you and another composer," who shall be nameless, and whose style is not in the least like mine, if you can call my style a style. But it was a peculiar choice, strange bedfellows, so to speak, and I couldn't quite make up my mind what the association would have been in this producer's mind, that he should pick on two such disparate styles. There have been cases, of course, where people have said to the composer, "I want this score to sound like so-and-so's." I don't know who gave him the answer, it may have been David Raksin—at least the statement was characteristic of the thing Dave might say—"Why, in this case, didn't you hire so-and-so, instead of asking me to write music like his?" And there we are.

★    ★    ★

FRIEDHOFER: Let's go in continuity. Have you got *Lydia Bailey*?

ATKINS: That wasn't released until '52.

FRIEDHOFER: I know that I undertook *Lydia Bailey* because it gave me a tax write-off, because in 1950 I had been down in the Caribbean and spent a little time in Haiti, and had picked up a lot of stuff about the African drumming and what not. I used that as an excuse to write off my trip, on the basis of my research, not only in Haiti but also in Cuba and Trinidad. My first encounter with the steel band. My ears are still ringing. But *Lydia Bailey* was not, truth to tell, a very good picture, although the original novel was very good. I don't know whether it was her first film, but it was the first time that I had ever seen a young lady by the name of Anne Francis. She couldn't have been more than eighteen at the time, a perfectly charming lady, incidentally.

*Two Flags West* was a Civil War story about Confederate prisoners of war who were given a sort of amnesty if they would assist in holding down the Indian uprisings. It had a very neurotic type commanding officer, played by Jeff Chandler. Joseph Cotten was in the picture and Linda Darnell. Not an altogether successful picture, but it was okay, as I recall. I know there was a lot of wagon train music in it.

ATKINS: Next is *Ace in the Hole*, also known as *The Big Carnival*. What was your rapport with Billy Wilder?

FRIEDHOFER: It was very good. I had met him when he first came to this country, through Franz Waxman. I think they came over at just about the same time. I mentioned a picture that he had made in Germany, *People on Sunday*, which was just a series of random shots, a fantastic documentary. He was so surprised that I knew the picture. I had seen it at the art house here that ran those things. Anyway, he was at all the recordings, and he made a remark that stays in my mind. We recorded the main title and he came over to me and said, "Why is it that composers always have the peak crescendo at the point where their credit comes on?" So I told him that if he didn't like what I had done, I would very gladly switch credits with him and he could have his credit over that so-called crescendo, and I would get down into a softer part of it. But unfortunately, the curve of the music demanded a peak right at that point, and that was it. But I think he was probably putting me on.

ATKINS: Musically, there's an interesting sequence where the camera is panning through the carnival, and the music changes as you approach the carousel. How was that done?

FRIEDHOFER: Oh, that took a lot of gluing together. It was made in separate sections, with overlaps. There was much in the picture that I doubt if I would do much differently today than I did then. It had a good stark, hard quality to it. I believe that Page Cook, in his long article that he wrote for a London publication, referred to it as the first picture that employed a very stark dissonance in the score. I like that sort of thing, even though I'm considered basically a neo-romantic composer, whatever that means. No, I liked it very much, and I was pleased with the fact that the score, as well as the film, attracted considerable attention in Europe and walked off with some awards at the Venice Festival. That was in 1951. There's another picture in there—

ATKINS: *Outcasts of Poker Flat?*

FRIEDHOFER: Yes.

ATKINS: That's Twentieth Century Fox.

FRIEDHOFER: Yes, that was the Bret Harte story about the people who are driven out of this mining camp and they get snowed in up at this lone cabin in the High Sierras. That was a rather difficult assignment for this reason: that any film where the principal action takes place in one location, or inside four walls, is always rough because there are so many places that you can find where you can start, but then you've got to figure, "How am I ever going to get out?" I think that George Adams and I ran that picture at least four times, which is kind of high for me, because I've generally managed to make up my mind at least by the second running. But every day I would come in with a new notion. Finally, at the end of the fourth running, we had our minds pretty well made up.

Oh, the opening was difficult, too, because we had a long dolly shot around this mining camp, which was loaded with saloons, and every saloon had either a banjo or a fiddle or an accordion or a beat-up piano. These things all had to be overlapped as you move away from one sound into another locale and sound. And then, on top of that, there was an influx of bad men intent on robbing the Wells Fargo safe, or whatever it was. So all these things had to be woven together. But it worked well, somehow, and we managed to get from the source music into scoring. I think we got into that, finally, as the safe blows up, which is a good place for a crossover. You can drop the source music quite naturally because the local musicians would have been startled by the explosion, and then we could go on into scoring pretty nicely.

ATKINS: Was your source music original or were they old tunes?

FRIEDHOFER: Some of it was original and some of it was the standard repertory of that time. I recall one hunk of stuff I wrote which I called The Pioneer Stomp, which has been used in other films—films that I had nothing to do with except that they would always drag this thing out where they needed that kind of source music. I know that

Urban Thielmann, who was at that time connected with the studio, used to lay out source music for composers who were otherwise busy. He would always drag in The Pioneer Stomp because he liked it, with all of a sudden odd beats or odd bars, that he kind of liked, and so he kept using it, which is naturally good for my performing rights. A nickel here, and a nickel there, and we have our old-age pension.

ATKINS: The film editor of *Outcasts of Poker Flat* was William Reynolds, who won an Academy Award for *The Sting*.

FRIEDHOFER: Bill Reynolds, yes. The cast was a good one, as I recall: Anne Baxter, Cameron Mitchell, and Dale Robertson, who was also in *Lydia Bailey*. I saw him just the other night in this very bad Bonnie and Clyde type film. I can't think of the name of it, but it was very obvious, even including this pestiferous trend towards the banjo-type thing, that started, really, with *Bonnie and Clyde*, that is beginning to bore the pants off me. It's fine, but enough, already. But that is one of the hangups in this business: the trend-followers, the copycats. A thing works fine in one film and right away they decide that they want the same thing. A case in point is *The Third Man*. All of a sudden everybody wanted a score done with one instrument, preferably a zither. A zither, to me, sounds like, as Dave Raksin once said, beating a birdcage to death with a broom.

But somehow or other they lose sight of the dramatic content of the film that is their own baby, and they want to slap something in it in the way of music that could very well completely destroy the mood of their own film, no matter how admirable it was in some other. In the case of *The Third Man*, I have no quarrel with that at all. I thought it was excellent. It had sort of that beat-up, post–World War II atmosphere of Vienna at the time. But that doesn't mean it would work as admirably in other places.

Anyway, after that film, I think I went back to Paramount.

ATKINS: Yes, there was *Just for You*.

FRIEDHOFER: Oh, that was a film that I came in to do. All the material was Harry Warren's. The score was all based on Harry and Leo Robin's songs. I know that Harry ran into some kind of difficulties over there. Some of the best things that he did were eliminated from the picture. He tried, and finally succeeded in getting the rights to certain tunes back.

ATKINS: Did you have any contact with Bing Crosby?

FRIEDHOFER: No. Naturally, I saw Harry over there a great deal, and Leo.

ATKINS: There's another Paramount film released the next year in 1953, but may have been done in 1952. That's called *Thunder in the East*.

FRIEDHOFER: Wow! I'll tell you about that one. It was a very strange picture. It had a pretty impressive cast, Alan Ladd, Deborah Kerr, Charles Boyer, and a French gal, Corinne Calvet. We took it down to Westchester for a preview and it was rather disastrous because the audience laughed at a couple of scenes. And it was disastrous for me because immediately they started blaming the score. But this is par for the course. It's happened, not to me, but to others more than once. They've got to find a scapegoat and it's generally a composer.

ATKINS: These screen credits are all mixed together—you must have been at every studio in Hollywood in this period. There's *San Francisco Story* at Warner Brothers.

FRIEDHOFER: I think that was Allied Artists.

ATKINS: Warners released it. Fidelity-Young Pictures.

FRIEDHOFER: I don't know, but I know we didn't score over there. We scored at the old RKO or RCA studios, south of Santa Monica Boulevard.

ATKINS: *The Marrying Kind*, at Columbia, and *Above and Beyond* at M-G-M.

FRIEDHOFER: That was just about the period when we were grabbing at anything that we could get because of the advent of television. Business was miserable for the composer and it remained so for some time. I did two films that were released by Warners. They were both Batjac productions—Bob Fellows, John Wayne, and company.

The first was a picture Bill Wellman directed, *Island in the Sky*, which was about the bush pilots up in Canada. The second one was *Hondo*, which I like very much as a picture. John Wayne had a pretty good leading lady in that one, too: Geraldine Page. Oh, she's a great actress. Let's face it, after Helen Hayes, this is the first lady of the theater. And she looked like a pioneer woman, for a change. The hairdo was not perfect, and she had that look—earthy.

ATKINS: I understand that *Hondo* was made in 3-D. How did that affect the music?

FRIEDHOFER: I saw it in 3-D, and there were a couple of shots in it that literally scared the hell out of the audience. There was one that I remember: John Wayne standing up in the back of this covered wagon, swinging a rifle. That rifle seemed to come right out into the audience. But I don't remember what it did to the music. As a matter of fact, I was so annoyed with those spectacles that they gave you to view 3-D, that I didn't pay much attention to anything. It was run in the Academy theater.

ATKINS: This was also at the time when several wide-screen processes were being tried out.

FRIEDHOFER: Actually, I think Darryl Zanuck is largely responsible for having saved the entire industry at that time, with *The Robe*, one of Lloyd Douglas's ecclesiastical lollipops, but with a stunning cast, and a real blockbuster of a score that Al did. It was wide screen and color. The cameraman was Leon Shamroy, one of my favorite cameramen of all time, one of the real experts in color. He was the first man to utilize color not to paint pretty pictures, but to create a dramatic mood. It seems to me that the follow-up on *The Robe*, which was *Demetrius and the Gladiators*, was offered to me. I didn't like the idea of—I would naturally have had to use a lot of referential thematic material out of *The Robe*, the story of which did not particularly appeal to me. So, through my agent, I asked for an exorbitant amount of money to do it—exorbitant by 1950s standards. Now it would be nothing. They turned my request down and that was the end of that.

ATKINS: There's another Robert Fellows film in that same year, *Plunder of the Sun.*

FRIEDHOFER: That was a film that had been shot and scored in Mexico. When they got it back up here, they decided that there was some of the score that they did not like too much. The score was written by a Mexican composer but they wanted a certain primitivism that the score did not have, so I did the main title and several key sequences in the thing. I wrote another kind of sultry bad girl with a heart of gold type love theme. I don't think I had screen credits on it. I had cue sheets credits, but not on the main title. Those credits are listed on the log because of obligations to performing rights societies. As a matter of fact, there are a few that I'd just as soon *not* have credit on. *Island in the Sky* was one of them—although *Island in the Sky* was the first album that I had. It was a ten-inch that Decca put out.

ATKINS: Was it an actual soundtrack?

FRIEDHOFER: Yes, it was. It was Emil Newman's idea. He got John Wayne to do some narration over the music in the album. I've never heard the album. Have you a credit listed for *Guilty of Treason*?

ATKINS: Yes.

FRIEDHOFER: That was the story of Cardinal Mindszenty. That was one of Jack Wrather's ventures into production on account of— who's the gal that he married—isn't it Bonita Granville, who played the bad child in the original version of *The Children's Hour*, called *These Three*? Mr. Goldwyn made it.

ATKINS: *Deep in my Heart* and *Vera Cruz* were done in 1954.

FRIEDHOFER: I had done one other picture prior to *Deep in My Heart*, at M-G-M, *Above and Beyond*, which was one of the few, if not the only, serious script that Norman Panama and Mel Frank wrote. It was about Lieutenant Colonel Tibbett, the man who trained the crew

Wedding photo of Paul and Eva Koenig Friedhofer.

Hugo Wilhelm Friedhofer, born May 3, 1901.

Hugo with one of his beloved dachshunds.

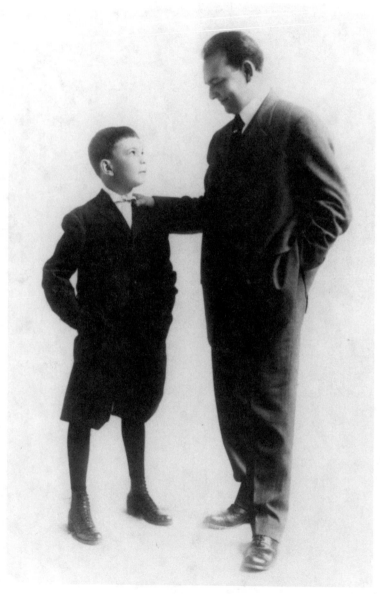

Hugo with his father.

Hugo as a teenager, with his cello.

Hugo and Elizabeth with baby Erica.

Elizabeth with Erica, and Karyl on her lap.

Portrait of Hugo.

Party at Al Newman's (from left to right): Franz Waxman, Alfred Newman, Bernard Herrmann, Ken Darby, Vinton Vernon, Alex North, Hugo Friedhofer.

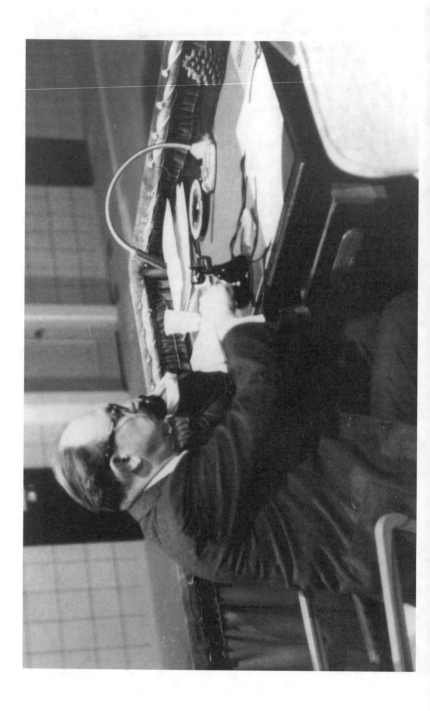

Hugo, clowning around.

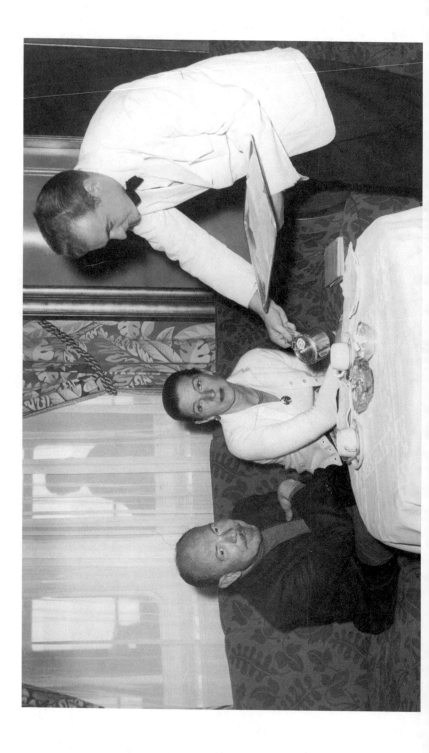

Production meeting, with George Stevens presiding.

Hugo with Earle Hagen (on right).

Hugo with Lionel Newman and Eddie Powell.

Tired composer, 1970s, demonstrating a theme.

for the Hiroshima thing. It was a very strong and very fine picture. The music was nominated for an Academy Award. Bob Taylor and a good supporting cast, including Eleanor Parker. The reason I like the picture so much was because it was not a flag-waver, which would have been pretty horrible in light of subsequent developments. The film was a study of character, of a man whose loyalty to his country and the whole circumstances went against the grain. It told of the fact that he lost friends and his wife, or almost, through having to keep this very tight security. It was a study of a man and his crew, rather than a war picture, and very well done.

ATKINS: I have a notation: "Music conducted by Andre Previn."

FRIEDHOFER: Yes. Andre had conducted at Metro and then he was called up to do his military service, which stationed him close to San Francisco. It was at the time that Leonard Bernstein had done some guest conducting with the San Francisco Symphony. He and Andre knew each other, and he asked Andre to play the piano parts in his symphony, The Age of Anxiety. Monteux was present, either at the rehearsal or at the final performance, and was very much impressed with Andre. Andre went to him and asked for lessons in conducting, and he used to spend his day of leave with Monteux. He naturally came out of it thoroughly equipped as a conductor. And he was lovely to work with. I don't know if I mentioned it in connection with *Body and Soul*, but Andre played in a jam session in a party scene, after a successful prize fight, in the film. We had an all-star jazz band. I had never met Andre up to that time, although I knew his uncle, Charles, very well. Then we used to see each other around town, but this was my first contact with him in a musical sense.

ATKINS: How did Andre Previn happen to appear in *Body and Soul*?

FRIEDHOFER: Rudy Polk recommended him. I don't think I'd heard about Andre before that, but I took Rudy's recommendation, and it turned out to be very good. I think Andre had barely gotten out of Beverly Hills High at that time, and I think it was concurrent with his signing with Metro. But that was the beginning of a very long association, socially. It's the only thing that he ever worked with me on, but as a result of this, we became very good friends. Right after his first marriage, he was living up in the hills near me. His wife,

Betty Bennett, was a jazz singer, and I've maintained a friendship with her through the years. She's a very, very nice gal.

There's a strange thing about *Above and Beyond*—It was held up for a long time. It wasn't released until 1953, and it was in the 1954 awards nominations. Bronnie Kaper picked up the Oscar for *Lili* on that.

On awards night, we were having dinner with Adolph Deutsch, who was musical director for the Sigmund Romberg story. In the course of eating dinner, before we went to the Paramount Theater for the Awards presentation, Adolph said, "Gosh, I'm in trouble on this Sigmund Romberg thing, *Deep in My Heart*. I need an arranger so badly. Who would you recommend?" So I said, "Well, Adolph, I'm not working. And you know how things are these days. I'd be glad to take it on." He said, "You really would?" I said, "Sure." So I did. And it was kind of a change of pace for me because I hadn't done a musical for Lord knows how long, and the results were very nice. Among the pleasant encounters on that picture was the one with Helen Traubel, who was such a fine musician, despite the fact that later she became what she called "a saloon singer." She got tired of Wagnerian operas, and she had a fine sense of comedy. She had a beautiful voice and she had a musician's ear. She would listen to the rehearsals of her orchestral background and analyze just where she fit in. And she talked about her contribution as a vocalist as if she were another instrument in the orchestra, which is the sign of real understanding and of a fine singer. I did all other vocal backgrounds as well as some for Tony Martin and for Howard Keel, and a ballet for Cyd Charisse, and the main title and odds and ends, all based on Sigmund Romberg's material.

ATKINS: There's a long list of "guest" stars in this film.

FRIEDHOFER: There was one singer, William Olvis, a very fine tenor, who insisted upon singing the big tune from *Student Prince* a half tone higher than Lanza sang it—and got away with it. He had a magnificent voice.

★    ★    ★

Right on top of that I was getting my feet wet in television with Herbert Spencer and Earle Hagen, who had left Twentieth and formed a partnership. They had their own outfit. It was called MSI— Music Service Incorporated. They did an awful lot of shows in there, and every once in a while they would get jammed up on work and I'd jump in and do things with them. Right around that time I did a pilot film for Samuel Goldwyn Jr., a science-fantasy kind of thing called *The Unexplained*. But it was just a little too early for that sort of thing. It was fun to do, but the pilot never sold. It was released as a one-shot and got very good reviews.

But right on top of that came *Vera Cruz*. I got a call from my agency, which was William Morris at the time, and went down and talked with Harold Hecht whom I'd known from way back in the days when he was an agent. We talked about the picture and ran what they had of it at the time. There was still some second unit stuff to be shot in Mexico. After talking with him, I believe I went down several weeks later, just an overnight trip to Mexico City to run the film and talk a little bit further about it. He said, "Gee, I'd like to have a theme song for this. Who would you suggest I get to write the theme song?" I got brash and I said, "Well, I've got to write the score, and to me, the theme song has got to be integrated with the score. Why don't you let me have a whack at it, and if you don't like it, we'll get somebody else." So Harold agreed to the idea and he asked me, "Who do you want for a lyric writer?" The name of Sammy Cahn popped into my mind. So we made contact and he came up to my place one afternoon to discuss the idea. And you know Sammy's idea of getting the title right into the opening phrase. He suggested starting with a statement: "Vera Cruz!" You know. So he left and came back a couple of days later. I had sketched out a few ideas. He came in and unpacked his typewriter and sat down. He said, "What have you got?" I played him the opening phrase. He said, "That's it," and went over to the desk. And in, I think, something like two hours, we had the song written. But he was very strange. He said, "I'm gonna stay here until you get this all down on paper. I don't trust songwriters' memories." So I immediately made a lead sheet. And the next day we went over to Radio Recorders. I had, in the meantime, contacted Bobby Tucker, who was rehearsal pianist and vocal coach out at Metro, and he got me a singer. I got hold of Andre Previn and Jose Carioca, who was one of Carmen Miranda's boys, and we went in and made a demo. Sammy was there, and he took the acetate and said, "I'll meet you at the Brown Derby in about an hour and a half." He took the demo up to Robbins, Feist, and Miller, and I was sitting in the Derby, all in a sweat, while working on my second or third martini. The phone rang and it was Sammy. He said, "I'll be right over. Relax. It's sold." It was a very happy experience. Shortly after that, I took off for Mexico to write the score down there.

ATKINS: Did you integrate the song theme into the score?

FRIEDHOFER: Oh, yes. The theme was just right for the picture, as a piece of instrumental music, and also as a main title. In that connection, there's a kind of disappointing and frustrating experience. I was down there writing the score for about fourteen weeks. In the meantime, Harold had gotten Tony Martin to sing the theme song over the title. Tony did it to a piano track, and then sent the clean vocal track up here, and I had to do the vocal background for the thing. The picture, in its original form, opened with beautiful scenic shots of all these various riders riding across the border, the defeated Confederates and the soldiers of fortune, drifting down into Mexico after the conclusion of the Civil War, over which you heard the voice of Tony Martin, singing. And then it went into an instrumental of the thing over the cast and credits. After the first preview, somebody, I don't know who—I believe it was a writer who had worked on the script—said to Harold, "You know, I get the feeling that we're going into a musical." And so, without my knowledge, the front half, the Tony Martin vocal, was cut out. But they didn't tell anybody because, by this time, Hy Kanter over at Feist, Robbins, and Miller had gotten seven recordings on the basis of the vocal in the film. I was just tipped off to it by an inside man who was working for Hecht at the time. He phoned me, terror-stricken. He said, "For God's sake, don't tell anybody that I told you, but the song is out." Oh, I know, I had called *him*, this man who had been second unit director on the film, about this hassle because I had gotten a call from Hy Kanter, who'd gotten wind, somehow, of this switch. It was a frustrating disappointment because the tune did very well despite that, but it would have done even better. I'm still getting royalties on it. It got several European recordings.

The strange part of it was that just before this switch about taking the song out, Harold offered me a lump sum for the performing rights to the song, ten thousand dollars. So I smelled a rat. He apparently had gotten used to the idea that it was a good song by that time. It's just pure conjecture on my part whether this was his kind of sneaky revenge or not. I don't know, and it doesn't matter at this late date. Good Lord! That's 1954 we're talking about. I think I've actually picked up more royalties than I would have gotten from a lump payment. But that, as I say, is water under the bridge. And who cares, anyway? It's only money.

ATKINS: We talked a bit about *White Feather.* You said the score was something like the one for *Broken Arrow.*

FRIEDHOFER: It was. Right after I got back from Mexico, I got this call from Twentieth to do the score for *White Feather.* In discussing it with Alfred Newman, he said, "Look, this is in essence the same story as *Broken Arrow.* Be smart. Use the material, or as much of it as you can, and save yourself a lot of work. I don't know if it saved me a lot of work or not, but at least it gave me a basis to go on. And also, as I said before, wide screen and color do something to music. I said once to somebody, jokingly, that I felt that music always sounded better in Technicolor. But the score was in the same bag as *Broken Arrow*'s. It was sort of an adaptation of the story. And even the female lead was Debra Paget, who had been in *Broken Arrow,* too.

ATKINS: Did you use themes from the other film?

FRIEDHOFER: Yes. I used the, you should pardon the expression, love theme, and some other material that I tailored for these situations, and also wrote a lot of original new material because it was a pretty hefty score, a much bigger score than *Broken Arrow.* And that got me planted at Twentieth Century again. I was approached immediately about a multiple deal out there that set me at Twentieth until 1959.

*Violent Saturday* was the first one after that. It was a very good little picture. The script was based on a *Saturday Evening Post* story. It dealt with a bank robbery in this little copper mining town. There was a good cast right down the line, starting with the three heavies, Lee Marvin, Steve McNally, and J. Carrol Naish. I know that the picture resulted in a very happy association with Dick Fleischer, which went on for only one other picture.

*Soldier of Fortune* was the next film. It was one of three or four pictures that all had Japanese or Chinese backgrounds. I scored that one; it was with Clark Gable and Susan Hayward. At the same time, Alfred Newman was doing *Love is a Many-Splendored Thing.* Leigh Harline was scoring *House of Bamboo,* and Vic Young was brought in to do the score for the Bogart film, *The Left Hand of God.*

ATKINS: Did you compare thematic material?

FRIEDHOFER: No, we didn't, except that Alfred used some background source material based on the kind of phonograph records they were making in India, which had a big market in Hong Kong. I didn't take any of this, but I listened to them very carefully to see what they were doing because I needed considerable source background, because apparently Hong Kong is littered with loudspeakers in front of every shop that blow this stuff at you. There were a couple of things that I did that Al liked, and I think he used them in similar sequences in *Love is a Many-Splendored Thing*.

After that was *Seven Cities of Gold*. That was Anthony Quinn, and Michael Rennie playing the part of Father Junipero Serra. The whole thing was the story of the founding of the San Diego Mission and that expedition up the coast. It was directed by Robert Webb. He's a very charming guy to work with, kind of a rough, rugged individual, but very sensitive to music.

ATKINS: Did you try to do anything within the period, musically?

FRIEDHOFER: No, it was Mexican-Spanish, that type of thing. It was another big, fat score. Richard Egan was very fine and Quinn was, as always, superb. He played the part of Portola, the leader of the expedition.

ATKINS: The next one I have, in 1953, is *The Rains of Ranchipur*.

FRIEDHOFER: Yes. I know that *Seven Cities of Gold* and *Rains of Ranchipur* were scored at a very crucial point in my life. I was stuck with the knowledge that my oldest daughter was dying of leukemia. And if it hadn't been for a workload that I assumed, I would really have gone out of my mind. She had three months to live, and in order to blot out this knowledge, which is not exactly comfortable because of the great helplessness that one feels at a time like this, I literally drowned myself in those pictures, both of which were very, very big jobs. Just before that, Dick Fleischer had another picture, *The Girl in the Red Velvet Swing*, that he was about to direct. He wanted me to do it but I think I got a couple of weeks of leave of absence just to pull myself together as much as I could. And by that time, they'd engaged Leigh Harline to do the score. Then I did those other two. But it wasn't a good time, let's say.

ATKINS: After those, there is *The Revolt of Mamie Stover* and a Columbia film, *The Harder They Fall.*

FRIEDHOFER: The scoring of *The Revolt of Mamie Stover* was a lot of fun because Buddy Adler said, "You've got to come up with a theme that is sort of the hooker with the heart of gold. And I did. In fact, that's published by Robbins or Miller or Feist. But they never did anything with it because they had put a lot of money into a song that Sammy Fain and Paul Webster wrote for the Ames Brothers, who sang it in one or two sequences in the picture, called If You Want to See Mamie Tonight. Oh, and to backtrack—the theme for *Soldier of Fortune* was also published as a song, with lyrics by Ken Darby. It didn't do much, although it's a nice tune. I'm sorry that nothing ever happened with it, but one can't expect miracles.

ATKINS: And *The Harder They Fall*, was that a Columbia loan-out?

FRIEDHOFER: Yes. Jerry Wald was the producer on it, and ordinarily, Morris Stoloff would have conducted, but he was ill. So Lionel Newman went over and conducted the score.

ATKINS: Phil Yordan is listed as the producer of that film.

FRIEDHOFER: Yes, he was the producer, but I don't know, somehow or other, Jerry was in charge of the thing. And like all Yordan scripts, it was a good, tough one. It was based on the Budd Schulberg novel. And it was Bogey's last film. Jan Sterling played the part of his wife and Rod Steiger was the heavy, the fight manager. And a big bruiser of a chap named Mike Lane, who'd been a professional wrestler at one time, played this dumb Argentinean who is set up as a pigeon. It was based on the story of a South American prizefighter who went through this same thing—oh, good Lord! I can't remember his name. I think my interest in prizefighting ceased when Max Schmeling was knocked out in the first round by Joe Louis. Max Baer Sr. played a very rough, tough part of the fighter who ultimately flattens our hero. It was a very strong and moving picture. I loved the thing and it didn't portray the fight game in a favorable light. I remember the director, Mark Robson, telling me that they were even having trouble renting sporting goods equipment and they couldn't get an auditorium to shoot the prizefight scenes in. And the cast was being threatened by unknowns. But somehow they bulled through the thing and came through with a very fine, strong picture, stronger, if anything, than *Body and Soul*, because the happy ending that *Body and Soul* had was an unknown quantity in this. It left you up in the air. It wound up with Bogart sitting at the typewriter, starting an expose of the whole fight racket.

ATKINS: Was Bogart threatened, among other people?

FRIEDHOFER: I imagine he was. Oh, and I got another song out of that—not a song, but an instrumental which was originally released as Cocktail Lounge. It was used as material for Bogart and Jan Sterling. Later on it was recorded by Howard Roberts, the guitarist. He had been playing the date, and heard the theme and came over to me and said, "Hey, man, I'm making an album and I'd like to use the tune." So he did. It was released under the title An Orchid for Miss Sterling.

*Between Heaven and Hell*, also released in 1956, was a very interesting picture to me. This was Dick Fleischer's. It was a very strong cast right down the line. It was a story about a rich southern kid's readjustment to life owing to the incidents in the war. It was a very strong picture, and I was pleased with one thing, as far as the music goes, that in a picture where the tendency on most everybody's part was towards blockbusters, here was a, comparatively speaking, unassuming little picture, that didn't have an intermission in it, and yet I managed to snag an Academy nomination on the thing. Of course, in the final shuffle it got lost, but I felt that the nomination was an accolade. And those are always nice to get. I'm enough of a ham to enjoy those things.

That film is also a sample of my fondness for the variation technique. Outside of the very short episode between Bob Wagner and Terry Moore, with kind of a love theme, practically the whole score was based on the famous plain-chant that goes way back, Dies Irae, Day of Wrath. It acted either as a foundation on which I built other things or stuck into the fabric somehow. Consequently, it glued the whole score together. But it was a very fine experience, very, very pleasant.

ATKINS: There's another film that was nominated for an Academy Award, the next year, *Boy on a Dolphin*.

FRIEDHOFER: I somehow managed to cross myself up by getting two nominations that year, one for *An Affair to Remember,* and the other for *Boy on a Dolphin,* both of which were extremely pleasant experiences. Did we talk about *Rains of Ranchipur?*

ATKINS: Just briefly.

FRIEDHOFER: I want to add something about *Rains of Ranchipur.* Some reviewer for *Films in Review* said that they had used the visual effects of the earthquake and the flood out of the original picture, *The Rains Came,* which was made way back, and they used the catastrophe directly out of the original film. In the first place, it's ridiculous, and this lad, whoever he was that was reviewing, wasn't particularly careful about it. He sort of fluffed the whole thing off. That catastrophe in the remake was a gigantic undertaking, and one of the best special effects jobs I've ever seen in my life. There was one shot that was kind of amusing to me. People outside of southern California wouldn't recognize it, but they used the Colorado Street Bridge. All of a sudden you see this bridge with all these fleeing Muslims and Hindus running over it, and this enormous tidal wave after them. And then you see the whole damn bridge crumble. My first thought on seeing it was, "How am I going to get over to Pasadena now?" But it was magnificent. It made the original look like a wind machine set over a bathtub.

The novel, by Louis Bromfield, was called *The Rains Came,* and they changed it to *The Rains of Ranchipur,* why, I don't know, except that they didn't want people with long memories to think it was just a reissue of the original. Usually the only names of novelists that stick in my mind are Hemingway, James Joyce, Mickey Spillane, Raymond Chandler, who is by far the best, and who also has a strange background. He was, one night, reading pulp detective stories and he threw one across the room angrily and said, "I can write better stuff than this," and so he proceeded to. A lot of his things have been done in film, of course. He created one of the best private eyes of all time, Philip Marlowe. His whole depiction of Los Angeles, the city—you can practically smell the dry rot and hear the termites gnawing away at the timbers, and the bums on skid row putting down their muscatel bottles, and the whole thing. And I daresay it's a Los Angeles that's not vanishing; it's expanding in certain quarters. It's a Los Angeles that I don't see very often, but I associate constantly in my mind with Ray Chandler and Humphrey Bogart, and others who've enacted the part of Philip Marlowe.

But the score turned out very well. It was highly romantic and it had some purely synthetic source music in it. I didn't use Ravi Shankar, or anything like it. As a matter of fact, nobody was using Ravi Shankar at that time except some people in India, maybe, who were making films. This was more of a commercial score, which is nothing to be ashamed of exactly. It was directed primarily at American audiences, for whom, at that time, you had to temper your ethnomusicology to a certain extent. Owing to a lot that has happened since then—since everybody, including the jazzniks, has gotten hooked on various aspects of Eastern music—that has changed.

ATKINS: Didn't you use ethnic music in *Boy on a Dolphin* ?

FRIEDHOFER: That, also, was largely things of my own invention, except for some source stuff that had been recorded over there. The thing that later became the love theme, was sort of a collaboration once removed by what's-his-name—the Greek composer—he's written a lot of popular music over there, Manos Hadjidakis. But it was sort of a half a tune, so I put it into a more commercial form. It did pretty well, too. I think. Oh, Julie London recorded the original main title on the thing.

ATKINS: What did Marni Nixon do in that film?

FRIEDHOFER: Marni did the sort of another world sound that I wanted. She did a vocalese in the underwater sequences when Sophia Loren first finds this statue that has been under water for two thousand years. Then later on in the picture, it came back again.

Julie London had made a commercial record, for Liberty, which we used in the main title. We dolled it up with strings and a few things. But to get back to Marni, whom I'd known since I was doing *Joan of Arc*, and she was in the Roger Wagner Chorale, she was sort of a godsend. She was just a kid, really, but I wanted a simulation of boy voices, and also the hard Medieval sound, which is without any vibrato at all. She got the idea right away, and the rest of the gals in the chorus, because we didn't have choir boys or castrati, they got it.

It was in the coronation scene in *Joan of Arc*, where I used a lot of plain-chant and one thing of Guillaume Dufay's. And the sound was just right. But Marni, who can do anything, practically, has not only a fine voice, but has absolute pitch like you wouldn't believe. She came in and recorded this vocalese. One was an overdub, which she read through once, with the track and the picture on the screen. She listened to it on the headset, and I believe it was the second take that was perfect. Then the next one she did, which was a much longer one, she did on one take, and just fantastic. I know that Sam Engel, the producer, was on the stage and fell madly in love with her on the strength of that.

ATKINS: She was in *An Affair to Remember*, too.

FRIEDHOFER: Yes, she was Deborah Kerr's voice double in that and, later, in *The King and I*. I know that when she worked with Deborah, she literally lived with her in order to get all the inflections of the speaking voice, and to translate those into the vocal field. Both those films are just about as good examples as I know, with the possible exception of *The Jolson Story*. There are places in *The King and I* where Deborah Kerr would start a vocal phrase, and then Marni would take over. And the switch is not perceptible to the ear. You'd have to know that it was there in order to suspect that there was something.

ATKINS: In *Affair to Remember*, I assume that everything was prerecorded. Would she then coach Deborah Kerr on the lip synching?

FRIEDHOFER: Yes, and *there* is a lady for whom I have the greatest admiration. She's not only a fine actress, she's a very fine person, and a thoroughly earthy sort.

ATKINS: There was all sorts of music in *Affair to Remember*: the school children—and the ballet.

FRIEDHOFER: The ballet was mine. The ballet sequence was a film clip from some musical. Lord knows how long ago it was made, and it was all in a long shot, which was in 2/4. And I had my music editor make me a click track in 3/4 because I wanted a kind of a Tchaikovsky—Glazounov waltz feeling in the thing, which I fortunately got. And it worked out just fine in that way. It was a deliberate, what you might call, musical forgery on my part without actually stealing anything from Tchaikovsky or from Glazounov. It was right in the vein of that imperial ballet type thing.

And then some of the source music on shipboard was mine, also. There's one tune that I'm still kind of fond of, called Pink Champagne. That was mine. In the score, I used pieces of Harry Warren's tune, fragmented. There's one scene that Harry was very fond of. It's when they go to visit Cary Grant's aunt in Europe, and Deborah goes into the chapel to pray. I referred to it, I said, "Harry, this probably sounds like an intermezzo from a not too successful Italian opera." That broke him up, because right in the middle of this thing, which was a churchy atmosphere, I introduced a strain of Harry's tune.

ATKINS: You both had Academy Award nominations and both lost out. I don't know about you, but Harry was very disappointed.

FRIEDHOFER: I wasn't. I took it as an inevitable happening. When you suddenly find yourself with two nominations in one season, that automatically splits your vote right down the middle and somebody else gets it. I can't remember from one year to the next who got it. I can't even remember what years I was nominated. The only two that I really remember were the first ones, *Woman in the Window* and *Best Years*, which was the one Academy night on which I was up with a nomination that I did not attend because I was working on a film up against my own deadline, because I wanted to get away to the Caribbean. I'd gotten a big fat refund from Uncle Sam and decided to spend it foolishly.

★    ★    ★

ATKINS: There were some other Fox films in 1957: *The Sun Also Rises* and *Oh Men! Oh Women!*

FRIEDHOFER: *The Sun Also Rises* was my own, but the other was Cyril Mockridge's and I jumped in and helped on it because it was one of those deadline things. I was without assignment, so I was asked to help Cyril.

ATKINS: There are several music credits on *The Sun Also Rises.*

FRIEDHOFER: Yes. It was Vicente Gomez who did the guitar work. And it also has the name of my dear friend Alexander Courage, who is a bullfight aficionado. He worked with me in laying out that whole second part of the film that dealt with the fiesta in Pamplona. From a technical standpoint, this was about as difficult a job as I've ever had, in that we had all these marching bands and fiesta music and the Basque—what they call "cxistu." It's a two-pronged fife and drum kind of thing. It's like a small timbale. And these two instruments are played by one man. They had these cxistu set-ups, and we couldn't find any, so we faked it. Sandy wrote some of it, and I wrote some of it. Then we made arrangements of this very famous thing that is always played at this Pamplona fiesta. I wrote a lot of marching band stuff. And this all had to be made with long overlaps because of the fact that you'd move from one area to another and have to cross-fade these things. This was all postscored. The whole Pamplona thing opened up with a religious procession. That moved into something else, and from there into something else again. Then there was the stuff that Vicente Gomez did. It started in a little pub in Pamplona where Tyrone Power leaves the lady who is very much intrigued with this bullfighter, who is now head of production at Paramount, Bob Evans.

ATKINS: He was in it?

FRIEDHOFER: He was the bullfighter. Zanuck picked him up and figured that he'd be a good type. It was the first thing that he'd done in films, I believe.

ATKINS: Was any music recorded in Spain?

FRIEDHOFER: No, we had to lay all that stuff in afterwards. You see, the picture was shot in two locations. Part was shot in Pamplona, and then the actual bullring stuff was shot in Mexico City, in the big ring down there. But it was a neat job of matching. We worked ourselves silly on it because, for some reason, we were dubbing at night. Sandy Courage and I would be over in my office working, and all of a sudden I would get a call from the dubbing stage. Henry King wanted to know about certain things, so I'd have to go in and give him an intelligent answer at eleven o'clock at night. But it all worked out fine and he was very happy with it. Everybody was. I still like the score. Incidentally, I got another tune out of that one, too, a thing called The Lights of Paris, which was published by The Big Three. The lyric was Charles Henderson's. I think I've still got a demo some-place around that was made by a gal who never got as far as she should have, Eileen Wilson. She was on *The Lucky Strike Hit Parade* for a long time and sort of wore out her welcome through overexposure. But she had a fine voice and could do anything.

ATKINS: Did you ever find that in the theater the sound was differ-ent from what you'd expected?

FRIEDHOFER: Let's say that I've been sixty percent of the time happy, and the other forty disappointed, and I won't say suicidally dejected, but let's just say unhappy. I think I mentioned the case of the film we ran at AFI, *The Big Carnival*. I was not at the first dubbing, for other reasons than an unwillingness to attend, because that is, to me, one of the most important parts of the composer's job. As Cop-land pointed out, that's where you not only learn your mistakes, but you've got to be there to defend your interests. He referred to the dubbing room as the "composer's purgatory." Much later on, Lennie Bernstein wrote a most amusing chapter in his *The Joy of Music*, about his experiences on the Brando film *On the Waterfront*. The chapter was called Upper Dubbing Ten, which was the name of the dubbing room over at Columbia on Gower Street. And it's most amusing, but a little petulant.

But it's true that you have to stand up on your hind legs and scream bloody murder, which is something that has happened to me on more occasion than one. And I scream very loudly sometimes. Fortunately, on this last tour of duty at Twentieth Century Fox, I had a very stalwart ally in Arthur Piantadosi, who had good ears and was musically inclined, anyway. Between the two of us we managed to get our way, so with that whole Twentieth output I was extremely happy.

There's another film such as *Oh Men! Oh Women!* that just comes back to me on which I was asked to jump in and work—*The Gift of Love*. I forget who the child actress was in that, but she was apparently a precocious little monster who got herself thoroughly disliked wherever she worked. The film was beautifully photographed around the Monterey Peninsula. But those two are relatively unimportant because my contribution was minor in both cases.

Then, I believe, came *The Young Lions*, which, in my estimation, was a darn good picture. It still is, I believe. Maximilian Schell played Marlon Brando's commanding officer and there's an interesting thing about him: he spoke no English at the time and he learned his part phonetically. Maria, his sister, had been over for some time, but he was a comparative newcomer. But it was a very strong picture, although they took considerable liberties with the novel. The Brando character, in the novel, was a thoroughgoing no-goodnik, but they softened him up considerably, made him the victim of circumstances, because he was not a very sympathetic character in the novel. Hardly anybody was. But it was a very well-made picture and the sad part of it was that the producer, Al Lichtman, a thoroughly nice guy to work with, did not live to see the final print. He died, of what I don't know, but it was very sudden and rather sad. He was a producer who was vitally interested in every aspect of the progress of the film and I know he came to every recording session. Outside of his charm, this was an extremely practical man. A story is told about him, that he would be able to take a script and sort of weigh it in his hand, the way that a fish merchant weighs a halibut or something, and determine the budget right down to the penny. It's an apocryphal story, but it's very funny. I knew another man who had that habit and that was the musical director, Louis Silvers. When you brought a score into him, he would do that same thing, as if it was smoked salmon or sturgeon, or something like that. I used to kid him about it all the time, as did other people. But apparently Lichtman was very, very shrewd about this sort of thing.

I recall a sneak preview of the film in San Francisco, which I attended. After the preview, there was a long session that went on for several hours in the Fairmont Hotel. There was a great deal of controversy about what was one of the strongest sequences in the picture. It was after the collapse of the German forces, and Brando is running around by himself and runs into this concentration camp at the same time as the arrival of the American troops. They run into this concentration camp and bust down one of the barracks. And you see these poor emaciated victims of the policies of the Third Reich.

Where they got these people I don't know, because it was not a documentary shot. I'm quite sure of that. If it was, it was some of the most stunning intercutting I ever saw in my life. But there was some talk about whether they shouldn't take that out of the picture. And on one of those occasions when I really got my dander up about something, I proceeded to make my views on the subject heard rather strongly. I said, "This is the sort of thing that nobody should ever be allowed to forget." I think Eddie Dmytryk sided in with me and perhaps somebody else, I don't know, and I think Lichtman. On the opposing side were Buddy Adler and Alfred Rogell, who by that time had become quite a power at Twentieth Century Fox. But our side won, fortunately, because it would have completely emasculated the picture and destroyed the whole point of it. So that's the way it went. But it was a very successful picture.

That was one of the few pictures for which I attended an invitational preview. As was the custom in those days, it was held in their then new, big auditorium, which was part of the new dubbing set-up. Stage One was the original recording studio and still is to this day. Stage Two, on the other side of it, had been redone as a dubbing stage. But that no longer proved adequate, so they moved over to this new dubbing building. I was very happy with the results on the picture. Afterwards, there was food and drink and hordes of people who had attended the preview. It was, all told, a very happy time.

*Young Lions* was the last picture that was actually scored by me or by anybody else at Twentieth Century Fox until the strike was over. There was this big fat exodus to Europe and to Mexico to score films. Mexico had been eminently satisfactory for some time, as I found out when I went down there in 1954 to write the score for *Vera Cruz*, which was also recorded down there. In that interim, apparently the sound equipment out at the studios, Churubusco, had deteriorated. I know that Lionel Newman, who went down there to record, was very unhappy with the results. Then he went to England. While he was in Mexico, however, this picture, *The Bravados*, came up. This was a score that Al Newman and I wrote, and Lionel is credited on the screen because he had to take the scores over to Munich and record them over there.

ATKINS: How long did the strike last?

FRIEDHOFER: I'm not certain about that because I was among a few who bolted the union at that time and joined the Guild.

ATKINS: Was that the Cecil Read group?

FRIEDHOFER: Yes. Some of us stuck with Cecil Read. But of course, as a composer, the union had absolutely no jurisdiction over me. As an orchestrator, yes; as a conductor, yes. And I think also as an arranger, they would have had jurisdiction, but as a composer, no, because that would have been in violation of the antitrust law if they had a completely monopolistic control over all musical activities. No, it involved players, arrangers, orchestrators, and conductors.

After *The Bravados* came *The Barbarian and the Geisha*. That was written over here, then the score was taken over to Munich and recorded at the Bavaria Sound Studios. The picture did an awful lot of traveling, in that it was shot in Japan, by John Huston. Remakes were done in Hollywood, by Leon Shamroy, who matched the photography in Japan so beautifully. They did some acting redos over here, with the girl who was in the picture—she was not Japanese, she was Manchurian—Eiko Ando, and John Wayne. I think it was the only thing she did do here. She didn't like it in California very much and went back home. But the bulk of that film was shot in Japan, and John Huston had a notion that the whole thing should be scored with ethnic Japanese music. I was assigned to the picture and went in to confer with Buddy Adler, who by that time had become head of production at Twentieth Century Fox. Buddy told me of this notion of Huston's. After seeing the film, I said to Buddy, who was all hopped up about this ethnic idea, I said—as gently as is possible for me—"We mustn't forget that this film will be shown largely in American and European countries, so the ethnic thing, no matter how authentic it might be, would, I don't think, be advisable because the story is not basically about the Japanese. It's about a pair of Caucasians who have been sent over as the first diplomatic representatives of the United States to Japan. The film is about the ambassador, Townsend Harris, who was rather an embarrassment to the United States government, so they shipped him over to Japan to get rid of him. Apparently he was an alcoholic and a general no-goodnik. In mentioning this whole thing to Buddy, I said, "The story, if you analyze it very closely, is *Madama Butterfly* all over again. So my personal feeling is that it should be about as Japanese as Puccini's *Madama Butterfly*. It should be a romantic, dramatic score, with certain ethnic overtones, but fundamentally something that wouldn't be puzzling to a European or American audience."

He said, "Well, let me think about it." So I went back to my quarters. Then, about two or three days later, I suddenly got a call on the phone. It was Adler, who said, "You know, I've been thinking about *The Barbarian and the Geisha*, and I think we ought to approach the score from the standpoint of Puccini's *Madama Butterfly*." Well, I counted a slow four, and said, "Buddy, I think you're absolutely right." He didn't mention the fact at all that I had implanted this idea in his mind, but that's characteristic, let's say.

So I went ahead and wrote the score, and took it to Europe and recorded it over in Munich. We had an arrangement for shipping back the tracks. A broker here would pick them up, and so on, and ship them to the studio.

ATKINS: Were they dubbed here?

FRIEDHOFER: Oh, yes. And it was dubbed while I was still over there sitting in the booth, listening to the scoring. So they had about four or five reels dubbed by the time I got home. That was another one I've not seen in the theater. I think I saw it once on television, which is always an annoyance. But I did get a pretty good recording on it, an album which is now, I understand, being fought for by soundtrack freaks, at prices far above what an album sells for. Now the collectors of this sort of thing are getting sums anywhere from fifty up to one hundred, in some cases up to one hundred twenty bucks a copy. And sometimes they're even auctioned off at I don't know what prices. I think I only have one album of the seven or eight or so that I've gotten soundtrack albums on. The other day I heard about a chap who has mint copies of all these albums, which he's hanging onto for dear life. But he is willing to make tapes of them. I don't know if he has a flourishing business at this, but I asked him what he would charge to make me tapes. He said he would make them for me for ten dollars a copy.

ATKINS: I think there's a going business in that sort of copying.

FRIEDHOFER: Oh, yes, and it doesn't do the composer any good at all, really.

★    ★    ★

ATKINS: Was *In Love and War*, released in 1958, made during the strike?

FRIEDHOFER: I think the strike was over by then. It was scored on this side. That was a Jerry Wald production, also with Robert Wagner and Hope Lange. It was another war picture about the regeneration of, well, he wasn't exactly a rotten kid, he was kind of no-goodnik. The picture was always amusing to me because Mort Sahl appeared in it, in just a cameo bit.

ATKINS: What was your experience with Jerry Wald?

FRIEDHOFER: Very pleasant. Very pleasant. I knew him slightly from Warner Brothers, back in the days when I was just an orchestrator or arranger over there. But I had never worked on anything that he produced there. My first contact with him was doing *The Harder They Fall*, at Columbia. Right after that he came to Twentieth. I used to see him on the lot a great deal. I did, as I say, *In Love and War* and *An Affair to Remember*.

ATKINS: According to Harry Warren, Jerry Wald had very little to do with *An Affair to Remember*. It was mostly Leo McCarey's work, he said.

FRIEDHOFER: Well, Jerry was smart in that he—some say that he used people. On the other hand, I think if he had engaged somebody whom he entrusted implicitly, he let them alone completely, which is, after all, one of the most important producer functions. It made Goldwyn a pretty important producer, you might say, as it also made Zanuck quite an important producer, and a couple of others.

ATKINS: What sort of musical taste did Jerry Wald have in his films?

FRIEDHOFER: He would question. When we were running a pre-scoring print, I, or whatever composer happened to be working for him, would make certain suggestions and Jerry would question them. And during screenings he was always scribbling notes, either to himself or in regard to questions he wanted to ask. If one made out a fairly good case for one's opinions or points of view, he would think about it and he'd wind up saying, "Okay, you know your business. I don't know anything about music. I just wanted to know. Go ahead and do it your way," which makes for a very pleasant working association, *if* you happen to be right. Of course, the composer for films is forced into the unfortunate position of having to be right the first time around. And if he isn't, it's kind of hard luck for him, because you goof on something and it's not forgiven or forgotten very easily.

In connection with *In Love and War*, a very amusing and slightly shattering thing happened. We were on our way to the Twentieth Century Fox commissary and I was driving over with Ted Kane, who was at that time executive head of the music department. We stopped by Alfred Newman's bungalow, that little thatched cottage, to pick up Al. Ted was driving a convertible and I had my arm flung over the back of the seat, sort of dripping down outside. Alfred got into the car, and he was saying something very jovial to me, and I wasn't paying much attention to his physical movements. And he reached behind him and slammed the car door on that finger, my—what is that one? "This little pig went to market, this little—." It was the roast beef finger. And he really slammed the door hard, so instead of going to the commissary, we went to the emergency hospital on the lot. Both Alfred and I went in, and when the nurse looked at us, she said, "Which one of you should I take care of first?" because Alfred was positively green, and in as big a state of shock as I was. She put a splint on it and stanched the bleeding, and then we went to the commissary and had lunch, believe it or not, after which I went to see my physician and an x-ray man. Apparently it had cracked up all the little tiny bones in the finger. So they put a good fat splint on it, and you can imagine the difficulties of trying either to play the piano or write under those circumstances. And it was unadulterated hell for a couple of days. They took another x-ray, and it was healing very satisfactorily, so they put on a short splint of some molded material. After that, while there was discomfort, I could go on writing.

When Alfred got home that night, right after the accident, and mentioned it to Martha, his wife, she looked at him and said. "What's the matter with you? Do you want to write all the scores on the lot?" which was a great joke, of course. As a matter of fact, Alfred wrote a couple of sequences for me on my material, to take some of the load off me. But I explained one time that it was the custom of Hollywood composers to act the way the citizens of a certain Chinese village did.

They solved the economic problem by taking in each other's laundry. But this is a common practice and it's happened so many times that nobody ever thinks about it. You're in a jam and you holler for help, or somebody else is in a jam, and they holler for help, and what do you do? Union and guild restrictions make this sort of thing an impossibility, you know. If you so much as breathe on a script, you're supposed to get screen credit as a writer—or as a composer. But that's beside the point.

ATKINS: The next film I have listed is *This Earth Is Mine.*

FRIEDHOFER: After *In Love and War,* I took a vacation. My wife had gone over to Brussels, to the World's Fair there, picked up a car, and met me in Genoa. I had taken a ship. I wanted really to relax and went over on one of the American Export Lines ships—I forget which one—either the President, or the Senator, or the House Un-American Activities Committee was the name of the ship. But fortunately I saw a great deal of Europe that I might not have seen if I'd flown over, stopping at various places, including Casablanca, where I didn't see Sidney Greenstreet, nor Peter Lorre, nor Humphrey Bogart.

While my wife and I were in Rome, I got a telegram from Mark Newman, who was my agent at the time, asking whether I would consider doing this picture at Universal, *This Earth Is Mine.* So when we returned to New York, I headed straight for the coast and went over to Universal and got everything squared away, and then wrote the score for the film. That was late in 1958 and early '59. The television slump, right around that time, was beginning to hit not only Twentieth Century Fox, but every studio in town. I had one more contractual commitment with Fox. If I had refused the commitment, they would have been obligated to pay me. And I would have felt uncomfortable about that. Don't ask me why. It's just my Teutonic conscience, which has a way of being very inconveniently ethical at times. So I took the picture. It was called *Woman Obsessed.*

That was a picture that had one of everything in it—really. Syd Boehm did the script on it, I believe, and I think Henry Hathaway directed. It had a forest fire. It had a snowstorm, a death, a rape, a miscarriage, and a few other things like that, including Stephen Boyd.

ATKINS: Did it have music under all these calamities?

FRIEDHOFER: Well, some of the calamities were so horrendous that there was no point in trying to write music for them. I don't remember much about the score, except that it was kind of a farewell to Twentieth Century Fox for me, to a certain extent, because that was the end of my contractual agreement. And in the meantime, Alfred had left Twentieth and had gone into semi-retirement. Lionel Newman had become head of the music department, but he was largely in charge of television.

Oh, hard on the heels of that came the remake of *Blue Angel.* It was released through Twentieth, but it was a Jack Cummings production. His associate was Saul Chaplin, whom I'd known from way, way back at Columbia when I first worked over there in 1945.

ATKINS: Was there much effort made to follow the previous *Blue Angel*?

FRIEDHOFER: Oh, yes. And I think the only song that was left out from the original Frederick Hollander score was Falling in Love Again. And the other things were written by Jimmy McHugh and Harold Adamson. The cast was not a bad one: Curt Jurgens, John Banner, Theodore Bikel, and Mai Britt. In the cast was also a gal who later on had considerable success in Hollywood as an actress. I think her first real bid to success was the *Little Abner* film—Carol Lynley. I spotted her as having a great acting potential, although she was just part of the lineup in this shabby little nightclub. But she did a couple of things by which I detected an instinct for the spotlight in her. She had a very neat and unobtrusive way of scene stealing.

ATKINS: The next film I have is *Never So Few.* This wasn't a musical, but what was your contact with Frank Sinatra?

FRIEDHOFER: I had no contact with him. He was in charge of everything on the film, including the wardrobe woman, probably.

ATKINS: This was an M-G-M release. Was it made on the M-G-M lot?

FRIEDHOFER: Yes, it was. And the score was written at the time of emotional stress on my part, but I got through it, somehow. It was kind of interesting to do because I had to fake an ethnic background for a lot of the scenes. The cast was—who the devil was in it?—

Sinatra, Steve McQueen, and Dean Jones, who became successful in their own right. The story was based on a factual novel, the name of which I forget. But the protagonist was a real-life character who was a sort of a maverick soldier who took things into his own hands when he got steamed up. That was the part played by Sinatra. Peter Lawford was in it. Naturally, one of the members of the rat pack had to be in it.

ATKINS: Did Sinatra have any active part as far as the scoring was concerned?

FRIEDHOFER: I had no association with him at all. In fact, I have no idea what even happened to the picture after I left Metro. That was in 1959, wasn't it?

ATKINS: Yes. The next picture, which is sort of a jump, is *One Eyed Jacks*.

FRIEDHOFER: That's right. There was a period in there when I was—how shall we say—unemployed. But not altogether because I had been starting to get my feet wet in television at that time. Mark Newman, my agent, came up with not one but two pilot films, one for a Western series—one of the first hour-long Westerns—called *Outlaws*, and another one, it being the centenary of the war between the states, which was originally called *The Blue and the Grey* and wound up being called *The Americans*. I did pilots on both of them and both sold. But I didn't want to tie myself up with the two, so I stuck with *Outlaws*. And before the selling of *Outlaws* as a series, Mark Newman came up with *One Eyed Jacks*. Directly upon finishing that film, I really got hooked into television.

But *Jacks* was, and is to this day, in its original—not its "original original" version, which I think ran for some seven hours—but the version that Brando edited down to I forget what length, and decided he couldn't get it any shorter, and then somebody at Paramount took over and got it down to something like two and a half hours, its final cut. I went in to look at it one night with my wife, and we literally both sat on the edge of our seats. And, mind you, it was in its final cut, but dissolves, et cetera, had not been put in. Certain sound effects were missing. Music was naturally not in the film. They hadn't done a preview score on it. We were both really gripped and deeply moved by the film. So that was my sole obsession for the next ten weeks.

ATKINS: You mentioned to me that there were certain changes made by the time it was released that you weren't happy about.

FRIEDHOFER: At the time of the first preview, everybody got their grubby little hands on it. (I was not asked to the preview.) You may have noticed an elision, a cut in the episode where Brando and Karl Malden had been pursued by the Mexican fuzz, the rurales, up to the top of this high peak, and were left stranded up there with only one horse. It was a long scene that played practically silent, except for the music. They decide which one of them is to go for fresh horses. And through a trick, Brando gets Karl Malden, who is practically a father image in his mind, to go for the horses. Malden's greed gets the better of him and he makes off with the loot, and Brando is left stranded, and captured by the rurales. But this whole episode, this feeling of warmth between these two men that you got, sort of gave credence to the terrific hatred that Brando had built up for Malden, and vice versa. If you've done somebody a dirty trick, your conscience, in order to save face, sort of instills in you a hatred for the person whom you've done dirt to. And with this elimination, a lot of things that happened afterwards didn't quite ring true, that is, to me. The thing was psychologically so right that it destroyed certain things in the film for me. And also, the change in the ending of the picture.

ATKINS: How many different endings did they have for the film?

FRIEDHOFER: Just two. The first one was the final shoot-out between Malden and Brando, as Brando rides out with the girl, who is Malden's stepdaughter. In his last shot, Malden fires after them and the girl is hit. They make it way out in the sand dunes of Monterey. She dies, and the picture winds up with Brando riding off into the— not the sunset, I hope—I don't remember now, but anyway, with the girl's body in his arms. That was somehow or other the apt ending for the film, because here was a man who had been an absolute stinker all his life. And he finds the one thing that is a sort of regeneration for him, and it's taken away from him—sort of a poetic *in*justice, shall we say. And certainly not a happy ending. But the other ending was as phony as a three dollar bill. They ride off. She hasn't been hit. They stop out on the dunes there, and he gives a long cop-out kind of speech about how he's got to get out. She's pregnant. And he says, "Well, don't you worry about that, baby. You go on home and your mother will take care of you. And one of these nights soon you'll hear me scratching at the back door, and we'll go away someplace." And so he rides off and leaves her gazing after him, which to me was a complete cop-out, and completely phony.

ATKINS: Whose decision was it to change the ending?

FRIEDHOFER: I don't know. Brando was away, and he'd left the lot. I think he was preparing to go to Tahiti to do *Mutiny on the Bounty*, and I think that by dint of a great deal of persuasion, they managed to get him to come back and change the ending. I'm really surprised that he did, but I think that by this time he was completely indifferent to what the fate of the picture would ultimately be. And I think that by this time, Marty Rackin had become head of production at Paramount. D. A. Doran had been in charge to a certain extent. But, at that time, Paramount was kind of a captainless ship, shall we say. It was this, plus an unsuccessful preview, plus the fact that there was no real strong deciding hand at the helm, that made for what turned out to be a semi-successful picture. And yet there were some performances in the thing that stayed very strongly fixed in my memory: the little girl, the Mexican actress, Pina Pellicer, was superb as this child whom Brando seduced, and Katy Jurado, who is one of my great loves in film, whom I've never seen turn in a bad performance anywhere. She's wonderful. Malden. An entirely new image was created for Slim Pickens, who had always been a kind of a clown in films, and became a supreme heavy as a result of this. And a very fine actor, Ben Johnson. And a very fine Mexican actor, Larry Duran, who comes into the film as Brando's cellmate.

But I always think of the film in its original form. I had an album of the original score, which I had edited myself. But they had made innumerable cuts in the film, in addition to these two story points that annoyed me so, so that they had the devil's own time bridging musical sequences that had been slashed into. The only way they could do it was by goosing up sound effects and lowering music levels. I saw the picture once, in the studio, after they had made these cuts and I walked away from it kind of ill. As a result of these cuts and all that, I might possibly have snagged myself another music nomination, but alas, no.

ATKINS: I wasn't as conscious of the music cuts as you would have been.

FRIEDHOFER: Unfortunately, I have this kind of recall for things, musical, particularly. A number of people, who hadn't been subjected to the kind of purely aesthetic flogging that I took, liked it. I got a very glowing letter from Gene Lees, among other people, who was at that time still editor of *Downbeat*. That was the beginning of a correspondence that wound up finally in a beautiful friendship that I still have with Gene.

ATKINS: There's another film, in 1961, with the famous William Castle.

FRIEDHOFER: That would be *Homicidal*. He's famous on account of—before that he was simply notorious—but he's famous now on account of *Rosemary's Baby*, which I consider an excellent score and an excellent picture. I think it has it all over the much-touted *Exorcist* like a tent. But these earlier efforts of his, he was not only producer; he was director on them. And he went in for all kinds of audience gimmicks. But I think *Homicidal* was the first film that he made which did not have—oh, yes, it did have one gimmick in it, near the end of the picture, where there was an announcement. A voice said, "If you've got a weak heart, you'd better leave the theater now." He did a lot of that, and he actually had electric shock installed under certain seats, and synthetic lobsters crawling up and down the aisles, pinching people on the ankles, and things like that.

But this film, I don't know how it came about—oh, I know. I was getting a little bit harassed by the weekly hour-long TV things, which were loaded with music, and which I, like an idiot, was trying to do in the same manner that I would do a film score. But these scores ran twenty, twenty-five, thirty minutes of music each. I finally wised up and pulled in my friend and associate Sidney Cutner. In a great many instances, I would write maybe two-thirds of the score, and sometimes less, and give him a roadmap and thematic material, and say, "This is the way it should go, so go." He also sat in the monitor booth and rode herd on what we were getting on the track. And this was my second, after a long period of time, excursion into a field that I had always shied away from, and that's conducting. This was a purely practical matter because I would have had to hire a conductor. I was doing the series on a weekly package deal, which meant that I paid for everything except the sound stage and the recording engineer and the projectionist. That would have meant X number of dollars that I wouldn't have been able to latch onto. So I figured, well, I might as well get my feet wet. And the first four or five episodes were sheer hell, not only physically, but mentally. And I will be eternally grateful to a number of playing musicians in this town, who not only bore with me, but pulled me through some rather shaky places, because they had a personal, as well as, I daresay, musical regard for me. But after that it got to be fun and I enjoyed it because it was a switch of activity from what was purely introvert—which writing is—to conducting, which is extrovert. Mind you, I don't mean to imply that I became a hell of a conductor. I didn't. But at least I knew what I wanted and was able, to a certain extent, to get it out of the orchestra.

Along towards the nineteenth or twentieth episode, I suddenly got this call from Bill Castle. I don't know who had told him about me, but he was interested in having me look at the picture. He said he didn't have a lot of money to spend on music, but he thought I might be interested. He wanted me to come over and look at it, so I went over to Columbia one afternoon and ran the film and was kind of fascinated with it, because outside of *The Lodger*, which goes all the way back to 1944, it was the first so-called horror film that I had ever done. I was interested in it and so I did the thing. In the meantime, I was juggling that and my TV series at the same time. I think I did the Castle score in about three weeks' time. I had left Sid in charge, but was giving him thematic material. And I think that if it hadn't been for the fact that 1961 was a political campaign year, and a lot of our time was being preempted by political things, we never would have gotten through, because the series went on the air in very, very bad shape from a standpoint of preparation.

ATKINS: About *Homicidal*, did you find this genre difficult?

FRIEDHOFER: No. I have always had at least a literary leaning towards the macabre and the supernatural and other-world type things. Back in my twenties, I used to be a reader of a magazine that has since become a collector's item, a magazine called *Wierd Tales*. There was also my early interest in Edgar Allan Poe, and I was a freak for Sherlock Holmes, too, and still am.

Bill Castle was very pleased with the score. He came to most of the recording sessions. And that, incidentally, was my first and only experience in conducting an entire feature film. It worked out all right. I sort of handpicked my orchestra. I forget who contracted it, but I got all the players I wanted. I had a rather peculiar orchestra set-up, the exact nature of which I don't recall now, but I got all the people I wanted. It was a strange mixture of jazzmen and legitimate musicians. I had a good brass section and excellent woodwinds and so who could ask for anything more? It was a relatively small orchestra, but a good one, that gave me everything I wanted.

The next film you must have on your agenda there was Chuck Conner's *Geronimo*. Right?

ATKINS: Yes.

FRIEDHOFER: And Irene, I must tell you quite honestly that this is an experience the like of which I have never gone through, with a production triumvirate, which was Levy, Laven, and Gardner, and I never want to go through it again. These were men who had come into theater film production by way of television. And their conception of how to score a television film was fairly primitive, in that one of them—I forget which one, and I prefer not to remember—was hooked on the Mickey Mouse technique. You had to catch every flick of an eyelid with what is known in the business as a "stinger," a dissonant chord of some kind that points these things up. I know that breaking the film down from a standpoint of scoring was done not in my usual fashion of getting away by myself and breaking the film down, and then coming to the producers with my notions, which they could either reject or accept or fight about. We ran the thing reel by reel, and not on consecutive days. We'd go in in the morning and spend the better part of the day on one reel. And then I had to fight not one, but three men, about mood, about where to start, where to stop. And in some cases, these things were ridiculous because one of them, who was more vocal than the others, would say, "No, I think maybe you should start four feet earlier," or "four feet later." And then we'd have to battle about that, and it got to be kind of a persecution. It took more time than I thought it would. In the first place, the film, which was supposed to be ready for me at the time that my first TV series was through for that break in the summer, when we'd go into reruns, sort of got fouled up and I think I had to wait about five or six weeks before the thing was ready for me. And the whole thing was a frantic hassle from then on. But we got through it somehow, just under the nose, before my second year of *Outlaws* was ready, a second season which I should not have accepted in the first place because there was a switch in producers. This producer, who shall be nameless, a very nice guy, and a brilliant man when it comes to dreaming up ideas for series, et cetera, but a producer who wanted to have his hands in everything, and who consistently fought with everybody in the company, including the story editor, the writers, the actors, the directors, et cetera. And when he finally ran out of people in that department to criticize and pick on, he started on me.

I'm perfectly willing to admit that I can bomb as readily as the next one, but—perhaps this is conceit on my part—but I cannot possibly bomb five television episodes in a row. So it got me down to the point where it actually affected my eyesight. I got what is known as "hot eye." I woke up one morning. My eye was bloodshot. It was psychosomatic. So I wound up turning in my badge for that reason. And lo and behold, two days later, the whole situation had cleared up. But more than that, the first time around, when I signed to do the series, I had, in addition to what I was collecting in front, I had the publication rights, which means a lot of money, principally because of the theme. The second time, because I didn't have anything in the offing, against my better judgment, I signed for another go at it. As I say, I think I did seven or eight, and then bowed out.

That rather left me stranded for a while there. But it would have probably resulted in a nervous breakdown or a massive coronary, or something like that because to have this kind of thing on top of the strain of trying to get these things out once a week is just a little bit too much, and there's no point to it. Lord, I've seen younger men than I am, who are involved with television, who come out at the end of the season looking like their own grandfathers. And how some of them manage to survive, I don't know. It's beyond me.

★    ★    ★

ATKINS: You went on and did some more television.

FRIEDHOFER: Heavens, yes. I did some work with Herbert Spencer who had a TV series at that time, *The Joey Bishop Show*. Also, Earle Hagen had a couple of shows, and I was jumping in and doing bits and pieces there. Then, actually, I orchestrated a couple of films for David Raksin. One of them was a film made for the Family Theater, a thing called *The Redeemer*, a beautiful film and one of the finest scores that David ever wrote, I think—and which the public will never see unless they want to go down to the basement of the local parish.

ATKINS: Wasn't that film released in the Latin American countries?

FRIEDHOFER: I don't know anything about the saga of it afterwards. Then I did another film for him, *Invitation to a Gunfighter*, with Yul Brynner and an assorted cast. I was about two-thirds of the way through that one when I suddenly got a call from the Corman outfit. The film was originally called *The Dubious Patriots*, but released finally under the title of *Secret Invasion*. This film was shot in Yugoslavia. I scored it in Germany. It was an interesting picture. Its basic premise was the same as that of *The Dirty Dozen*. In fact, we later got to refer to it as "The Dirty Half-Dozen," because there were only six people, and six very good people, too. I know it actually held up production on *The Dirty Dozen*—which was a picture of much broader dimensions and more production—for a good two years because I think there was a legal hassle about it, and also I think the people who were making *The Dirty Dozen* wanted the minor impact of *Secret Invasion* to die down.

ATKINS: There's a great deal of music in *Secret Invasion*.

FRIEDHOFER: Oh, it's *loaded*. It was one of those pictures that I did on a package deal and came out of it with practically nothing but the satisfaction of having done a good job. But it sort of made up for itself. My contractual deal called for either fifty or twenty-five percent of world publication rights. That meant theater film outside of the United States, and all television performances, which I finally managed to collect from United Artists because they had put their copy

of the contract away in a drawer someplace. I don't think it was deliberate on their part, but I finally had my attorney get on their backs,
and everything has been very nice in that connection since.

ATKINS: It's been on television several times.

FRIEDHOFER: Oh, yes, it has. So, that was in 1964. And then
came another long and very pleasant stint in television, on a series
called *I Spy*. On that, I jumped in first as a sort of an unknown quantity with Earle Hagen. While Earle had done innumerable television
shows, he'd never been up against the problem of doing an hour
show. Both he and Sheldon Leonard had the idea that there was no
more difficulty in doing an hour show than there would be in doing
two half-hour shows. But the opposite proved to be true. So Earle
called me in and we were finally alternating episodes. Hence all the
screen credit that I have on that show. It was one of those things
where we worked more or less in collaboration. Whoever got
through first would call the other one and say, "Do you need any
help?" And that's the way it worked. The show had a three-year run
and it should have run longer, but it unfortunately didn't, on account
of certain internal strife on the part of one of the principals in the cast.
But that's none of *my* business.

  After that came one unfortunately very short stint in TV, also
with Earle, on a series called *My Friend Tony*. In that, Sheldon had
brought over a young Italian that he'd used in one of the *I Spy* episodes. He sort of supported him for a year while he was learning English. It was a series starring James Whitmore as a criminology profes-
sor, and this boy as his leg man, sort of like Nero Wolfe. This boy
played a sort of Italian Archie to Whitmore's Nero Wolfe. We
thought it was a good show, but somehow or other it didn't catch on.

  Then, after that, Sheldon produced one of the most delightful
shows ever to hit television, *My World and Welcome To It*, with that
beautiful actor, William Windom, who is capable, by gollies, of doing
anything, but Thurber seems to be very close to his heart. I saw him
in a talk show just the other night, where he did a couple of Thurber
episodes that were just delightful. But that was the end of the TV
thing for me—for the time being.

ATKINS: We passed by a film—1965, *The Greatest Story Ever Told*.
There have been so many stories about Alfred Newman's problems
on that film.

FRIEDHOFER: I'm sorry that you brought it up because it was a disastrous experience for almost everybody involved. And I daresay that it contributed to the death of Alfred Newman.

ATKINS: Not to be macabre, but I thought you might have something to say from the musician's standpoint.

FRIEDHOFER: I have a lot to say about it. George Stevens Sr. is a very strange man who has almost a hypnotic effect upon everybody with whom he works. If somebody finds fault with something, as Harry Cohn did on a couple of occasions, George just sits back, clams up, and does not say a word. So in the end, the producer or whoever shrugs his shoulder and walks away and George continues. He has made some beautiful pictures, and he has made some that are not so beautiful.

In the case of *The Greatest Story Ever Told*, it was, as far as I'm concerned, and as far as many others are concerned, a complete *mess*. George had the effrontery in some cases to try to rewrite the New Testament. And the casting was ridiculous. He had all these cameo bits with well-known Hollywood figures, including Ed Wynn among others. And poor Alfred, who accepted the assignment only because of a friendship of long standing with George, was really hamstrung on the thing because for months and months he wrote a tremendous amount of music, not against film, but against the script, itself. The stalling, and the reshooting, and the recutting went on and on and on, until finally United Artists lowered the boom on George and said, "Look, we've got to have this thing out of here by December. So get off the dime." So George transferred this information to Alfred, who said, "Look, if that date is the right one, I am going to need help. Don't forget that I have as yet not seen a foot of film in its final length, and it's just impossible." So George said, "Okay, who do you want?" And he told him, and he called in Fred Steiner and myself, and Shuken and Hayes were orchestrating for him.

So I was on that picture for either ten or eleven weeks, in which I wrote somewhere in the vicinity of twenty-five minutes of music, five of which wound up in the final cut of the picture. Very, very expensive, that sort of operation. And then, after it was finally finished, George, instead of using the music that Al had written for the way to the cross, and the hallelujah accompanying the raising of Lazarus, used part of the Verdi Requiem and the Hallelujah Chorus from Handel. I think he had done some tracking with it. By this time, Alfred said, "To hell with it. I've had it. Goodbye." And his friend and associate, Ken Darby, actually did those two sequences. He conducted them. And that is the story of the greatest story that should never have been told.

Al's last picture was *Airport*, and he was frightfully ill all through that. There again, he called me in to do some writing, and to arrange a couple of things for him. But it's a source of great joy to me, in a way, that I did wind up doing however little it might have been on Al's last picture. And had I had a voice in the Academy, which I didn't because I had kind of given up on the Academy, I would have strongly suggested to the Music Branch that Al should be awarded an Oscar posthumously for this, his last score, and also a sort of musical Thalberg for his great contribution in the years from 1929 up to and through 1971. I think that considering all that he had done for the promotion of film music, and the betterment of it, that honor should have really been paid him. But nobody else seemed to think of it and I was in no position to open my face about it, except by means of an open letter written to the trades, and that's expensive.

But to wrap up my own film ventures and bring them up to date, in 1971, another Corman venture came along called *Von Richtofen and Brown*, which was kind of a total loss as far as I was concerned, although I don't know. I've never seen it since. I don't think it's hit TV yet. It was scored in Germany, which perhaps the Guild wouldn't approve of, but look, if you can't get anything to do over here, you go over there and do it.

And then the last one was *Private Parts*, which was Gene Corman's first solo flight as a producer. He had always worked in collaboration with his brother Roger, but this was his own baby. I talked about my predilection for horror films, of which I've done very, very few. That was one of the principal reasons why I undertook *Private Parts*. It was a departure from the usual sort of thing that I've been associated with—if I've been associated with any particular style of film. I honestly don't think so. I think that in my tour of duty I've covered just about every imaginable type of film. But it was only the third in this particular type of film that I have done. Consequently it was fun and—so to speak—a shot in the arm. I enjoyed it thoroughly. Metro was a trifle shocked by the picture. I don't know under what name it was finally released—some associate of Metro's. It's that kind of corporate thing that leads ultimately to a kind of tax shelter. I don't know. The ins and outs of the business are completely foreign to me.

But *Private Parts*, outside of the sneak preview, which I saw here, has strangely enough not been heard of since. I don't know why exactly. I felt it was, of its kind, a very, very good picture. Page Cook reviewed that and Bernard Herrmann's film, *Sisters*, and he put them in the same category and said that they were two of the best film scores of that particular year.

ATKINS: Did you try for something special, as far as horror music was concerned?

FRIEDHOFER: Yes. Except for a couple of episodes that were source, and a couple of things that were purely atonal, the entire score was based on one tone row. It was serial, actually, but pushed around in all kinds of ways, some of them unorthodox, some of them quite orthodox. And I think I can account for every permutation of that row in the film—not that I'm going to bother, because it doesn't make any difference, but just for my own purely intellectual satisfaction. For that reason, I enjoyed doing it very much, because in the last four or five years that has become more of an interest to me, the serial techniques. In this film, I used a regular twelve-tone row, but I have done pictures—I think I used a five- or six-note row in *Violent Saturday*, and a seven-note row in *One Eyed Jacks*, not throughout, but it was sort of a binder to the whole score.

ATKINS: Would the average moviegoer who wasn't familiar with serial music be aware of what you were doing musically?

FRIEDHOFER: I don't think so, in view of the fact that motion picture music is absorbed almost, you might say, through the pores, or subliminally. But I think that they still are aware of a certain feeling of continuity, a certain binder that winds through the thing. Having been thoroughly indoctrinated in my student years with the values of the variation techniques, I tend to move along those lines because it gives a certain solidity and continuity to the score, instead of being just a series of chopped up shorter things or a good college try for an album, consisting of a number of songs which are not particularly relevant to the film itself. And that is, to my way of thinking, a destruction of the true purpose of a film score, in that a score has got to relate, somehow, to the film. It's got to integrate. A series of instrumentals, largely jazz oriented, to which I have no objection at all under the right circumstances, have no continuity. It may be fun to listen to as an album, but as far as the film is concerned, trying to view the whole thing objectively from an audience standpoint, I don't dig it. There's no character delineation, no continuity in the thing. One feels it's fragmented to the point that, as far as theater music—drama—is concerned, it's utterly meaningless. It gives me to wonder what audiences really are interested in in the way of film music, whether it's an association item in the minds of the viewer, or not.

You find a younger generation, a great many of whom weren't born at that time, when you go back to the forties and the fifties, who have this tremendous interest in not only the music, but the films of that period. Perhaps it's a form of escapism for them, from the vicissitudes of life today, but they not only see the films; they go out and look for the soundtrack albums, which become increasingly harder to come by. And perhaps this is indicative of a return to that kind of thing, naturally updated, with more contemporary techniques, compositionally speaking. And that is maybe a hopeful sign. Of course, film music depends so much on the content of the film. One certainly couldn't score a film like *American Graffiti* with a Korngold type score, or an Alfred Newman type score. That is purely source, and used very adroitly in that film, as it is in *The Great Gatsby*, and other films of that nature.

But the dramatic film, even the film that isn't based on the principle of the good guys and the bad guys, and the maiden who is pure of heart, whatever that means, is naturally not part of screen writers' thinking nowadays, and calls for a different and more subtle approach to music. Unfortunately, the approach so far has not been very subtle. You've been hit over the head with something that the producer, and the producer's publisher affiliate, and the recording companies hope will yield a gold record for them. But that, to me, is not the purpose of film music as it was originally intended. And mind you, this is not a manifestation of sour grapes on my part. I've had it, and had it very nicely. So who am I to complain. But, as Dave Raksin put it, "Nowadays it seems that the more you know, the less employable you are." That sounds a little bitter, but it's the truth.

ATKINS: You mentioned a film that you're preparing.

FRIEDHOFER: I am about to embark upon a documentary for the Macmillan Lumber Company, up in British Columbia. It promises to be a very interesting assignment for me.

ATKINS: What direction would you take for that?

FRIEDHOFER: This particular thing is a thirty-minute documentary with wall-to-wall music and very sparse narration. It is not an industrial film in the ordinary sense. It doesn't deal with the heavy industry aspects of lumbering, but rather with the aspects of nature through the four seasons. It's called *A Walk in the Forest.* It's simply taking you through the four seasons in the forest, with all the plant life and some of the microscopic plant life that nobody ever sees if they're just strolling along. What I've seen of the film is delightful and the music will sort of fall into what you might almost call a little four seasons sinfonietta. That should be fun to do because it can almost add up to absolute music, however relevant to the film. I'm looking forward to that. And that is, to date, the gamut of my activity in this business.

ATKINS: It's a pretty prestigious gamut.

FRIEDHOFER: Well, having seen it from practically the inception of sound, and having done a tour of duty as a cellist in pit orchestras back in the silent days, I think it's not necessarily prestigious, but, for me, a very educational trip.

★    ★    ★

ATKINS: You said you wanted to take note of some of the musicians with whom you've worked.

FRIEDHOFER: I wanted to speak not only of instrumental musicians, but arrangers, orchestrators, conductors, who have all contributed their share to the development and advancement of the art and the techniques of film scoring. Let's start with the instrumentalists.

When I first arrived in Hollywood, the influx of first-rate instrumentalists from all over the country had not really started yet. In the field of one instrument in particular, namely the French horn, there was one truly great French hornist in town and that was the very great Alfred Brain, who had played with various symphony orchestras in London before he came to this country. After coming over here, he literally trained a generation and a half of fine hornists, so that now you can pick almost anybody and not go wrong. There are some outstanding men like Vincent Derosa and Arthur Maebe and a host that are right in that same category. And they all had this wonderful training, just as many did from the now retired clarinetist who was over at Metro for years, D. H. McKenney, whom I met shortly after I came down here. He was the teacher of a whole generation of clarinet players. Then we have men of the character of Arthur Gleghorn, the flutist, who was Sir Thomas Beecham's number one man for many years before he came over here. And there are cellists of the calibre of Kurt Reher, who is about to retire from the L. A. Philharmonic, and Edgar Lustgarten and a number of others. Fine, not to say great, cellists seem to come in bunches like bananas. Many of them were trained by Piatigorsky, after his arrival on the Hollywood scene. And you find pupils of Heifetz sitting in the violin sections, and so on down the line.

And wonderful percussionists: Hal Rees, who has been at Twentieth for years and who has been a recording artist; and an amazing man named Emil Richards, who has probably the most complete and comprehensive collection of percussion instruments from all over the world, and who's written a book about them, describing the potentials of each instrument. He's done practically everything. He's done avant garde music. He was an associate of that very wild and strange American composer who is just now coming into his own, Harry Partch. Partch is also an inventor of musical instruments, many of them microtonal in character. Emil has worked with him, and when Partch did a concert down here, Emil was a standby on that. In addition to his interest in all sorts of oddball percussion instruments, Emil is a performer of the first rank. His work on pitched percussion, marimbas, xylophone, et cetera, is utterly fantastic. He was associated with Mr. Hagen and myself on the *I Spy* show. He was one of our two percussionists. You could always depend upon Emil to come up with the kind of sound you wanted. All one had to do was to get on the telephone and say, "I want something that sounds like so and so," and you'd go into a vague description of what you wanted, and Emil would invariably show up with a raft of stuff that would work for you. Among other things, he built a microtonal marimba-xylophone type thing, out of random lengths of hardwood left over from a patio floor that he was installing. I think it's built in quarter tones, and is a very, very fine adjunct to the percussion section. I've used it on several occasions, and always with good results. Anything you want from Emil, you can get.

There are several others around just like him: Larry Bunker, who started as a jazzman, and a very good one, is now one of the mainstays of the Monday Evening Concerts, with their avant garde stuff. Excellent man. And the list is literally endless. You can go down the line, and you don't find a spoiled apple in the barrel. I am very grateful to all these men, because when I first got my feet wet as a conductor, I believe it was at my first recording session that I started by saying, "Fellows, all I want to say to you is one word: 'Help!' " And they did, bless them. I'll never forget them. I'll be eternally grateful to them for that.

I want to mention some of the various brilliant—and I use the word advisedly—orchestrators and arrangers who have contributed more than a little for music of films. In the case of the arrangers, men like Ray Heindorf, Edward Powell, Herbert Spencer, Earle Hagen, Conrad Salinger, Andre Previn really should get medals from practically all of the songwriting profession who have worked in films, because while it is true that there are songwriters who are capable of making a respectable piano part, and there are even some who are capable of orchestrating very well, for the most part their talents—which are brilliant—are confined to one thing, and that is playing their music. A great deal of them are not even capable of notating it. And if it were not for the arranger, they'd really be out of luck. It's a fact that does not manifest itself in gratitude on the part of the songwriter, for the most part. They rather resent it, but that's beside the point.

Then there's the third category that I wanted to mention, and that is the orchestrator who works with the composer of background music, and who is highly necessary because of the tremendous pressures brought about by deadlines and by everything having to be done in a hurry. The film composer is, in the main, capable of making his own orchestration, and has, but the time pressure is so great. Naturally, this is a practice that is frowned upon by the so-called serious composer, in this country particularly, and it's frowned upon by composers who've never had a film to write. They find out differently after that. In Europe, the custom is accepted. Prokofiev had his assistants. Going way back in history, Richard Wagner had his assistants, too. Just the business of writing out the harp parts in the beginning of *Rhinegold* was a back-breaking job. But over there, nothing was thought of it. Faure used Charles Koechlin, who was Conrad Salinger's teacher when Conrad went to Paris.

ATKINS: I think it's worth noting that you left Warners because you were tired of being known as an orchestrator, did become known as a composer, but that you didn't do your own orchestrating.

FRIEDHOFER: After that, I don't think there are more than four films that I orchestrated myself—the Corman things, and a few others here and there. But for the most part, I relied on orchestrators. The orchestrators that I worked with were all competent, and willing to submerge their own personalities. There's a question of rapport there, just as there is for an arranger to become the songwriter's alter ego, and forget about his own personality.

ATKINS: Who are some of the outstanding orchestrators?

FRIEDHOFER: Edward Powell, Herbert Spencer, Earle Hagen, and Arthur Morton, who is one of the best in my estimation. I feel to a certain extent responsible for Arthur working both sides of the street now. He operates as an orchestrator for various people like Jerry Goldsmith and Lawrence Rosenthal on occasion, and I think he has also done much for Lalo Schifrin in television. But as I say, I was responsible for Arthur devoting a great deal of time to composition. He did a charming television series with Shirley Temple acting as narrator. It was kids' fairy tales, and he did some charming things for that. He did the bulk of that interminable nighttime soap opera, *Peyton Place,* and many other things. I think he's also orchestrated film scores of Nelson Riddle's, and Lord knows how much else. Nobody could ask for a better collaboration than with a man like Arthur. After perhaps two or three assignments, he would sense, instantly, just exactly what you wanted. That, naturally, takes a load off one's own mind because you have the feeling that he can be trusted not to monkey around, not to try to improve anything, even though it may need improving.

You see, to begin with, I work from a completely well-organized, I hope, orchestral sketch, of anywhere from four to six lines. In the course of discussion, there have been occasions when I've been in a quandary about where this thing should go orchestrally, and his suggestions have been extremely helpful and valuable. And if they weren't the right suggestions, at least they have helped me to make up my own mind. And that is a help also.

Leo Shuken and his former partner, now deceased, Sidney Cutner, and Leo's present partner, Jack Hayes—all of them are competent. Of course, everybody in Hollywood now orchestrates well. The reason for that is that you get to hear what you've done, either as a composer, arranger, and/or orchestrator, practically before the ink is dry on the parts. So the result is that you never make the same mistake twice. And if you do make a mistake, you know how to fix it on the stage. There are no hangups there, and daren't be any, for purely economic reasons, because we are the tail end of the operation—in the words of Dore Schary, the "mop-up," which I mentioned. Not a nice thing to say. But I must say, in the words of one of the few civilized Germans I know, Wolfgang Goethe once said, "Against stupidity, the gods themselves strive in vain."

Let's see—who else? Oh, I don't know, there are so many who are all competent. In the field of theater, we have men like the legendary Robert Russell Bennett, who worked for Irving Berlin, did an awful lot of work for Jerome Kern, and was always admirable. He even worked for Richard Rodgers without losing his temper.

ATKINS: Robert Russell Bennett worked in Hollywood, too.

FRIEDHOFER: Yes, he was at RKO for a while. That's where I had my first meeting with him. I had known his work from the time I was a pit musician and used to play these Jerome Kern medleys from the famous Princess shows that he did with Guy Bolton and P. G. Wodehouse. They were charming, all of them, and I was always struck with this name: "orchestrations by Robert Russell Bennett."

As far as conductors go, there is one in this business who is pre-eminent and who is sort of a legendary figure, and that is the late lamented Alfred Newman, who was in measure largely responsible for my so-called career as a composer of film music, rather than merely an arranger or orchestrator. So I am, and always will be, very much indebted to him. Not that my music sounds anything like Al's, any more than it sounds like Steiner's or Korngold's, two other men to whom I owe much. But they were sort of catalysts for what is jokingly known as my own style.

ATKINS: How would you describe Alfred Newman's rapport with the orchestra?

FRIEDHOFER: Al had what you might call a Napoleonic command. He was never a martinet unless certain things would happen. Occasionally somebody would be inattentive. Then the fire would start to flash—not for long—but he could cool down an orchestra that was perhaps a little inattentive or tired, or what not, and do it with the minimum of expenditure of temper and profanity—nothing of that sort. He had a way of just looking. I know I've seen him do it in the case of an arrangement or an orchestration that didn't quite come off. He would literally turn his back on the orchestra and glare at whatever culprit had defected, let's say. And it was a kind of expressionless fish eye. And you knew right away that something was definitely wrong. And he might call for a ten-minute break, and say to whoever was responsible, "What in the hell's the matter with you, anyway? That's not right. The voice-leading there is terrible." And he was justified.

And Al had such good ears for what went on in the orchestra. A clumsy harmonic progression or bad voice-leading would drive him right out of his skull. He was particularly sensitive to that sort of thing. If one can find any fault at all, it's that he sometimes would fall so in love, in an arrangement, with an inner line, with a counter-melody, that it would completely swamp the melodic line. That has happened on a couple of occasions, but not often. But it showed his tremendous interest in the structuring of a piece of music.

Alfred was at his ease and at his best in two departments as a conductor. One was in the confines of the sound stage and the other was when he was working with children, which he did—I saw him conduct brilliantly the UCLA band in Royce Hall, and also the Merenblum Orchestra, when he was doing the picture with Heifetz for Goldwyn, *They Shall Have Music.* With his own men Al was perfectly at ease, no white tie and tails, or anything like that, and with men that he knew and had worked with and had fostered over the years, he was magnificent. It's almost blasphemous even to mention it, but he would get extremely nervous in public. Not that anything ever went extremely wrong, but one felt that he didn't have the magnificent control that he had when he was working within the studio. But God bless him, everybody in the business owes something to Alfred.

And I think on this note, we can wrap the thing up. I think I have rambled on just about enough about my life and times in the film business. But I've seen quite a lot. I've been there and back, and I'm quite content, and also, in a strange sort of way, honored to have been asked to contribute this oral history. And in the words of a not particularly favorite stand-up comic of mine, I kid you not.

ATKINS: I don't know what I can add to that, except that I'm glad you had the time to do this. And I'm glad you're still "at it," to use that expression.

FRIEDHOFER: Well, I'm on the threshold of my seventy-third birthday. And it doesn't hurt in the least, somehow. I feel very good. Maybe now I can get down to writing some music on my own. And I hope to do an occasional film or something like that. And thank God for ASCAP and BMI, and all that sort of thing. So economically, I have no problems. After all, I don't want to buy any yachts, or live in Trousdale or any place else. I prefer to stay mobile, with the idea of doing some traveling.

And now, I think we can give this the final downbeat, or the cutoff, or, a long hold, let's say.

# LIMERICKS, HUMOROUS RHYMES, AND SKETCHES

## SONG AGAINST AUSTERITY

Music by Piston or by Sessions
  Never inflames the baser pessions

A string quartet by Quincy Porter
  Will not debauch one's virgin dorter

The same holds good for Douglas Moore
  Whose muse is ultra-ultra pure

And as for Randall Thompson, he does
  Nothing at all for our libidoes

So let's give ear to Richard Strauss
  And seek the nearest bawdy-hauss!


## LINES

Thematic metamorphosis
  (that favorite ploy of Berlioz) is

Labored and procrustean
  and very largely fustian.

Moreover, it is Lisztian
  and vulgar, and unchristian.

(Written after hearing still another performance of the "Symphony Fantastique")


## MEHR DICHTUNG ALS FARENHEIT

The temperature's low in Cologne
And I'm glad that I'm living alone
  Since those intimate parts
  Used in amative arts
Function best in the tropical zone

(Written while working on "Best Years" suite in Cologne, September 1972)

B is for Bison;—long ago
   He roamed the Western plains
Until the Railroads came, and so
   The Bison simply had to go
Lest he delay the trains.

A conference was held, and then
   They summoned Buffalo Bill
And other expert riflemen
   To whom they said, "Don't trifle, men—
But shoot—and shoot to kill!"

With maximum efficiency
   As in a total war
They killed; that's why we seldom see
   Outside of movies on TV
The Bison any more.

MORAL
(which may be optionally by-passed)

Resistance by minorities
   'Gainst young aggressive nations
Is futile, say the histories;
   The Bison outwardly agrees
But keeps his Reservations.

ANNO DOMINI
1 9 4 1

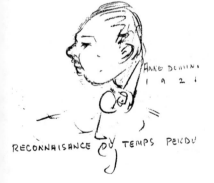

ANNO DOMINI
1 9 2 1

RECONNAISANCE DU TEMPS PERDU

ANNO DOMINI
1 9 6 1

# ·4·

# Correspondence with Page Cook

$\mathcal{H}$ugo Friedhofer was a marvelous correspondent. He belonged to that sadly diminishing body of people who enjoy writing letters and who express themselves with style and eloquence. Those who received letters from him usually kept them.

Of those with whom he enjoyed a long correspondence, the most important for the purposes of this book was the late Page Cook, who from 1963 to 1992 was the film music commentator for *Films in Review.* His actual name was Charles Boyer, but for obvious reasons decided upon a pseudonym. Cook was an astute critic and a man of firmly stated likes and dislikes. He most certainly liked Friedhofer, and a correspondence sprang up between them when the composer replied to a column Cook had written in 1965. It became a warm postal exchange in which they wrote frankly about the art and craft of writing music for films. Sixty-three of the Friedhofer letters to Cook are contained in the Friedhofer archives at Brigham Young University in Provo, Utah. Here are excerpts from some of them.

7974 Woodrow Wilson Drive
Los Angeles 46, California

22d March, 1965

Page Cook
c/o Films in Review
31 Union Square
New York 3, N.Y.

Dear Mr. Cook:
　　With reference to your comment on TV film music in the current issue of FIR, I am inclined, on the whole, to agree with

you. Nevertheless I feel that in the interests of justice, fair play and all that sort of rot, I must take it upon myself to enlighten you on a few points and also to differ with you (however mildly) in a couple of your critical evaluations.

In the first place I should point out to you that Lionel Newman does not conduct the score of "12 O'clock High." He is credited with "Musical Supervision" for reasons I cannot fathom since he has, actually, about as much to do with the show as I have with the Missa Papae Marcelli, or perhaps even less. As for the quality of the music, I can only tell you that it is exactly what the producer wants, and Frontiere is like the rest of us disinclined toward the oft-proven fruitless pastime of windmill tilting.

Perhaps the music for "The Rogues" could be better, but so could the series, at least in my estimation.

You speak of North as having, for once, eschewed cacophonies in his music for "FDR." I must confess to never having found North's music in the least cacophonous, but then I suppose that one man's dissonance is another man's schmaltz.

As for "Daniel Boone" I don't believe that Lionel Newman ever scored a segment of the series outside of the pilot. The music for this flaccid piece of pseudo-Americana has been written by a number of composers, among them Fred Steiner, Van Cleave, Alexander Courage, Cyril Mockridge and Irving Gertz. As for Newman's theme song, this again is the producer's baby.

As for my own contribution to "Voyage to the Bottom of the Sea," I must admit to being in complete accord with your evaluation. It is not only "not memorable" as you say; in addition, it is damn near inaudible. The producer of this waterlogged epic is so sound-effects happy that the show might just as well be scored with an infinite series of variations on "Asleep in the Deep" for all the difference it would make.

Waxman's theme for "Peyton Place" I would hardly call "exquisite" as you seem to find it. To me it sounds like "Alice Blue Gown" sideways. It is scarcely out of Waxman's top drawer. The published song version is rather ineptly titled "The Wonderful Season of Love." "The Wonderful Season of Rut" would be a title more in line with the bi-weekly goings-on. Again I must inform you that the producers of this sexy soap opera are delighted with Morton. To his everlasting credit be it said that Morton is not delighted. Far from it. To him it's just a chore, and the prospect of a sizable residual income, since the show will most likely run until doomsday on the network and ultimately will be sold for syndication.

"Valentine's Day" has been scored mostly by Jeff Alexander, excepting of course the pilot and the title music which were by Lionel Newman.

I am in total agreement with you as regards vinyl music for the Hitchcock Show. It is excellent, as was Lyn Murray's, last season. One must naturally take into consideration the fact that Hitchcock turns out a consistently fine, imaginative show. If only he would refrain from those sickeningly coy personal appearances.

Taking into consideration the assembly-line conditions under which the music for TV is ground out, I am astonished, actually, that it is as competent (not to say good) as it is, regardless of the fact that the larger portion may strike you as a lot of cliche-ridden mediocrity. Deadline pressures, producer vagaries, badly written teleplays and miserable sloppiness in the dubbing room are hardly inspirational. Add to this the fact that the financial rewards, barring performing rights fees, are far from lavish. The average running time of a score for a theater film is in the neighborhood of 40–45 minutes. An hour-long TV segment often has as much as 30–35 minutes of music. Top money for an hour show is roughly about one tenth of what the composer earns for writing not much more music for a theater film. On top of all that, the TV product has to be gotten out in much less time than is generally allotted to the creation of music for theater film. Ten days is considered a luxury; generally it's 7–8 days from the time a composer sees a segment, to the recording session. Which means that the composer works over weekends, and generally puts in at least one 22 hour day. This makes for a sketchy home life, twitching nerves and a jaundiced outlook. And there's not an awful lot that one can do about it. One must eat, and the show (such as it is) must go on. Or so I've been told.

Most sincerely yours,
Hugo W. Friedhofer

P.S. I trust that you will keep this letter strictly confidential. If that sounds "chicken" I'm sorry, but I am in no position to leave Southern California at this writing, much as I would like to.

HWF

Hugo Friedhofer
7974 Woodrow Wilson Drive
Los Angeles, Calif. 90046
6/8/1971

Dear Page Cook, alias Charles Boyer (or is it the other way around?):

Thanks for your continued interest, as well as your nice letter. However, I must ask you, as a very special favor, to say as little as possible (if anything at all) about the score to Von Richtofen and Brown. Knowing you to be an honest and fair-minded critic, you would be forced to say nothing commendatory about it. Under more favorable conditions, it probably wouldn't bother me very much, but since my current status in the music business is fairly shaky, an unfavorable review could well be the kiss of death. Hollywood is, as I'm sure you're aware, a strange town, one in which you are only as good as your last score.

Frankly, I don't believe that I have ever written a worse film score than this one. The fact that the film is also pretty bad is no excuse. I have written scores which I consider better than just adequate for some pretty bad films in the past, but this time there isn't any difference 'twixt the score and the film. They are in my estimation both pretty godawful.

I had grave doubts about the film from the beginning, and had I been fortunate enough to have anything else going for me at the time, I would have declined the commitment. But there wasn't anything else, so I took on the job, regardless. I could of course find plentiful excuses for the lack of quality in the score, some of them quite legitimate and justifiable, such as the bad dubbing job, for one, only it would sound like a cop-out, and that is hardly my style. Anyway, bad film or not, I should have done better. Maybe I'll do better next time, should there be a next time. Anyway, I must ask you again to kick the score under the rug, so to speak. But should you be forced to comment upon the score, be as gentle and tolerant as your integrity will permit.

One thing more. Are there any more copies of the October '65 issue of FIR available? I was given four at the time of issue, all of which seem to have disappeared. If it were possible for me to obtain a couple of spares I would gladly pay for them. Please let me know about this. It was most warming to hear from you again.

Most sincerely yours,
Hugo Friedhofer

P.S. I'll appreciate your keeping the contents of this letter strictly confidential and entirely off the record, please!

HWF

6th July, 1971

Dear Charles:

Your letter of the 30th June came this morning. Thanks, it provides me with a valid excuse for taking a breather from the endless Sisiphyean chore of putting my house in order; i.e., filing and cataloging scores, manuscripts, recordings, sketches, etc., etc. What a mess! It's a blessing that I haven't hung on to all the notes I've written since 1921, when I first got the itch to be something more than just another cellist, otherwise I would be obliged to build an annex to my working quarters.

In 1944 when I was auditioning some classes which Nadia Boulanger was holding in Los Angeles, she had occasion to warn her students about the danger of ever throwing anything away. Very sound advice, as I subsequently found out, but it does make for a lot of undecipherable clutter at times, and I am afraid that my musical remains will (in the event that posterity finds them of sufficient importance) give some editor severe eye strain and nervous fidgets.

Nevertheless, I can think, offhand, of two occasions when a piece of material I had dreamed up did come in handy. In 1933 I was improvising at the piano and hit upon a sort of far-out valse lente strain which struck me as being fairly attractive, so I straightaway made a piano copy of the thing. Upon reading through it, the thought flashed across my mind that I had had some pretty discouraging experiences with tone-deaf executives before, so I filed it away and promptly forgot all about it. Fade-out 1933 and Fade-in 1958, the year of "The Young Lions." You may recall the scene between Brando and May Britt. The episode was giving me considerable trouble, since I couldn't seem to hit upon the proper amalgam of sexy romantic decadence the episode demanded. Everything sounded like "luv-music" which would have been all wrong.

After two days of scratching in vain I was just about ready to give up in despair, when I suddenly awakened from a sort of nightmarish sleep with the 1933 valse lente strain sounding in my mind's ear. I got up, staggered down to my work-room and plowed through a two-foot high stack of manuscript and there it was, at the very bottom of the stack. The miraculous part of the thing was that it was exactly the right length to cover the scene. All I had to do was to discuss the orchestration with Earle Hagen and I was, so to speak, home free. Entitled "The Captain's Lady," it's enshrined in imperishable vinyl, Side 1, Band 4, of the sound-track album.

"Michael's Theme" from the same film, is a piece of material written in 1951, that also came in handy some seven years after the fact. The Stagecoach Montage in "Broken Arrow" was based on some random doodles put down while soaking up some sunshine during a weekend in the desert, some eight or nine years before the film was even thought of. The waltz theme for Constance Bennett in "Topper Takes a Trip" was another such a lucky find. Written in 1934, it lay in a desk drawer for three years before finding a home in the "Topper" film. There are other instances far too numerous to cite, which lend considerable weight to Mlle. Boulanger's homily.

Sergei Prokofieff used to write down everything which came into his mind. Occasionally he would examine his sketchbooks and when he felt that there had been a sufficient assemblage of usable ideas, out would pop another symphony, or piano sonata, or concerto or ballet or what have you. I figure that if it was good enough for Sergei, I could do much worse than to follow his example.

I do have my original sketches of practically everything I've written from 1942 on. In addition to my commercially issued soundtrack albums I have a complete set of acetates of the "Bishop's Wife" score (1947) "The Adventures of Casanova" (1947) "So Dark the Night" (1945) and portions of perhaps a half-dozen or so others. I do have the Bernstein recording of the "Broken Arrow" music, reorchestrated by me for the rather out-of-balance instrumental combo used in the album. Also a recording of the theme from "The Rains of Ranchipur" in an album made by Jack Shaindlin with the Symphony of the Air on Roulette (R-25023) in '56 or '57. Incidentally, about 95% of the Korngold album recorded by Lionel Newman for Warner Bros. Records, was my orchestration, some of which dates back to the mid 30s and early 40s. You know, sometimes I get the feeling that I really should have been put out to pasture, long ago, particularly when I consider the fact that all but three or four of my friends in the business weren't even born in '29, when I first arrived in Hollywood.

I have heard the Herrmann recordings of his music from "All That Money Can Buy" and "Psycho." I think that they are both stand-outs. In "Psycho" some of the devices of the Polish avant-garde, i.e. Penderecki and Lutoslawski, were anticipated by quite a few years. I have a great weakness for Bernard, despite the fact that, at times, he can be a pretty thorny and difficult character. At least 75% of the time we don't get along at all, but no matter. Anybody with that much talent, knowledge and craftsmanship is entitled to an eccentricity or two.

I have been trying (naturally in vain) to get a tape of the "Lancer" episode with Jonathan Harris and Stephanie Powers. If you could possibly copy your tape I would be deeply grateful since I was rather happy with the score. The love theme is a very free adaptation of a tune I found in the Petrie Collection of Ancient Irish Music.

Thanks for sending me your "doodle" for a projected Fried-hofer album. I'm afraid that the costs involved would be on the astronomical side, but it's a nice thought . . .

Best, as always,

8/19/72

I have just returned from Munich and the recording of a film score for a little goodie produced by Gene Corman entitled, be-lieve it or not, "Private Parts"—very sick and altogether revolt-ingly decadent. Anyway, the score is like nothing of mine you've ever heard. It may be you won't like it but I must confess that I consider it to be as good a score as I have ever turned out, barring some source music of the rock persuasion and a couple of very dis-sonantly harmonized hymn tunes. The score is strictly serial, or rather, post-serial. Anything less would have been entirely out of key with the film. The score runs close to 50 minutes. It was com-posed, orchestrated and recorded in 29 days flat. And if I had to do it over again in that short a time span, I wouldn't.

All this is by way of warning you as to what is in store. I imag-ine that my youthful excursions into the realm of the macabre via

Edgar Allen Poe and such like are largely responsible for my lean-
ings toward the far out and the weird.


11/17/73


My music is difficult to play because of a built-in transparency
which makes a wrong note or a faulty balance stick out like one of
Franz Liszt's warts. I'm not implying that what I do is better; it's
just trickier. I haven't spent a lot of years immersed in Mozart,
Mendelssohn, Mahler, Debussy and Ravel without having a little
of the aforementioned gentlemens' approach to the orchestra rub
off on me. "Toujours la clarte!" as Mmselle Nadia Boulanger used
to say, a truly great musician and truly fine lady. American music
owes her much.


HUGO FRIEDHOFER
1545 NORTH BRONSON AVENUE #309
HOLLYWOOD, CALIFORNIA 90028


14th July, 1974

My dear Charles:
Your letter of the 17th last really deserved an immediate re-
sponse. I'll spare you any apologies or explanations since any such
would be no more than flimsy cop-outs; cover-ups for sheer unadulterated indolence. I loaf about in the sun, listen to phono records, read a lot (mostly contemporary scores), and dither about at
the keyboard in search of new cliches in an effort to get my somewhat rusty creative machinery moving. My documentary, which
was promised for mid-June, won't be completed before the end of
this month because of the unpredictable British Columbian cli-
mate. Evidently there's a preponderance of wet weather in those
parts which has slowed up production considerably. I hope that the
first of August will find me hard at work. I've had my belly-full of
deadlines over the past 45 years, and at age 73 one tends to slow
down a bit. This is regrettable but inevitable. Also, there's an ever-
growing tendency toward self-criticism and nit-picking. My
shrink, who is not really a shrink, but a consulting psychologist of

the Jungian persuasion, assures me that my spooks are a lot of nonsense, and that I can look forward to at least another ten years of creative activity. All I have to do is to get it all together and push on regardless.

I refrain from dwelling upon the current trends in film music except to say that I am somewhat saddened thereby. As for TV, the larger part of what I hear is either rock, electronic, or the kind of serialism which sounds as though it was run up on the computer. There are a few exceptions, like Lyn Murray, David Shire and Billy Goldenburg. Also Larry Rosenthal, who should by rights be writing for theater film. His scores for Raisin in the Sun, Requiem for a Heavyweight and Becket (to name but three) are right out of the top drawer.

I am currently involved with editing my Oral History of Film Music. The typescript runs to 400 pages, which is a hell of a lot. Your article in the '74 International Film Guide acted as a sort of mnenomic prod on several occasions when I was afflicted with limping recall. I shudder at the contemplation of all the notes I have committed to paper between 1929 and 1972, not to mention the spate of stage-band arrangements I concocted 'twixt 1923 and 1928 during my tour of duty as cellist and arranger, before celluloid acquired a voice. And so it goes. Do keep well, and let me hear from you, however briefly.

As always,


11/3/74


As for your concern over the fact I'm not writing music for today's better films, don't let it concern you too much. I've had perhaps more than my share of good years in the trickiest and most unpredictable of all media, as well as my share of opportunities missed because of my inability to put up with stupidity, arrogance and utter incompetence. Naturally, I'd like to do more than I've done in the past few years, but only on my own terms. This, perhaps, is asking for the impossible, since composers in their 70s aren't exactly sought after. In a letter from J. S. Lasher written a couple of years ago, he mentioned the fact that quite a few people he knew were surprised that I was still alive! Small wonder, since

1929 to 1974 is a fairly long life span in this demented, nerve-racking business.


HUGO FRIEDHOFER
1545 NORTH BRONSON AVENUE #309
HOLLYWOOD, CALIFORNIA 90028

30th July, 1974

Dear Charles,

In answer to your query, I am feeling very well indeed. In addition, I'm enjoying (as you say) a most comfortable summer. The weather, at least up to last week has been of the best, but then the temperature started rising, also the humidity, plus the damned smog. However, my apartment is air conditioned and the building boasts a communal pool which, with the exception of Saturdays and Sundays, is practically unused by all the tenantry except for a couple of lazy loafers like me. On weekends it's a veritable Coney Island but fortunately there's a 10 o'clock curfew, so it's really not bad at all.

As for my tendency in the direction of self-criticism, don't worry about it. Self-criticism, so long as it's kept under control, and doesn't hamstring the creative impulse at the outset, is actually a blessing. Without it, the composer, no matter how gifted, tends toward smugness and complacent self-satisfaction. Believe me when I tell you that I am thoroughly aware of the fact that I am a good composer. But I know as well that without the constant and vigilant surveillance of my critical censor, I could easily degenerate into a slovenly hack. It's only the unending search for something new, something different from anything I've ever done before, that keeps me young and ever-curious at an age when most men have either given up trying and just coast along on the formulae which they have either invented or borrowed, quite oblivious to the fact that what may have once been fresh and exciting will, because of unthinking repetition, ultimately become flat, stale and utterly without interest to the auditor. You recall that I once spoke of the dread I felt at the notion of being victimized by my own cliches. If I ever felt that it was happening to me, I'd give up and bend my efforts in the direction of other areas of self-expression. So then, this should serve to convince you that I am far from being as modest and self-effacing as I sometimes appear to be. It's just that I'm an arrant snob who tries to avoid being pigeon-holed along with the spate of strutting little egos who are only concerned with exploiting their minimal talents by way of public relations, socializing, and making as much money as is possible in the easiest possible way. I wish them well, but their methods are not my methods and never have been, nor will they ever be. So much for that.

You spoke of your friend, the Delius freak. I must confess that when I was in my late teens and early twenties, I too went through a period of swooning admiration for some of the Delian harmonic writhings. Strangely enough, it was hearing the "Florida Suite," "Koanga," and the "Paris Symphony" which ultimately turned me off. However, I can take his "Dance Rhapsody," "Brigg Fair," "The Walk to the Paradise Gardens" and the two truly lovely miniatures, "On Hearing the First Cuckoo in Spring," which some joker rechristened "On Cooking the First Hero in Spring," and its companion piece "Summer Night on the River." Even at the outset, a certain lack of rhythmic vitality coupled with his over-lush and sticky chromaticism troubled me. It got to be the tonal equivalent of floundering waist-deep through a sea of molasses, so I bade old Freddie a not-so-fond farewell, and haven't listened to him, except in my mind's ear, since that time.

My old friend and colleague Cyril Mockridge had an amazing talent for perpetrating Delian forgeries. Many of the luscious treatments of thematic material in Alfred Newman's scores were contrived by Cyril when he was on staff at 20th Century Fox. Most, if not all, film composers are eclectics. The exigencies of film require a familiarity with a number of musical styles and/or idioms. This has little if anything to do with creativity. It's simply a matter of technique, craft, and a wide acquaintance with the literature of music. On quite a number of occasions I've come up with fairly reasonable facsimiles in the style of Brahms, Wagner, Debussy, Ravel, Richard Strauss and others. The trick is to remain well within the boundaries of whatever style you have chosen to simulate. Otherwise one runs the risk of starting—let's say—in the manner of Aaron Copland, only to wind up in a welter of Wagnerian schmaltz, something which is to me nothing less than abominable.

I finally heard from Elmer B. about his recording project. Like you, I cannot see how a revival of the "King Kong" score can be anything other than harmful to Steiner, as well as to Elmer's project. I told him as much, suggesting that there were other early-vintage Steiner scores far more worthy of exhumation. Today, the "Kong" score sounds like a compilation of all the worst platitudes to be encountered in film music. I yield to no man in my respect and admiration for Steiner's massive contribution to our craft, and I recall my tour of duty (1936–1946) as his arranger-orchestrator and occasional ghost-writer, with feelings of great warmth. Nevertheless, my love and gratitude for all that which I learned from him, has not befogged my critical acumen, nor my ability to differentiate between first-rate Steiner, run-of-the mine Steiner, and some (but very little) downright bad Steiner. One of these days I'll give you a critical study of what might be titled "The Three Faces of Maxie" as a sort of counterbalance to the sloppy adulatory mouthings put out by the Max Steiner Society. This will be a little something for *your eyes alone*, since I'm not anxious to have some short-sighted idiot jumping to the conclusion that my opinions are the result of envy or bitterness over the fact that Max's name and reputation far overshadows mine, as far as the public is concerned. I fancy you know me well enough to believe me when I tell you that this is a matter about which I couldn't care less!

But let's return to Elmer. His idea of a record club for the salvaging and perpetuation of hitherto unrecorded film scores is a good one, and merits careful consideration. However, it entails a monumental amount of work, if it's to be done with integrity. There is so little of the material available in full score, owing to the fact that most of the one-time major studios have rid themselves of both the full scores and the orchestra parts. I am fortunate in having kept most of my original sketches, dating as far back as 1942, as well as bound photostatic copies of the conductor scores of some forty-odd films, but when I think of the labor involved in reorchestrating as well as recomposing (a la Bernard Herrmann), i.e., trying to give some manner of substance to much that was (of necessity) mere padding; valid enough as background music in the film but quite lacking in substance and/or listening interest when divorced from the film itself. While it's true that music adds life and substance to the visual image, the properly integrated film score, heard out of context, is no more than the gravy for the roast beef which isn't there! Of course, there are film scores which hold up fairly well as pure listening music, but even these could use a little repair work, here and there.

Last Saturday I was presented with a copy of the album containing the suite from "The Bandit of Sherwood Forest." This is really the most flagrant and shameless example of piracy as I've ever encountered, the album being a dub from a miserable out-of-balance air-check performance in the Hollywood Bowl, in the summer of 1946. I was given one at the time, and after playing it once, I straightaway chucked it into the trash bin. It wasn't a very good performance to begin with, owing to lack of rehearsal time, plus break-neck tempos which ruined a lot of carefully contrived detail in the orchestration. I must say though, that it's not too bad a piece, if one can ignore the sloppy performance, etc. It's a bit frightening to hear one's work after a lapse of twenty-seven* years. Incidentally, "The Bandit" was the fourteenth original score on which I received proper screen credit, and where in God's name have the years gone????

I've run out of words and idle maundering reminiscence.

Please keep well,

*twenty-eight

8/6/75

"This Earth Is Mine" no longer strikes me as being overloaded hyper-romanticism of the sort which was, at the time, a source of embarrassment to me. Now I find it, perhaps immodestly, just right, both in the film and out of it. Moreover, it's well-organized in that the Cahn-Van Heusen theme is so integrated with the score that it never sounds like an interpolation, rather, all of a piece. I won't belabor you with a tiresome account of how this was accomplished—someday, perhaps, but not now. Nor will I divulge the circumstances which brought about my change of heart, except to say that they are of a piece with those which make a score of AWITF what it is. Oh yes, my good friend, I do have my moments of conceit, but not very often and perhaps too far long after the fact. So now you know but don't ever tell on me please.

P.S. Returning briefly to "This Earth Is Mine," I believe that my pet scene is the longish episode titled "Confessional" in which Claude Rains bares his soul to his granddaughter, the lovely Jean Simmons. Yeah, I dig that lady as much as you do. I used to see her on occasion at my doctor's office but always got too tongue-tied to give vent to my admiration. Shyness do have its drawbacks.

8/18/75

My dear Charles,

I was quite frankly overwhelmed by your reaction to the WITF tape. My ego and my self-assurance both have a way of going underground far too often, leaving me quite naked and defenseless against the onslaught of self-doubting and creative insecurity. At such times I am obsessed with the notion that nothing I've ever written is worth a damn as generally happens when I am on the eve of embarking on a new venture. Randall Hood's new script now titled "Deadly Companion" is so good that I'm positively terror-stricken at the possibility of not coming up to scratch and the resultant feeling of total sterility isn't easy to live with—something like an 11-month pregnancy. Off hand, I can only recall at the most 3, possibly 4, film scores which came easily and with a minimum of blood, sweat and tears. I have a theory that most of us go through the same travail but just won't own up to it. I'm not including the hacks who solve their problems by writing the same score over and over. I name no names.

All this is by way of saying that your letter has acted as a confidence-restorer and I am no end grateful.

As ever,
Hugo

P.S It might interest you to learn that "Soldier of Fortune" was one of the scores which came easily. I attribute this to the fact that I have a passion for Chinese food. The main theme, with a lyric by Ken Darby is published. If I can unearth a copy, I will send it on to you.

11/11/76

All in all, the period between 1954 and 1956 was for me, a singularly happy time—happy because of an upsurge of creative assurance the likes of which I'd never known before—no doubts, no hangups—above all, no fear that my experiments might meet with disapproval up front. Nine sizable scores in a trifle over two years is a lot considering the fact that speed was not exactly my forte. Here's the roster: Vera Cruz, White Feather, Violent Saturday, Soldier of Fortune, Seven Cities of Gold, The Rains of Ranchipur, The Revolt of Mamie Stover, The Harder They Fall, Between Heaven and Hell. 1957–1960 was fairly productive but the output over the following 15 years (even making allowances for my involvement with the idiot box) is embarrassingly small—only 7 films. Still, nothing lasts forever and sooner or later everyone and everything is relegated to the limbo of the forgotten. You'd be astonished at the number of people who think that I've been long-dead and I have days when I'm almost certain that they're right.

> Blessings and benedictions,
> Hugo

# ·5·

# Epilogue

### by Gene Lees

$\mathcal{D}$avid Raksin called that morning, May 17, 1981, and said simply, "Hugo is gone," and my eyes misted, even though we had known he was going to die. He was eighty, he was arthritic, and as his daughter Karyl said later, "he was tired."

Dave asked me to handle the press. I called the *New York Times.* The editor of the Arts and Leisure section had never heard of Hugo Friedhofer, and so the *Times,* which takes a Brahmin pride in being an American historical record, ignored the fall of one of the most important orchestral composers the United States ever produced, even though all his music was designed to enhance the emotional content of movies, some of which did not deserve the dignity of his genius. It is unfortunate that he did not write symphonies, but he didn't, and that's that, and it is some compensation to remember that he was so uncertain of his talent that had he not been given the workaday assignments of movie scoring, he might never have written any music at all.

I got off the phone after that conversation with the *Times,* cursed, and said, "Must we be forever at the mercy of amateurs promoted from the city desk?"

I tried to explain my feelings to myself. I loved him like . . . a father? Hardly, Hugo was too childlike for that analogy. Like a brother? No. He was far my superior and senior not only in his knowledge of music but of many things.

Suddenly I understood something I had long felt, in an unformulated way: sex and love have nothing to do with each other. When men love other men, they append "like a brother" or "like a father" to the verb out of their fear of the Big Taboo. And in that moment of grief I knew that I simply loved Hugo Friedhofer. Not as a brother or as a father but as my friend. Just about the last thing he ever said to me, in one of our interminable telephone conversations, was something about "our friendship, which incidentally, as time goes on, grows increasingly dear to me," following which, embarrassed by his admission of emotion, he changed the subject very swiftly.

In any case, were my inclination towards men, I doubt that Hugo would have been to my taste. He was not tall and slim, and he had a small chin that a thin goatee poorly concealed, a stooped posture ("composer's hump," he called it), and enlarged fingertips stained with nicotine. Men are poorly equipped to judge the looks of other men: they admire the likes of Tyrone Power whom women dismiss as "pretty." But women found Hugo terribly attractive. They say it was his mind that excited them.

And so there he was, my dear friend Hugo, standing there now in sudden memory, gone. This man I loved so much, not just for his talent, although certainly I reveled in his musical genius. I used to phone him whenever I wanted to know something (or had discovered something) about music because, as composer Paul Glass put it, "Hugo always knew." The depth of Paul's loss can be measured in a remark he made to me in a phone conversation from Switzerland that might sound arrogant but which I found touching and lonely and devastated: "Now that Hugo's gone, I may know more about orchestration than any man alive." Paul lost his teacher. So did I.

A footnote to that: Hugo told me he had studied with Paul Glass. Paul told me he had studied with Hugo.

In September 1981, four months after Hugo died, I went to the Monterey Jazz Festival. Hotel rooms were scarce and so, at the suggestion of Hugo's daughter, Karyl Gilland-Tonge, I stayed with her daughter Jennifer, whose husband, Jeff Pittaway, was then an Army helicopter pilot, at their home in Fort Ord. Jeff was just back from a tiring flight mission and wanted to spend the evening at home. So I took Jennifer as my "date" to the festival. As we were progressing in a crowd across the grass of the Monterey fairgrounds, Jennifer said she had always loved the Modern Jazz Quartet. By exquisite coincidence, John Lewis was walking two or three paces ahead of us, unbeknownst to her. I reached out and grasped John's elbow to halt him and I said, with the people flowing around us, "John, I would like you to meet Jennifer Pittaway. Jennifer is Hugo Friedhofer's granddaughter." And John beamed that gentle and shy smile of his through his beard and said, "How do you do. I am honored to meet you," and made a great and elegant fuss of her. Later, backstage, I introduced her to musicians who told her stories about her grandfather, and as we were driving back to Fort Ord she said, "But how do people like John Lewis know my grandfather's music?"

"Jennifer," I said, "everybody in music knows your grandfather's music. And it doesn't matter whether it's classical music or jazz. The name Friedhofer will open just about any door in the musical world for you."

Toward the end of his life, Hugo lived in a two-room apartment on Bronson Avenue in Hollywood. Hugo's apartment building surrounds a central courtyard in which there is the usual small Hollywood swimming pool, its bottom painted blue. It is a three-story structure, pleasant enough but slightly gone to seed, of the kind you encounter in Raymond Chandler novels. If you walk along that balcony around the U shape of the building, you come to the apartment of Jeri Southern, a fine pianist and one of the great singers and song stylists. Jeri was the last love of Hugo's life and, though he was twenty-five years or more her senior, she loved him more than any of us, and took care of him. Jeri remained incommunicado for a week after he died, sitting for long periods in her bedroom staring at the floor. Jeri is more musician than anybody knows. She orchestrated Hugo's last movie.

In those late years I was, aside from Jeri, with whom Hugo had breakfast every morning, one of the few people who could pry him out of his apartment. "How come," he said to me once on the phone, "you can always lift me out of my depressions?" "Because," I said, in jest, "I am the only one you know who is a worse melancholiac than you are." I used to have lunch with him often but irregularly at Musso and Frank's on Hollywood Boulevard, that great old movie-business restaurant that is now an island of the past in a sea of porno movie houses, hookers, passing police cruisers, tee-shirt shops, and freaks. And when I wanted him to hear some piece of music, I would make a tape of it and drive very slowly and play it on my car stereo.

Claus Ogerman was coming to Los Angeles from Munich, and he wanted to meet Hugo. Composer after composer wanted to meet him, and since it was known that I knew him, they frequently solicited me to arrange an introduction. "I'm getting tired of being your social secretary," I told him. It was untrue of course. They delighted in what was in his head, and I delighted in opening the door for them to breach his reclusion.

Anyway, Claus was arriving and Hugo was unfamiliar with his music; therefore I made a tape of Claus's *Three Symphonic Dances* and played it on the way to Musso and Frank's, driving slowly enough to get arrested. Hugo gave a running analysis of its harmonic structure. But after a while he ceased listening and began to hear the music. Finally he said, "That kraut friend of yours has a melancholy streak."

"That kraut friend of mine?" I said. "What about this kraut friend of mine?" He responded with one of his worst puns, "Two's company, three's a kraut."

Someone once called Hugo "a real giant among film composers," to which he retorted, "No, I'm a fake giant among real pygmies." All the composers in Hollywood should have hated him for that remark, but instead they quoted it with relish, and they still do.

Along with critic Page Cook, I was always fighting for Hugo's recognition, even though he was, as Raksin told him, "complicit in your own ignoring." Once I took him to Musso and Frank's to interview him for an article for the *Los Angeles Times* or the Canadian Broadcasting Corporation or something—Page and I wrote a lot of pieces about him. I am always careful, in interviews, to save my hot questions for the end, so that I don't come away with empty hands if the interviewee gets furious. And so at last I said to him, "How is it that with all those superb film scores behind you and the respect of colleagues around the world, you have all the emotional security of a twenty-two year old?"

"Oh, you son of a bitch!" he said. And then, sinking into a pensiveness, he said, "Well, there are among the composers in this town some really fine craftsmen. If you want a certain thing done, you have only to tell them. They have done it before and they can do it again. And I have a very real respect for these men. But if you feel about music as I do, you are always working at the outer periphery of your abilities. And that makes you insecure.

"Look," he said as we were finishing our coffee, "I've got my personal estimate of what I know and what I don't know. But I am also acutely conscious of four or five hundred years of musical culture staring over my shoulder, and that makes for a genuine humility. As opposed of course to a false modesty."

He was the gentlest and shyest and, secretly, the most romantic of men, and he literally could not harm a fly. One morning Jeri Southern was killing ants with a sponge on the drainboard of her kitchen sink. Hugo watched in silence with a baleful expression and then said at last, "I hate the part where the Red Cross arrives." Jeri didn't get it for a moment, and then burst out laughing, and later, when he was gone, she suddenly remembered the incident and laughed for the first time in weeks.

Hugo had a steadfast integrity about music and everything else. I do not recall our ever talking about politics, but he recommended that I read the books of Carey McWilliams, which I did. This leads me to believe he was a California socialist, a unique breed with pioneer roots, of the Upton Sinclair stripe. He was German in the thorough discipline of his approach to his music, which was, however, in its airy clarity, rather closer to the French, I thought, than to the German. In personality he was more American than German and more Californian than anything. And he shared with Allyn Ferguson and Jerry Goldsmith a curious distinction: he was one of the very few American film composers actually born in California. Insofar as the politics of Hollywood were concerned, he was a canny observer and trenchant commentator. And I think every composer in the industry not-so-secretly wanted his approval.

He was in his way a revolutionary film composer. Because the scores to silent films were almost continuous, the early producers of talking pictures, who had not yet grasped the differences between the two media, expected the new scores to be like them. Hugo was perhaps the first to argue for less music. "The trick in film scoring," as Henry Mancini said, "is knowing when to cool it." Hugo, in scoring his first film, *The Adventures of Marco Polo,* already knew. He was thirty-six when he worked on *Marco Polo.* All the Friedhofer characteristics were already in place: the restraint, the perfect orchestral balance, the beauty of line, the sensitivity, and something that is indefinably but recognizably him.

There is another way in which he was revolutionary; he was the first Hollywood composer to write distinctively American scores. The significance of his *Best Years of Our Lives* score is generally considered to be its recognizably American quality. His friend Aaron Copland's scores for *Of Mice and Men* (1939) and *Our Town* (1940) preceded it, but Copland was not a mainstream "Hollywood" composer. Friedhofer's probably had the greater influence on other film composers. Prior to *Best Years* and in spite of the two Copland scores, Hollywood movie music had a European flavor, no doubt because so many of the composers were born and trained in Europe. The early film moguls imported them wholesale, as they imported directors and actors and costume designers. And I would have to point out that Hugo was imparting his American quality to scores well before *Best Years*, and for that matter *Of Mice and Men*. One need only listen to his music for *Marco Polo* to observe this.

Is it proper for a film about an Italian in China to sound American? Verdi wrote *Aida*, which is set in Egypt, and Puccini wrote *Madama Butterfly*, which is about an American in Japan, in their own Italianate styles. Hugo had every right, as they did, to approach his subject matter in his own idiom. He was amazing at this. In *Boy on a Dolphin* he writes in a Greek style and sounds like himself. In *Vera Cruz* he writes in a Mexican style (of which he was enamored; he loved Mexico) and sounds like himself. In *The Young Lions* he wrote in both American and German styles and sounds like himself. In any of his films it is fascinating to observe how much the music adds to the power of the story, and how unobtrusively (unless you're watching for it) it achieves its effect. And how distinctive the style is! Someone—Somerset Maugham, I think—said, "The greatest style is no style at all." Hugo never strove for style; he simply had it.

"One of the factors," Dave Raksin said once, "is his conception of melody and harmony, which maintains the traditional idea of what is lyrical and conjunct. The problem with most melodic writing, outside the obvious banalities of contemporary pop music, which is at the level of finger painting, is that in the effort to avoid what has been done, composers too often avoid what should be done. Hugo manages to be lyrical without being sentimental. His music has dignity to it. He is a sophisticated and thoroughly-schooled musician fully conversant with twentieth-century music who also happens to know that the tonal system is far from dead."

Which brings us to another of Hugo's worst puns. The music he wrote for one scene in *The Companion* was in three keys. "This was

inspired," Hugo said, "by the parrot in the scene. It's Polly-tonality."
He used to make these outrageous jokes even in the music itself.
Many years ago he was assigned to score a picture about the French
Revolution. There is an old and angry maxim among film composers:
everybody in Hollywood has two areas of expertise, his own and
music. The producer on this picture was a self-important jackass of
the old school. Striding into the room during the music conference,
he said, "Friedhofer, this is a film about the French Revolution, so I
think there should be lots of French horns in the music."

Hugo found this so hilariously stupid that he did in fact use "lots
of" French horns in the score. And as he neared the end of the picture, he put a capper on his joke. In the last scene, when the escaping
lovers espy the cliffs of Dover, he reprised the melody with solo English horn.


I turned up one day at the little apartment on Bronson Avenue
to go with him to lunch. In it were an upright black Steinway, a small
black Wurlitzer electric piano, four swivel chairs, a big round coffee
table on which reposed his typewriter and stacks of the correspondence he was always in the process of answering, a tape recorder, and
shelves of records and books. Everything was functional, and there
was no chair you could honestly call comfortable. He owned not one
copy of the albums of his film scores.

On the wall above a work table, on which was piled his score
paper, was a display of plaques commemorating those of his scores
nominated for Academy Awards. "Where," I asked, "was the statue
for *The Best Years of Our Lives*?" "In storage somewhere," he
grumped. "Let's go to lunch." He always maintained that an Academy nomination was more honor than the award, since only the
music division voted on it, while the award itself derived from the
votes of actors, producers, directors, and others who might or might
not know what music is all about. And anyway, he had resigned from
the Motion Picture Academy, which he despised, many years before.

"I have seen," Hugo once said, "two authentic geniuses in this
industry, Orson Welles and Marlon Brando. And this town, not
knowing what to do with genius, destroys it."

We were discussing his score for *One Eyed Jacks*, the one film
Brando ever directed and for which Brando was raked across beds of
broken glass by studio executives, their lackey press agents, and—in

supine obedience to the moguls—the newspapers. Brando was made to look the self-indulgent *enfant terrible* for his meticulous shooting of the picture, when in fact he was seeking that evasive goal of perfect craftsmanship. But the picture has now taken on a sort of cult status. Mort Sahl has seen it twenty times or more; I've seen it about ten times, partly for the pas de deux acting of Brando and Karl Malden, partly for the performances Brando elicited from Ben Johnson and Slim Pickens, partly for the cinematography, and partly for Hugo's splendid score. How heartbreaking that main lyrical theme renders the morning scene on the beach, when Brando tells the girl he has been lying to her and has shamed her. Hugo used a distantly lonely solo trumpet in front of strings, one of his favorite devices. He loved jazz and jazz musicians, and that trumpet solo is by Pete Candoli.

"I had ten weeks to work on that score," Hugo told me, "longer than I've had on any other picture."

"Brando had cut the film to about four and a half hours, and then it had been cut further to about two hours and fifteen minutes, at which point it was turned over to me for scoring. When I saw it at that length, it was without doubt the goddamnedest different western I have ever seen, and I loved it. They sneak-previewed it somewhere in the hinterlands on a Friday night with the kids and the popcorn and all that, and it bombed. They tried this and that and the other and cut it again, and it went out in a very much bowdlerized form. In fact they even butchered the music. Whole sequences I had designed for one scene were shoved in somewhere else. So the score is best heard in the UA record album, which I had the opportunity to edit. That is the real score of *One Eyed Jacks*, minus about forty-five minutes of music."

"By the way, in Brando's cut, the girl dies in the end. The studio didn't like that."

*One Eyed Jacks*, in which Hugo's genius is fused to Brando's, is a broken masterpiece. And as for the UA album of that score, if you can find a copy of it, it sells for $150 or more.

A few months after the LP of *The Best Years of Our Lives* was released, Jack Elliott and Allyn Ferguson assembled what they called The Orchestra, later renamed the New American Orchestra—a virtuosic organization of more than eighty-five of the finest studio, symphony, and jazz musicians in Los Angeles. I suggested that they perform *Best Years* in concert. Hugo at first refused to attend, as he had previously refused to attend a retrospective of his movies. But Jeri Southern prevailed, and we went.

The orchestra gave a shimmering performance, all its members knowing he was there. Most of them had worked for him at one time or another and revered him. Partway through the first section, Hugo said to me in that sepulchral voice of his, "The tempo's a little fast."

"Oh shut up," I said.

And when it was over, the audience cheered as at a football game, and Hugo had to stand up and take a bow. It was, as far as I know, only the second time in his life he had heard his music played in public and received the applause he deserved. And I think it was the last time he heard his music played anywhere.

I had come into a habit, whenever Hugo and I went anywhere, of hovering over him, in a surreptitious way. His step had become faltering and slow, and I was always afraid he would fall. He used a beautiful cane of dark wood that Jeri had given him, which he treasured. Once he left it in my car and he was frantic until he reached me and found that it was safe. As we left Musso and Frank's that day and were crossing a street, I reflexively and involuntarily took his arm. He gave me a withering stare, and I never made that mistake again. But my hands were always ready to catch him if he stumbled. The tragedy was that his body was failing and his mind was not.

He had a spot on his lung that turned out to be malignant, and he underwent chemotherapy. He smoked far too much all his life. He used to say that he needed the cigarette in his left hand to balance the pencil in his right. And then, as I had feared he would, he fell, and broke his hip. He was taken to the hospital for surgery. Ginda came up from Mexico and began making arrangements to put him in a home. Pneumonia set in, and he lost the power of speech, this most articulate of men.

Jeri sat by his bedside all one afternoon. He looked at her and silently formed the words, "I love you."

After Jeri had gone home, exhausted, a nurse entered the room to make him comfortable. He opened his eyes. Miraculously, the power of speech came back to him and he got off a last line that, days later, set off gales of consoling laughter, because it was so typical of him. He said, "You know, this really sucks." And he died.

When a great tree falls, it makes quite a crash. Without the help of *The New York Times* or *The Hollywood Reporter* (which printed about four lines on his death), the news traveled by mysterious means all over the world. Paul Glass called Roger Kellaway from Switzerland, desperate to know whether Hugo's scores were safe and where they were, saying they would be invaluable to music students for generations to come.

I became agitated about the scores when Dave Raksin told Ginda he was planning a memorial service for Hugo, and she said, "But who'd come?" Whether his full scores still existed in dusty studio archives I did not know, but I knew the whereabouts of his meticulous six-stave "sketches," so complete that Gene DiNovi once said, "When you orchestrate for Hugo—" and Gene proudly did at one time "—you are a glorified copyist." These were still in the apartment on Bronson Avenue. Everyone kept saying that something would have to be done about them. And at last it dawned on me that I would have to do it.

I felt a kind of shock when I entered that familiar silent apartment, knowing he would never be there again. Then I went to work. I knew where all his scores—each of them bound in hardcover, the film titles imprinted with gold leaf—were stored, and I hauled them out in great armfuls and heaped them on a flat-bed cart I had brought. In six minutes and three trips, I stripped that place of his scores, rushing along the U of the balcony and dumping them in a huge pile in the middle of Jeri Southern's living room carpet. I left Jeri's key to his apartment on her coffee table, went home, called Roger Kellaway and told him to tell Paul Glass the "sketches" were safe. A few days later Karyl took them home with her; later she donated them to the University of Utah, where they are now available for study. Lawyers say they are worthless. Musicians say they are priceless.

We held the memorial service in a small sunny chapel in Westwood. Dave Raksin conducted a chamber orchestra, made up of musicians who loved Hugo, in a recital of Bach and Brahms.

Elmer Bernstein and Leonard Rosenman and Dave and I made little speeches, and the service was not remotely sad. Indeed the conversation before and after it was full of laughter. Jeri didn't come, which I thought appropriate: somebody had to uphold Hugo's tradition of not attending affairs in his honor.

No life of course is long enough, but Hugo's was, as lives go, fairly long, and it was brilliant, and he left us with a thousand funny stories and a mountain of music whose worth has yet to be fully evaluated.

# ·6·

# In Memoriam

## by David Raksin

$\mathcal{O}$n May 23, 1981, a memorial service was held in Hugo Friedhofer's honor, at which David Raksin spoke the following words:

> The remarkable man whose life and career we are gathered here to celebrate was a paradoxical figure. On the one hand, he was surely one of the most learned, most accomplished members of our profession: a fine composer, a master of the orchestra, quick to perceive what was required of the music for a film, and sure-footed in providing that music. This was the Friedhofer that film audiences knew, the formidable musician who composed so many wonderful scores.
>
> But there was also the man who knew too much, the virtuoso of self-doubt who never seemed to have learned to take "Yes" for an answer. Somewhere during his early days something must have given one twist too many to the mechanism through which he viewed the world. I sometimes thought that he might have acquired this pessimism from his father, a man of mordant wit. You will recognize the son in one of his father's characteristic remarks. "Any man who remarries," said Friedhofer pere, "doesn't deserve to lose his first wife." On one appropriate occasion I reminded Hugo of that.
>
> He was notorious for an attitude toward the world that seemed to magnify its shortcomings while appraising its blessings as though from the wrong end of a telescope—but we all enjoyed him for that. When you were around Hugo you often got the feeling that to him, when life was at its best it was no better than an itch that needed scratching. I once said of him that he had managed to sustain a dark view of everything despite personal successes that

185

might have tempted lesser men toward optimism—and he enjoyed that.

Hugo was far from the ordinary, garden-variety misanthrope, but sometimes it seemed that the only time life lived up to his expectations was when it disappointed him. How much of that was "style" or affectation, and how much was real?

I believe that the self-disparagement that was so characteristic of Hugo was his way of dealing with the extreme anxiety that arose out of his exaggerated sense of his own fallibility and frailness. "Fallibility" and "frailness" are not the words ordinarily applied to patriarchal figures—and in his profession that was the position which Hugo achieved. But his intimates knew that in moments of great stress he often became obsessed with delusions of inadequacy. Through many of those nights of painful struggle that are so typical of the composer's life this obsession would persist, until the glorious sound of the music he had just composed filled the recording stage next morning, and told him in terms that could not be denied that his talent had not deserted him.

Still he would persist in judging his work according to arcane criteria that would, if indiscriminately applied, sink just about everybody else in sight. But he was wrong, and he must have known he was wrong. No one produces a body of work such as his out of anything less than talent, technique—and love. Long ago I wrote: "If Friedhofer likes to pretend that his art is other than of a high order, so be it. But for the rest of us to disregard the evidence of our own senses would be absurd. Besides, it would be foolish to be unaware that Hugo's antipathy toward praise was only skin deep, that the man who said, 'I'm just a fake giant among real pygmies!' was not really averse to being loved—as long as it was in spite of himself."

Hugo seems to never have resolved those contradictory traits: they argued within him to the end. But he knew that nothing he could say or do could drown out the testimony of his music, in which is revealed the beauty of spirit he was so determined to hide.

It is fitting that some of his friends and colleagues have joined us to honor him by performing some music of Bach and Brahms, composers with whom Hugo felt a special kinship. He loved to recount the parting shot delivered by Brahms on leaving a party, when he turned in the doorway and said he wished to apologize to anyone he had forgotten to insult.

Lucky as we were to have had Hugo among us, we must not

risk offending him by overdoing our praise—which he is even now trying his best to wriggle out of somewhere in time. Let us take comfort in that Olympian disdain for everyday hypocrisies, and for his unwillingness to be assuaged in his war against the unwelcome aspects of life. Fear not, dear Hugo: if there is anyone around who has earned the right to be insulted, and whom you have forgotten to insult, you are forgiven.

Peace be yours at last, dear friend. Sleep well.

# · 7 ·

# Hugo Friedhofer Filmography

*compiled by Hugo Friedhofer, Clifford McCarty,
and Tony Thomas*

## AS ORCHESTRATOR, ARRANGER, AND
CONTRIBUTING COMPOSER

1929  SUNNY SIDE UP (Fox)
Songs by B. G. DeSylva, Ray Henderson, and Lew Brown

1929  SEVEN FACES (Fox)
Music by Hugo Friedhofer and Arthur Kaye

1930  THE BIG TRAIL (Fox)
Music by Hugo Friedhofer, Reginald Bassett, Jack Virgil, and
Arthur Kaye

1930  THE DANCERS (Fox)
Music by Hugo Friedhofer, James Monaco, and Cliff Friend

1930  A DEVIL WITH WOMEN (Fox)
Music by Richard Fall

1930  THE GOLDEN CALF (Fox)
Music by Hugo Friedhofer, Arthur Kaye, and Jean Talbot

1930  HAPPY DAYS (Fox)
Songs by Con Conrad, Sydney Mitchell, and Archie Gottler

1930  JUST IMAGINE (Fox)
Music by Hugo Friedhofer and Ray Henderson

189

1930   MEN ON CALL (Fox)
Music by Hugo Friedhofer

1930   THE PRINCESS AND THE PLUMBER (Fox)
Music by Hugo Friedhofer

1930   SCOTLAND YARD (Fox)
Music by Hugo Friedhofer and Arthur Kaye

1931   ALWAYS GOODBYE (Fox)
Music by Hugo Friedhofer

1931   DADDY LONGLEGS (Fox)
Music by Hugo Friedhofer and Arthur Lange

1931   DELICIOUS (Fox)
Music by George Gershwin

1931   HEARTBREAK (Fox)
Music by Hugo Friedhofer

1931   THE MAN WHO CAME BACK (Fox)
Music by Hugo Friedhofer and Arthur Kaye

1931   SKYLINE (Fox)
Music by George Lipschultz

1931   SPIDER (Fox)
Music by Hugo Friedhofer and Reginald Bassett

1931   TRANSATLANTIC (Fox)
Music by Hugo Friedhofer and Reginald Bassett

1931   THE YELLOW TICKET (Fox)
Music by Hugo Friedhofer and Reginald Bassett

1932   ALMOST MARRIED (Fox)
Music by Hugo Friedhofer, Reginald Bassett, and Peter
Brunelli

1932 AMATEUR DADDY (Fox)
Music by Hugo Friedhofer

1932 CARELESS LADY (Fox)
Music by Hugo Friedhofer

1932 DEVIL'S LOTTERY (Fox)
Music by Hugo Friedhofer

1932 THE FIRST YEAR (Fox)
Music by Hugo Friedhofer

1932 MYSTERY RANCH (Fox)
Music by Hugo Friedhofer and Arthur Lange

1932 PAINTED WOMAN (Fox)
Music by Hugo Friedhofer and Arthur Lange

1932 A PASSPORT TO HELL (Fox)
Music by Hugo Friedhofer and Arthur Lange

1932 REBECCA OF SUNNYBROOK FARM (Fox)
Music by Hugo Friedhofer and Arthur Lange

1932 SHERLOCK HOLMES (Fox)
Music by Hugo Friedhofer and Reginald Bassett

1932 THE TRIAL OF VIVIENNE WARE (Fox)
Music by Hugo Friedhofer and Reginald Bassett

1932 THE WOMAN IN ROOM 13 (Fox)
Music by Hugo Friedhofer

1933 BONDAGE (Fox)
Music by Hugo Friedhofer and Samuel Kaylin

1933 BROADWAY BAD (Fox)
Music by Hugo Friedhofer

1933   DANGEROUSLY YOURS (Fox)
Music by Hugo Friedhofer

1933   THE FACE IN THE SKY (Fox)
Music by Hugo Friedhofer, Peter Brunelli, Reginald Bassett,
and J. S. Zamecnik

1933   THE GOOD COMPANIONS (Fox)
Music by Hugo Friedhofer and Arthur Lange

1933   IT'S GREAT TO BE ALIVE (Fox)
Music by Hugo Friedhofer

1933   MY LIPS BETRAY (Fox)
Songs by William Kernell

1933   SECOND-HAND WIFE (Fox)
Music by Hugo Friedhofer

1933   ZOO IN BUDAPEST (Fox)
Music by Hugo Friedhofer, Peter Brunelli, and Louis
DeFrancesco

1934   AS HUSBANDS GO (Fox)
Music by Hugo Friedhofer

1934   CHANGE OF HEART (Fox)
Music by Hugo Friedhofer

1934   COMING OUT PARTY (Fox)
Music by Hugo Friedhofer

1934   GEORGE WHITE SCANDALS (Fox)
Songs by Jack Yellen, Irving Caesar, and Ray Henderson

1934   NOW I'LL TELL aka NOW I'LL TELL YOU and WHEN
NEW YORK SLEEPS (Fox)
Music by Hugo Friedhofer, Arthur Lange, and David Buttolph

1934   ORIENT EXPRESS (Fox)
Music by Hugo Friedhofer and Arthur Lange

1934   SERVANT'S ENTRANCE (Fox)
Music by Hugo Friedhofer and David Buttolph

1935   CAPTAIN BLOOD (WB)
Music by Erich Wolfgang Korngold

1935   CURLY TOP (Fox)
Songs by Ray Henderson, Ted Koehler, Edward Heyman, and
Irving Caesar

1935   DANTE'S INFERNO (Fox)
Music by Hugo Friedhofer, Reginald Bassett, and Peter
Brunelli

1935   GEORGE WHITE SCANDALS (Fox)
Songs by Jack Yellen, Ray Henderson, Herb Migidson, Cliff
Friend, and Joseph Meyer

1935   HERE'S TO ROMANCE (Fox)
Music by Hugo Friedhofer

1935   THE LITTLE COLONEL (Fox)
Music by Hugo Friedhofer and Cyril Mockridge

1935   NAVY WIFE (Fox)
Music by Hugo Friedhofer and David Buttolph

1935   ORCHIDS TO YOU (Fox)
Music by Hugo Friedhofer

1935   WAY DOWN EAST (Fox)
Music by Hugo Friedhofer

1935   THE WORLD MOVES ON (Fox)
Music by Hugo Friedhofer, Reginald Bassett, and David
Buttolph

1935   LAST OF THE PAGANS (M-G-M)
Music by Hugo Friedhofer, Karl Hajos, and William Axt

1935   LAST DAYS OF POMPEII (RKO)
Music by Roy Webb

1935   A MIDSUMMER NIGHT'S DREAM (WB)
Music by Mendelssohn, arranged by Erich Wolfgang Korngold

1935   REDHEADS ON PARADE (Fox)
Songs by Don Hartman and Jay Gorney

1935   THE CHARGE OF THE LIGHT BRIGADE (WB)
Music by Max Steiner

1936   GOD'S COUNTRY AND THE WOMAN (WB)
Music by Max Steiner

1936   THE GREEN PASTURES (WB)
Music by Erich Wolfgang Korngold

1936   ROSE OF THE RANCHO (Paramount)
Music by W. Franke Harling and Hugo Friedhofer

1936   THE PRISONER OF SHARK ISLAND (Fox)
Music by Hugo Friedhofer and Reginald Bassett

1936   THE TRAIL OF THE LONESOME PINE (Paramount)
Music by Hugo Friedhofer and Gerard Carbonara

1936   SINS OF MAN (Fox)
Music by Hugo Friedhofer and Reginald Bassett

1936   WHITE FANG (Fox)
Music by Hugo Friedhofer and Charles Maxwell

1937   ANOTHER DAWN (WB)
Music by Erich Wolfgang Korngold

1937   GREEN LIGHT (WB)
Music by Max Steiner

1937  KID GALAHAD (WB)
Music by Max Steiner

1937  THE LIFE OF EMIL ZOLA (WB)
Music by Max Steiner

1937  LOST HORIZON (Columbia)
Music by Dmitri Tiomkin

1937  THE PRINCE AND THE PAUPER (WB)
Music by Erich Wolfgang Korngold

1937  THE PRISONER OF ZENDA (United Artists)
Music by Alfred Newman

1937  YOU ONLY LIVE ONCE (United Artists)
Music by Alfred Newman

1938  THE ADVENTURES OF ROBIN HOOD (WB)
Music by Erich Wolfgang Korngold

1938  THE DAWN PATROL (WB)
Music by Max Steiner

1938  FOUR DAUGHTERS (WB)
Music by Max Steiner

1938  GOLD IS WHERE YOU FIND IT (WB)
Music by Max Steiner

1938  JEZEBEL (WB)
Music by Max Steiner

1938  VALLEY OF THE GIANTS (WB)
Music by Adolph Deutsch

1939  DARK VICTORY (WB)
Music by Max Steiner

1939    FOUR WIVES (WB)
Music by Max Steiner

1939    GONE WITH THE WIND (M-G-M/Selznick)
Music by Max Steiner

1939    INTERMEZZO (United Artists)
Music by Max Steiner

1939    JUAREZ (WB)
Music by Erich Wolfgang Korngold

1939    MADE FOR EACH OTHER (United Artists)
Music by Hugo Friedhofer, David Buttolph, and Oscar Levant

1939    THE OLD MAID (WB)
Music by Max Steiner

1939    DUST BE MY DESTINY (WB)
Music by Max Steiner

1939    TOPPER TAKES A TRIP (United Artists)
Music by Hugo Friedhofer

1939    THE PRIVATE LIVES OF ELIZABETH AND ESSEX,
       aka ELIZABETH AND ESSEX and ELIZABETH THE
       QUEEN (WB)
Music by Erich Wolfgang Korngold

1939    WE ARE NOT ALONE (WB)
Music by Max Steiner

1940    ALL THIS AND HEAVEN, TOO (WB)
Music by Max Steiner

1940    CITY FOR CONQUEST (WB)
Music by Max Steiner

1940    A DISPATCH FROM REUTERS (WB)
Music by Max Steiner

1940    THE LETTER (WB)
Music by Max Steiner

1940    THE SEA HAWK (WB)
Music by Erich Wolfgang Korngold

1940    DOCTOR ERLICH'S MAGIC BULLET (WB)
Music by Max Steiner

1940    VIRGINIA CITY (WB)
Music by Max Steiner

1940    THE WESTERNER (United Artists)
Music by Dimitri Tiomkin and Alfred Newman

1940    SANTA FE TRAIL (WB)
Music by Max Steiner

1940    THE MARK OF ZORRO (Fox)
Music by Alfred Newman and Hugo Friedhofer

1941    DIVE BOMBER (WB)
Music by Max Steiner

1941    THE GREAT LIE (WB)
Music by Max Steiner

1941    KING'S ROW (WB)
Music by Erich Wolfgang Korngold

1941    ONE FOOT IN HEAVEN (WB)
Music by Max Steiner

1941    REMEMBER THE DAY (Fox)
Music by Alfred Newman

1941    THE SEA WOLF (WB)
Music by Erich Wolfgang Korngold

1941    SERGEANT YORK (WB)
Music by Max Steiner

1941    SHINING VICTORY (WB)
Music by Max Steiner

1942    THE BLACK SWAN (Fox)
Music by Alfred Newman

1942    DESPERATE JOURNEY (WB)
Music by Max Steiner

1942    THE GAY SISTERS (WB)
Music by Max Steiner

1942    IN THIS OUR LIFE (WB)
Music by Max Steiner

1942    NOW, VOYAGER (WB)
Music by Max Steiner

1942    THEY DIED WITH THEIR BOOTS ON (WB)
Music by Max Steiner

1943    CASABLANCA (WB)
Music by Max Steiner

1943    THE CONSTANT NYMPH (WB)
Music by Erich Wolfgang Korngold

1943    THE GANG'S ALL HERE (Fox)
Songs by Harry Warren and Leo Robin

1943    MISSION TO MOSCOW (WB)
Music by Max Steiner

1943    WATCH ON THE RHINE (WB)
Music by Max Steiner

1943   ARSENIC AND OLD LACE (WB)
       Music by Max Steiner

1944   BETWEEN TWO WORLDS (WB)
       Music by Erich Wolfgang Korngold

1944   THE WOMAN IN THE WINDOW (RKO)
       Music by Hugo Friedhofer and Arthur Lange

1944   FOUR JILLS IN A JEEP (Fox)
       Music by Hugo Friedhofer and Cyril Mockridge

1945   ALONG CAME JONES (RKO)
       Music by Hugo Friedhofer and Arthur Lange

1945   THE CORN IS GREEN (WB)
       Music by Max Steiner

1945   THE MAN I LOVE (WB)
       Music by Max Steiner

1945   MILDRED PIERCE (WB)
       Music by Max Steiner

1945   ROUGHLY SPEAKING (WB)
       Music by Max Steiner

1945   SAN ANTONIO (WB)
       Music by Max Steiner

1946   CHEYENNE (WB)
       Music by Max Steiner

1946   DEVOTION (WB)
       Music by Erich Wolfgang Korngold

1946   OF HUMAN BONDAGE (WB)
       Music by Erich Wolfgang Korngold

1946   A STOLEN LIFE (WB)
Music by Max Steiner

1947   ESCAPE ME NEVER (WB)
Music by Erich Wolfgang Korngold

1954   DEEP IN MY HEART (M-G-M)
Songs by Sigmund Romberg
Orchestrations by Hugo Friedhofer, Alexander Courage, and
Arthur Morton

1965   THE GREATEST STORY EVER TOLD (United Artists)
Music by Alfred Newman


HUGO FRIEDHOFER COMPLETE FILM SCORES

1938   THE ADVENTURES OF MARCO POLO (United Artists)

1942   CHINA GIRL (Fox)

1943   CHETNIKS! (Fox)

1943   THEY CAME TO BLOW UP AMERICA (Fox)

1943   PARIS AFTER DARK, aka NIGHT IS ENDING (Fox)

1944   THE LODGER (Fox)

1944   LIFEBOAT (Fox)

1944   ROGER TOUHY, GANGSTER, aka THE LAST
GANGSTER and ROGER TOUHY (Fox)

1944   HOME IN INDIANA (Fox)

1944   WING AND A PRAYER (Fox)

1945   BREWSTER'S MILLIONS (United Artists)

1945  GETTING GERTIE'S GARTER (United Artists)

1946  THE BANDIT OF SHERWOOD FOREST (Columbia)

1946  GILDA (Columbia)

1946  SO DARK THE NIGHT (Columbia)

1946  THE BEST YEARS OF OUR LIVES (Goldwyn)

1947  BODY AND SOUL, aka AN AFFAIR OF THE HEART
        (United Artists)

1947  WILD HARVEST (Paramount)

1947  THE BISHOP'S WIFE (Goldwyn)

1947  THE SWORDSMAN (Columbia)

1947  A SONG IS BORN (Goldwyn)

1948  ADVENTURES OF CASANOVA (Eagle-Lion)

1948  BLACK BART (Universal)

1948  SEALED VERDICT (Paramount)

1948  JOAN OF ARC (RKO)

1948  ENCHANTMENT (Goldwyn)

1949  BRIDE OF VENGEANCE (Paramount)

1949  ROSEANNA McCOY (Goldwyn)

1950  GUILTY OF TREASON (Eagle-Lion)

1950  THREE CAME HOME (Fox)

1950   CAPTAIN CAREY, USA, aka AFTER MIDNIGHT
       (Paramount)

1950   NO MAN OF HER OWN (Paramount)

1950   BROKEN ARROW (Fox)

1950   EDGE OF DOOM, aka STRONGER THAN FEAR
       (Goldwyn)

1950   TWO FLAGS WEST (Fox)

1950   THE SOUND OF FURY, aka TRY AND GET ME
       (United Artists)

1951   QUEEN FOR A DAY (United Artists)

1951   ACE IN THE HOLE, aka THE BIG CARNIVAL
       (Paramount)

1952   RANCHO NOTORIOUS (RKO)

1952   THE MARRYING KIND (Columbia)

1952   THE OUTCASTS OF POKER FLAT (Fox)

1952   LYDIA BAILEY (Fox)

1952   JUST FOR YOU (Paramount)

1952   ABOVE AND BEYOND (M-G-M)

1952   FACE TO FACE (RKO)

1953   THUNDER IN THE EAST (Paramount)

1953   ISLAND IN THE SKY (WB)

1953   HONDO (WB)

1954   VERA CRUZ (United Artists)

1952   THE SAN FRANCISCO STORY (WB)

1955   THE WHITE FEATHER (Fox)

1955   VIOLENT SATURDAY (Fox)

1955   SOLDIER OF FORTUNE (Fox)

1955   THE RAINS OF RANCHIPUR (Fox)

1956   THE HARDER THEY FALL (Columbia)

1956   THE REVOLT OF MAMIE STOVER (Fox)

1956   BETWEEN HEAVEN AND HELL (Fox)

1957   OH MEN! OH WOMEN! (Fox)

1957   BOY ON A DOLPHIN (Fox)

1957   AN AFFAIR TO REMEMBER (Fox)

1957   THE SUN ALSO RISES (Fox)

1958   THE YOUNG LIONS (Fox)

1958   THE BRAVADOS (Fox)

1958   THE BARBARIAN AND THE GEISHA, aka THE
           TOWNSEND HARRIS STORY (Fox)

1958   IN LOVE AND WAR (Fox)

1959   WOMAN OBSESSED (Fox)

1959   THIS EARTH IS MINE (Universal)

1959   THE BLUE ANGEL (Fox)

1959   NEVER SO FEW (M-G-M)

1960   ONE EYED JACKS (Paramount)

1961   HOMICIDAL (Columbia)

1962   GERONIMO (United Artists)

1962   BEAUTY AND THE BEAST (United Artists)

1964   THE SECRET INVASION (United Artists)

1971   VON RICHTOFEN AND BROWN, aka THE RED
       BARON (United Artists)

1973   PRIVATE PARTS (M-G-M)

1974   A WALK IN THE FOREST (Documentary)

1974   THE COMPANION, released as DIE SISTER, DIE
       (M-G-M)

# Index

*A Song Is Born*, 55
*Above and Beyond*, 13, 112–114
*Ace in the Hole,* (*The Big Carnival*), 107, 126
Adler, Buddy, 119, 128, 129–130
*Adventures of Casanova, The*, 164
*Adventures of Marco Polo, The*, 10, 48, 52–53, 56–57, 179, 180
*Adventures of Robin Hood, The*, 57– 59, 82
*All This and Heaven, Too*, 45
*Along Came Jones*, 81
American Film Institute, The, 20, 27, 28
*An Affair to Remember*, 13, 121, 123– 124, 131
Andrews, Dana, 56, 86–87
arranging, 67, 82, 114, 123–124, 125, 150, 153
Atkins, Irene Kahn, 27

*Bandit of Sherwood Forest, The*, 82, 171
*Barbarian and the Geisha, The*, 129–130
Bassett, Reginald, 34, 61
*Battle of the Midway, The*, 79, 104
*Ben Hur*, 86
Bennett, Betty, 114
Bennett, Robert Russell, 152
Berlioz, Hector, 6
Bernstein, Elmer, 38, 169–170, 184

Bernstein, Leonard, 52, 113, 126
*Best Years of Our Lives, The*, 11, 12, 13, 18, 53, 63, 72, 81, 87–88, 90, 124, 180, 181, 182–183
Best Years of Our Lives, The, audio recordings of, 24, 182
*Between Heaven and Hell*, 13, 120, 173
*Big Carnival, The,* (*Ace in the Hole*), 107, 126
*Birth of a Nation*, 34
*Bishop's Wife, The*, 13, 53–54, 89– 91, 164
*Blue and the Grey, The*, 15, 135
*Blue Angel, The*, 134
*Body and Soul*, 53–54, 89–90, 113, 120
Boulanger, Nadia, 99, 163, 164, 166
*Boy on a Dolphin*, 13, 120–121, 122, 180
Boyer, Charles (see Page Cook)
Brain, Alfred, 149
Brando, Marlon 14, 127, 135–137, 163, 181–182
Brandt, Carl, 17, 21, 22
*Bravados, The*, 128
Brescia, Dominico, 5, 30
*Bride Came to Yellow Sky*, 103
*Bride of Vengeance*, 95, 98
*Broken Arrow*, 100–101, 117, 164
Bunker, Larry, 150
Buttolph, David, 55

Cahn, Sammy, 115, 171
Candoli, Pete, 14, 182
Capra, Frank, 63
*Captain Blood*, 10, 39–41, 57–58, 67
*Captain Carey, USA*, 95–96
Carmichael, Hoagy, 87–88
*Casablanca*, 75
Castle, William, 74, 138, 139
Chandler, Raymond, 121–122
Chaplin, Charlie, 69
*Charge of the Light Brigade, The*, 41, 44
*Chetniks*, 73–74
*Cheyenne*, 81
*China Girl*, 71, 73–74
Churain, Jaro, 38–39, 43
*Companion, The, (Die Sister, Die)* 22, 23, 172, 180
composing, concert, 13–14, 18–23, 51, 58, 84, 95, 146, 164
conducting, 15, 36, 74, 89–90, 96, 138, 139, 150, 153–154
Cook, Page, 18, 20, 21, 22, 23, 24, 146, 159–173, 178
Copland, Aaron, 13, 14, 84, 98–99, 126, 169, 180
Corman, Gene, 142, 145, 165
Corman, Roger, 142, 145
Courage, Alexander, 74, 125, 160
Curtiz, Michael, 65
Cutner, Sydney, 138–139, 152

Darby, Ken, 119, 145, 172
Davis, Bette, 46, 65
Day, Richard, 55
de Havilland, Olivia, 57–58
Debussy, Claude, 6, 23, 85, 169
*Deep in My Heart*, 112, 114
*Delicious*, 48–49
Delius, Frederick, 169
*Demetrius and the Gladiators*, 111
DePackh, Maurice, 61
Derosa, Vincent, 149

*Desperate Journey*, 70
Deutsch, Adolph, 45, 61, 114
*Die Sister, Die*, (see *The Companion*)
directors, working with, 13, 21–22, 35, 75, 79–80, 84–86, 97, 98, 115–116, 118, 144–145
*Dispatch from Reuters, A*, 46
Dorsey Brothers, 55
Duke, Vernon, 50
Duning, George, 15, 16, 89

*Edge of Doom*, 56
Elinor, Carli, 34
*Enchantment*, 54, 94
Engel, Sam, 79, 123

Ferguson, Allyn, 179, 182
film scoring
    click tracks, 43, 92–93, 123
    composing, 13–14, 18–23, 38, 49, 58, 61–66, 75, 84, 91, 96, 100, 107, 108–109, 120, 125, 129, 146–147, 148, 163, 168–169
    methods, 42–44, 64–66, 87–88, 91–93, 95, 103–104, 107, 108–109, 125, 138–139
Findlay, Hal, 42
Finston, Nat, 38
Fleischer, Dick, 117, 118, 120
Flynn, Errol, 57–58, 70
Forbstein, Leo, 10, 39, 41, 44, 67, 69–70
Ford, John, 79
Foy, Brynie, 78
Friedhofer, Hugo
    Academy Awards and nominations, 11–14, 47, 72, 80, 85, 87, 89, 90, 97, 114, 120–121, 124, 138, 181
    as student and teacher, 5–6, 19, 20–21, 28–30, 73, 99–100, 176
    colleagues' commentary on, 3, 12,

14, 15, 16–17, 20, 24–25, 179–180, 184, 185–187

letters, 16, 18–20, 22–24, 159–173

philosophy of film and television scoring, 13–14, 15, 17, 20–21, 109, 126, 129, 132, 146–147, 167, 168, 169

reviews of, 11–13, 21–22, 71, 82, 146

Fromkess, Leon, 85

*Gang's All Here, The*, 78
Geronimo, 140–141
Gershwin, George, 27, 48–51, 77, 94
Gershwin, Ira, 9
*Gilda*, 82
*Give Us This Night*, 39
Glass, Paul, 19, 176, 184
Gleghorn, Arthur, 149
Goldenburg, Billy, 167
Goldsmith, Jerry, 151, 179
*Goldwyn Follies*, 48, 50
Goldwyn, Sam, 11, 12, 13, 37, 48, 53–56, 62, 72, 81, 85, 131
*Gone with the Wind*, 37, 60, 63–64
Goodman, Benny, 56
*Greatest Story Ever Told, The*, 143–145
Green, John, 24, 68
*Green Light*, 45
*Guilty of Treason*, 112

Hagen, Earle, 15, 16, 17, 68, 74, 93, 114, 142, 143, 149, 150, 151, 164
Hall, Jon, 38, 48
*Harder They Fall, The*, 119–120, 131, 173
Hartford, Huntington, 104
Hathaway, Henry, 79
Hawks, Howard, 55

Hayes, Jack, 144, 152
Hayworth, Rita, 82–83
Hecht, Ben, 53, 55, 72
Hecht, Harold, 115–116
Heindorf, Ray, 33, 40–41, 45, 66–67, 150
Herrmann, Bernard, 3, 24, 36, 146, 165, 170
Hindemith, Paul, 14
Hitchcock, Alfred, 75, 161
*Home in Indiana*, 79
*Homicidal*, 74, 138, 139, 140
*Hondo*, 111
House Un-American Activities Committee, 72–73
*Hurricane*, 48, 80
Huston, John, 129

*I Spy*, 17, 93, 143, 149
*In Love and War*, 131–132
instrumentalists, 148–150, 182–183
*Invitation to a Gunfighter*, 142
*Island in the Sky*, 111, 112

*Joan of Arc*, 13, 97–98, 122–123
Johnson, Nunnally, 80, 100
*Jolson Story, The*, 16, 82, 123
*Just for You*, 109

Kahn, Gus, 27
Kanitz, Dr. Ernest, 99, 104
Kaper, Bronislau, 24, 25, 114
Kay, Arthur, 34
Kerr, Deborah, 123, 124
*Kings Row*, 67
Korngold, Erich Wolfgang, 3, 10, 24, 39–45, 57–61, 70, 147, 153, 164
Koster, Henry, 53–54

Lange, Arthur, 33, 67, 77, 80–81, 102
*Last Days of Pompeii, The*, 37

*Last of the Pagans*, 38
Lawrence, Maurice, 29
Lees, Gene, 138
Leonard, Sheldon, 143
*Letter, The*, 65
Levant, Oscar, 9, 49–50
Lewis, Joseph, 83
Lichtman, Al, 127, 128
*Lifeboat*, 75
Lipschultz, George, 7, 31
Lipstone, Louis, 96–97
Liszt, Franz, 58
*Lodger, The*, 78, 139
Loesser, Frank, 55
Lustgarten, Edgar, 149
*Lydia Bailey*, 106

Maebe, Arthur, 149
Mancini, Henry, 3, 24, 179
Mandell, Danny, 11, 55
Mahler, Gustav, 40–41
Malden, Karl, 136, 137, 182
Maxwell, Charles, 33
McCarty, Cliff, 46
McKenney, D. H., 149
*Midsummer Night's Dream, A*, 39–40, 58
Mockridge, Cyril, 124, 160, 169
Moross, Jerome, 13, 97
Morton, Arthur, 73, 151, 160
Morton, Lawrence, 31
Murray, Lyn, 167
music departments, 7, 9–10, 32–34, 44–45, 69–70
music editing, 91, 92–93, 97, 123
musical directors, 31, 34, 36, 81, 82, 85, 89, 96–97, 114
musicals, 32–33, 78, 79, 114, 152

*Never So Few*, 134–135
Newman, Alfred, 3, 10, 12, 15, 18, 21, 24, 36, 41, 45, 48, 52–53, 55, 61, 62, 67, 69–72, 75, 77, 81, 93, 104, 111, 117–118, 128, 132, 134, 143–145, 147, 152–154, 169
Newman, Emil, 56, 81, 85, 89–90, 101, 112
Newman, Lionel, 119, 128, 134, 160, 161, 164
Newman, Mark, 133, 135
Nixon, Marni, 122–123
North, Alex, 24, 105, 160
*Now, Voyager*, 47

*Of Human Bondage*, 45
*Oh Men! Oh Women!*, 124, 126
*One Eyed Jacks*, 14, 15, 135–138, 181–182
orchestration, 13–14, 17, 43–44, 49–52, 58–64, 68–69, 77, 83–84, 86–87, 97, 142, 150–152, 164, 166
*Outcasts of Poker Flat*, 108–109
*Outlaws*, 15, 135, 141

*Paris after Dark*, 78
Parker, Dorothy, 55, 72
Parks, Larry, 82
Parrish, George, 44
Partch, Harry, 149
*Plunder of the Sun*, 112
Powell, Edward, 41, 44, 50, 67–68, 150, 151
Previn, Andre, 113, 115, 150
*Private Parts*, 18, 145–146, 165
*Prizoner of Zenda*, 48, 93
producers, working with, 35–37, 46–47, 54–55, 62–63, 80, 104, 105–106, 127, 129–130, 131–132, 140–141, 179, 181
Prokofieff, Sergei, 164
Puccini, Giacomo, 52
Purcell, Henry, 6

*Queen for a Day*, 101, 102

*Rains of Ranchipur, The*, 118, 121, 164, 173

Raksin, David, 3, 14, 24, 50, 67–69, 73, 75, 106, 109, 142, 147, 175, 178, 180, 184

Rathbone, Basil, 57

Ravel, Maurice, 6, 51, 169

Rees, Hal, 149

Reher, Kurt, 149

Respighi, Ottorino, 5, 6

*Revolt of Mamie Stover, The*, 119, 173

*Rhapsody in Blue*, 94

Richards, Emil, 149

Rimsky-Korsakov, Nicolai, 52, 85

*Robe, The*, 111

Roder, Milan, 59, 66

Roemheld, Heinz, 44–45

*Roger Touhy, Gangster*, 76, 103

Rogers, Will, 76

Romberg, Sigmund, 114

*Rose of the Rancho*, 37

*Roseanna McCoy*, 55

Rosenman, Leonard, 184

Rosenthal, Lawrence, 151, 167

Rozsa, Miklos, 86

Salinger, Conrad, 41, 67–68, 73, 150, 151

Schary, Dore, 37, 152

Schifrin, Lalo, 24, 151

Schoenberg, Arnold, 50

*Sea Hawk, The*, 65, 67

*Sea Wolf, The*, 66

*Sealed Verdict, The*, 95, 96

*Secret Invasion*, 142

*Secret Sharer*, 103, 104

Selznick, David O., 62

Setaro, Andrea, 30, 37

*Seven Cities of Gold*, 118, 173

Shamroy, Leon, 111

Sherwood, Robert, 11, 53, 55

Shire, David, 20, 24, 167

Shuken, Leo, 144, 152

silent films, 6, 7, 29–31, 62, 104, 179

Silvers, Louis, 127

Sinatra, Frank, 134, 135

Skiles, Marlin, 82, 102

*So Dark the Night*, 83, 164

*So Red the Rose*, 37

*Soldier of Fortune*, 117, 119, 172, 173

*Son of Fury*, 71

Sondheim, Stephen, 52

*Song of My Heart*, 77

songs and songwriting, 32–33, 52, 96, 98, 104, 110, 115–116, 119, 120, 124, 126, 134, 150

sound
  early use of, 32, 34
  recording, 35, 63–64

*Sound of Fury*, The, 101

soundtrack recordings, 14–15, 18–19, 24, 112, 115–116, 130, 137–138, 146–147, 164–165, 169–171, 182

Southern, Jeri, 19, 177, 179, 183, 184

Spencer, Herbert, 15, 50, 67–68, 73, 74, 114, 142, 150, 151

Steiner, Fred, 144, 160

Steiner, Max, 3, 10, 18, 24, 41–47, 59–61, 69–70, 88, 153, 170

Stevens, George, Sr., 144–145

Stoloff, Morris, 82, 83, 89, 119

Stravinsky, Igor, 14, 50–52, 85

*Sun Also Rises, The*, 124–126

*Sunny Side Up*, 33

*Swordsman, The*, 89

Talbot, Irvin, 96–97

Tchaikovsky, Peter Ilich, 77, 123–124

television scoring, 15–17, 74, 92, 93, 114–115, 133, 135, 138–139, 140–142, 143, 151, 159–161, 165

*They Came to Blow Up America*, 74

*This Earth Is Mine*, 133, 171
Thomas, Tony, 18, 46, 70
*Three Came Home*, 100
*Thunder in the East*, 110
Tiomkin, Dmitri, 44
Toch, Ernst, 99
Toland, Gregg, 55, 79
*Topper Takes a Trip*, 164
*Tovarich*, 46
*Trail of the Lonesome Pine, The*, 38
Traubel, Helen, 114
*Two Flags West*, 106

Van Heusen, Jimmy, 52
*Vera Cruz*, 14, 112, 115–116, 128, 173, 180
*Violent Saturday*, 117, 173
*Virginia City*, 66
*Von Richtofen and Brown*, 18, 145, 162

Wagner, Richard, 169
Wald, Jerry, 77, 119, 131–132
*Walk in the Forest, A*, 20, 21, 148, 166, 171, 172

Warren, Harry, 109–110, 124
Waxman, Franz, 3, 24, 107, 160
*We Are Not Alone*, 46
Webern, Anton, 23
Webb, Robert, 118
Webb, Roy, 37
Welles, Orson, 181
Whale, James, 103
*White Feather*, 101, 117, 173
*Wild Harvest*, 88–89
Wilder, Billy, 13, 85, 107
*Wing and a Prayer, A*, 79
*Wintertime*, 77
*Woman in the Window, The*, 10, 13, 80, 124
*Woman Obsessed*, 133
Wurtzel, Sol, 49, 78
Wyler, William, 11, 12, 13, 84–86, 98

Yordan, Phil, 56, 119
*Young Lions, The*, 13, 127, 128, 163, 180
Young, Victor, 3, 36, 117

Zanuck, Darryl, 37, 62, 80, 111, 131

# Contributors

LINDA DANLY is a composer and film music historian. A graduate of Northwestern University in radio, television, and film, she studied film music with Walter Scharf and Earle Hagen. She composed music for thirty-nine episodes of the television series *Jim Henson's Mother Goose Stories* and scored several children's recordings for Caedmon Records. She is on the board of The Film Music Society and teaches the history of film music at the University of Southern California.

GENE LEES has twice won the Deems Taylor ASCAP Award for his work as a music journalist and author. He is the publisher of the monthly *Jazzletter* and is the author of *Inventing Champagne: The Worlds of Lerner and Loewe, Oscar Peterson: The Will to Swing, Meet Me at Jim and Andy's: Jazz Musicians and Their World*, and *Singers and the Song*, a 1987 Oxford University Press book that contains a chapter on Hugo Friedhofer, a man for whom Lees clearly felt great respect and attachment. In a slightly abridged form, it is here used with the author's consent.

DAVID RAKSIN is a film composer whose theme for the 1944 film *Laura* has become one of the most performed and recorded melodies in popular music. Other notable film scores include *The Bad and the Beautiful, Forever Amber, The Redeemer*, and *Will Penny*. David Raksin and Hugo Friedhofer met while working at Twentieth Century Fox and were colleagues for thirty years. A friendship between the two witty and talented composers was inevitable. Raksin teaches in the Film Scoring Program at the University of Southern California and is past president of The Film Music Society.

TONY THOMAS was a renowned writer, soundtrack and television producer, broadcaster, narrator, and the author of thirty books on film. He is considered to have been a leading historian of film music. His biographies featured such personalities as Errol Flynn, Busby Berkeley, Marlon Brando, Gregory Peck, Ronald Reagan, Olivia de Havilland, and James Stewart. His book *Film Score: The Art and Craft of Movie Music* surveys the careers of twenty-five leading film composers in Hollywood.